ALWAYS COMPETE

Also by Steve Bisheff

John Wooden: An American Treasure

Fight On!: The Colorful Story of USC Football
(with Loel Schrader)

ALWAYS COMPETE

*An Inside Look at Pete Carroll and
the USC Football Juggernaut*

Steve Bisheff

St. Martin's Press ≈ New York

www.stmartins.com

Book design by Michael Collica

Library of Congress Cataloging-in-Publication Data

Bisheff, Steve.
  Always compete : an inside look at Pete Carroll and the
USC football juggernaut / Steve Bisheff.—1st ed.
      p. cm.
  ISBN 978-0-312-56022-5
  1. University of Southern California—Football—History.
2. Southern California Trojans (Football team)—History.   3. Carroll, Pete, 1951–
I. Title.
  GV958.U57B57 2009
  796.332'630979494—dc22
  [B]

                                                          2009013187

First Edition: September 2009

1 2 3 4 5 6 7 8 9 10

For Wes, who has brought so much
joy and wonder into our lives

Contents

ALWAYS
COMPETE

Introduction

He doesn't work in South Bend, Indiana, and give rousing "Win One For The Gipper" speeches. He isn't a craggy-faced legend wearing a houndstooth hat who speaks with a thick, Southern twang. He'll never be mistaken for a tough, hard-nosed bully of a man who can get so carried away he'll take a swing at an opposing player on the sideline.

Pete Carroll is something altogether different. In both appearance and style, he has little or nothing in common with the Knute Rocknes and Bear Bryants and Woody Hayeses of the past.

He is college football's coaching icon for a new age, and he has clearly built the No. 1 program in America.

Carroll bristles with as much energy as ambition, exudes more enthusiasm than kids one-third his age. "Always compete" is his mantra, and he isn't kidding. He competes every day, every hour, almost every minute. He doesn't observe from a private practice tower overlooking the field like Bryant did. He stands on the 50-yard line and fires perfect spirals downfield to his receivers. He isn't a grandfatherly figure as much as a cool, computer-hip friend who keeps up with all the latest trends and gadgets. Seriously, how many fifty-seven-year-old grandfathers do you know who can twitter?

Carroll has the kind of smiling, charismatic presence that has made him an appealing celebrity, even in star-conscious Southern California. He is tan and lean with blue eyes and tousled gray hair that makes him boyishly handsome enough to elicit flirtacious "We love you, Pete" catcalls from members of the women's swim team who practice nearby. He is also a workaholic who adores what he is doing. He is the No. 1 recruiter in the sport—some say no one except maybe Florida's Urban Meyer is even close—but never can be heard whining about the long hours or the fickle teenagers who tend to change their minds. His practices are noted for their ferocious intensity, but also for the head coach who sets the fun-loving tone by pulling off pranks or diving into a pile of flailing, emotionally charged players.

To truly appreciate what Carroll has become and what he has achieved in the eight short years he has been at USC, you have to understand the depressing state of the program when he arrived back in 2001. After the glory years of John McKay and John Robinson, after national championships and Heisman trophies piled up one after another in the 1960s and '70s, Trojan football all but fell off the national map in the ensuing two decades. Doomsayers were claiming reality had set in and skeptics were reminding everyone that scholarship limits had conspired to make it impossible to recapture those wonderful seasons of Charles White and Marcus Allen and Ronnie Lott.

Then Carroll showed up, not even among the first three choices in Athletic Director Mike Garrett's original search for a new head coach, and almost immediately the program was invigorated and energized by his California cool approach. Practically before you could say, "Student Body Right," he reestablished the Trojans not only as the dominant football team in the Pac-10, but as the pre-eminent program in the country. After his first, rebuilding 6-6 season, Carroll embarked on a seven-year, 82-9 binge that has included two national championships, a thirty-four-game-winning streak, an NCAA-record seven Bowl Championship Series (BCS) bowl appearances, and an unprecedented eleven victories each season, while finishing in the top 4 in the Associated Press poll a remarkable seven consecutive years. Heading into 2009, he is the winningest active coach in the amateur sport at 88-15 (.854).

If those eye-popping numbers don't unanimously qualify him as the current head of college football's coaching royalty, let's just say they won't be planning a coronation for anyone else in the near future. It's also why, when pushed, Carroll somehow manages not to sound arrogant when he describes his formula as "a little bit John Wooden, a little bit Bill Walsh, and a little bit me."

What this book will show is how he operates the No. 1 college football program in America, from spring practice all the way to when the final seconds tick off in the Rose Bowl, and then on to National Signing Day. It will take you inside the coaching offices and the locker room and out onto the daily practice field, demonstrating how Carroll works with his players and his assistant coaches. By following the just completed 2008 season week by week and often day by day, you will get a sense of how Carroll has to deal with the inevitable ups and downs and the injuries that invariably occur; how he has to be part CEO, part PR man, and part football strategist; how he has to mix and match both his time and his effort; and why all of it seems to fit so much better for him at USC than it ever did in the NFL.

It also will provide insights into an intensely competitive man far more complex than his public persona would lead you to believe. Trying to cover Carroll on a regular basis is a little like trying to track a butterfly. He flits here and darts there, always moving, never pausing for more than a few seconds. One day, as you speed-walk through campus with him, he'll look up and ask, "How's the book going?" The next day, he'll look right through you. Somehow, he never comes off as rude, only preoccupied. His mind seems to run on some kind of photographic shutter speed, surprisingly alternating between football and deeper, more meaningful pursuits. Not that he'll let you get too close to find out. Just as someone mentions that the coach can play "a mean piano," another friend advises, "Check out his spiritual side sometime. You might be surprised by what you find." Others say his conversation can drift to Indian philosophy, parapsychology, and religious mysticism. Something other than football obviously is in his head, or he wouldn't have taken time out from his busy schedule to go on an eleven-day trip to Egypt and Israel in the summer days leading up to the 2008 season. You ask him about it one day after practice. "Oh yeah," he says, "it was so cool. It was one of the greatest things I've ever done for a lot of reasons." You wonder if it had something to do with his spirituality. "It's hardly as simple as that," he says, and then he gives you that grin, the one that means he isn't about to allow you in any deeper than that.

While he can be mysteriously elusive in some ways, he also can be surprisingly accommodating in others. Because he and his staff were gracious enough to give us rare access, we will not only provide an in-depth chronicle of a typical USC season, we will intersperse chapters that offer you different looks into Carroll, the man and personality. You'll find out about his San Francisco Bay Area and coaching roots and why he continues to be such a free spirit. You'll discover how his hiring at USC was part accident and part old-fashioned luck. You'll learn what made him king of college recruiters and how he gets along with the large, diverse media that cover the Trojans as intensely as they used to cover the long-departed Rams and Raiders in L.A. You'll find out why the alumni consider him unique and how he also manages to stay so clued in to the younger generation that he has his own page on Facebook and even his own, on-campus Web chronicler. And yes, you'll also discover he is not perfect. He makes mistakes just like the rest of us, and despite his glowing record, he still has his share of critics out there.

You'll meet the quiet, but obsessed, activist side of Carroll, who, without much fanfare, has become a vigorous organizer and advocate of "A Better LA," a nonprofit foundation consisting of community leaders who are working to reduce gang violence, especially on the mean streets of Los Angeles. You'll walk the streets with him for an L.A. rally and meet former gang members-turned-activists, some of whom have taken the coach on midnight rides through the toughest neighborhoods in town, as chronicled on CBS's *60 Minutes*, trying to talk to current gang members and create a community voice and presence that didn't exist before the foundation took action.

You'll learn why Carroll and USC football have combined to help bring the city together. We'll take you to the sold-out games at the 93,000-seat L.A. Coliseum, where you can see a wide cross-section of fans of every ethnic variety. USC football games aren't limited to the rich, corporate types who dominate the season ticket holders in the NFL, or sit courtside for Lakers games at the Staples Center. No, they come en masse to see the high-scoring Trojans, from the chic West Side to the earthy East Side, from the affluent suburbs of Orange County to the blue-collar neighborhoods of the Inland Empire.

They come because Carroll wins and because, in a city without an NFL franchise since 1994, USC football has muscled its way up there with, if not past, the Lakers, Dodgers, Angels, and UCLA basketball at the very top of the Southern California sports entertainment chain. "I'm thrilled people are having so much fun with it and love the Trojans and like what we're doing," he says. "I'm thrilled to bring them that kind of joy. I hope it lasts forever. Let's keep it going."

Clearly, Pete Carroll *is* college football in Los Angeles, and for the past eight years, he has become the dominant figure in the sport nationally.

Hopefully, when you finish this book, you will be quick to agree on his rocketing status. Knute, "The Bear," and Woody have all had their day, but now some added room will have to be found on those glory-filled, championship pages of college football history.

A New Age coaching icon is about to join the party.

I

Excitement Amid a Fragile Spring

It is one of those almost-too-good-to-believe, 75-degree Los Angeles afternoons in late March, and the usual large, cardinal and gold–clad crowd spills through the sun-splashed gates at Howard Jones Field for the first day of USC spring football practice. The veterans among the spectators are dressed comfortably but are carrying Windbreakers or sweaters, well aware that the brisk spring winds will come rattling in about the same time the early evening shadows creep onto the manicured lawn before practice is over.

The head coach doesn't seem concerned with any of that. Pete Carroll, wearing a thin, white, form-fitting, long-sleeved shirt and khaki pants, sprints onto the field, clapping and chirping, flashing a smile as wide as the L.A. Coliseum tunnel. Carroll, with his face seemingly more tan than ever and his gray hair blowing in the breeze, looks like a kid who can't wait to open his new, gift-wrapped PlayStation 3. His bouncy enthusiasm is infectious, and several of the players look up and grin at him as they begin their calisthenics.

Thanks to Carroll, USC football is an institution again in L.A., the happy, winning substitute for the nation's No. 2 market that is still incredulously without an NFL franchise. Instead of Rams or Raiders merchandise, everyone can now be seen wearing USC gear at the malls and theaters and casual restaurants around this sprawling megalopolis. The Trojans have become the city's biggest winners, more consistent than the Lakers, more successful than the Dodgers, and clearly overshadowing the basketball exploits across town at UCLA.

It is not just all the winning, it is the style and caliber of players he has developed at USC. In his first seven years on the job, Carroll produced thirty All Americans and eleven first-round NFL draft picks, including four in the 2008 draft. It is a remarkable record, and the steady stream of victories has created a rare comfort zone for Carroll, who seems to tease the USC faithful every off-season by listening to an assortment of NFL head coaching offers. Few, if any, college coaches have less job pressures than he does. Still, you can sense a rustle of discontent from some boosters and alumni who have been spoiled by all the Trojans have achieved. They point out it's been four years since they won their second of two national titles under Carroll and three years since they've been back to the BCS Championship Game. They're hungry to wave those large cardinal colored foam fingers in the air and proclaim "We're No. 1" again.

Last season ended much like the one in 2006, with USC semi-grudgingly accepting a bid to the game that once was its ultimate goal, the Rose Bowl, where it systematically whipped yet another overmatched Big Ten opponent, this time Illinois. Back-to-back, 11-2 bowl-winning seasons would be cause for celebrations at most universities, but not here, where the bar has been raised to a whole different level. Maybe that's why there is an undercurrent of uneasiness about the start of this spring practice. Or maybe it's just the fact that, for the first time since a tall, left-handed kid named Matt Leinart squeezed out the job at the end of spring, the Trojans aren't sure who their quarterback will be in the opener at Virginia on August 30.

Once Leinart took control as a sophomore, he held onto the position for three glory-filled years, going 37-2, leading the team to those two national titles and winning the Heisman Trophy along the way. When he left for the NFL, everyone knew that John David Booty, who'd been waiting patiently, would take over. Booty quarterbacked the team for two seasons, and although he never matched Leinart, he had a nice, two-year run, losing only three games he started and directing the team to consecutive Rose Bowl victories.

Now, at least publicly, Carroll and his coaches are saying the job is open. "We want to take our time, and hopefully get a real sense of someone we can count on at the position," Carroll tells me in our first real one-on-one interview of the season. "We want to do it right. We're not necessarily going to go for the biggest, strongest arm. We'll go for the quarterback we think will help us win."

Still, those who've been around the program the longest quietly believe the choice has all but been made already. They have come to trust Carroll and his instincts. They should. He picked Leinart over Matt Cassel, the backup to Tom Brady who eventually took over when Brady was injured with the New England Patriots, even when the two quarterbacks were basically even coming out of spring practice. He said he sensed something special in Leinart. Whether he senses the same thing in Mark Sanchez is difficult to know, but one thing is clear: Carroll has never had a quarterback controversy in his previous seven years at USC, and he certainly isn't looking for one now. So the sense is that Carroll wants Sanchez, the fourth-year junior who's been around the program for three seasons, to win the job, despite the challenge he knows is coming from flashy Mitch Mustain, the much-hyped transfer from Arkansas.

Around the rest of the country, on ESPN and in most L.A. area newspapers, this has been proclaimed as the hottest spring quarterback duel in college football. These are, after all, two kids who were national prep players of the year their senior seasons in high school. Most of the ardent boosters and alums think this is about which of the two quarterbacks proves to be a better leader and more accurate, mistake-free passer. In the quiet reality of the

USC coaching chambers, however, it's about more than that. It is about a philosophy and some off-the-field politics that are understood but never openly discussed, even in the staff's private meetings in Heritage Hall.

Carroll values experience more than anything else, and Sanchez has spent much more time learning the offense than Mustain, who was the scout team quarterback, running opponents' offenses, not USC's, in his first year after transferring from Arkansas. Then there is the potential recruiting fallout involved. Sanchez is from the same rich Orange County pipeline that produced Leinart and Carson Palmer, another Carroll-coached Heisman Trophy winner. Already, the next highly decorated Orange County quarterback, Mater Dei's Matt Barkley, the national prep player of the year as a junior, has committed to USC. Carroll has to be careful not to do anything that would besmirch his reputation among future SoCal quarterback prospects, like maybe choosing a transfer from Arkansas over a highly regarded local kid who had been waiting three years for his chance.

So, although Carroll keeps insisting the position is wide open, it's clear early on in the spring that it is Sanchez's job to lose. The only way he wouldn't be named the starter at the end of spring practice was if, one, he completely screwed up, or, two, Mustain was so spectacular that he thoroughly outplayed him. Both of those options were long shots, especially since the plan was for Sanchez to take 80 percent of the practice snaps with the first-team offense, while Mustain and Aaron Corp, still another Orange County hotshot, would split time taking the majority of their snaps with the second team.

Steve Sarkisian, Carroll's bright, young offensive coordinator, smiles and talks about how much he likes all the quarterbacks, but when you press him, he shrugs and admits what most already know. "Yeah, I'd have to say Mark is ahead going into this," he says, "but we're excited to see what they can all do." What makes this quarterback choice more intriguing is that it's the first time Carroll and Sarkisian have had to make a decision of this magnitude since Norm Chow, the former offensive coordinator, left to accept the same job with the Tennessee Titans. Widely regarded as an offensive genius, at least at the collegiate level, Chow molded both Palmer and Leinart into Heisman winners and did the same for Ty Detmer at BYU. He left USC under a smoggy cloud of controversy when Carroll wanted to move him, or, as Chow's friends contend, "demote him," to quarterbacks coach, taking away his cherished role as a play caller.

The Trojans's program under Carroll seemed at its pinnacle when the head coach was directing the defense and the creative Chow was calling the plays on offense, although the presence of Leinart and Reggie Bush, still another Heisman winner, obviously had something to do with it. Chow had a strong voice and he wasn't afraid to use it, even if he disagreed with Carroll or others on the staff. Some felt it was the kind of creative tension that made everything work on offense. Others weren't so sure. Whatever was going on, the tenseness had begun to grow on the coaching staff. What happened from there still remains somewhat fuzzy. Some felt Chow started receiving what fellow staff members felt was a little too much credit in the media for the offense. At the same time, the role of Lane Kiffin, a young, ambitious assistant and son of Carroll's best friend, Tampa Bay defensive coordinator Monte Kiffin, started to magnify. Carroll wanted the thirty-something Kiffin, who starts this season as the Oakland Raiders head coach, to have more input in the offense, and Chow quietly, or not so quietly, resented it.

Before this season, and this book, is finished, I intend to get Chow and Carroll to corroborate what really happened, what led to Chow departing for the NFL Tennessee Titans, and Carroll moving Kiffin up and hiring Sarkisian, naming them co-offensive coordinators, putting his own stamp on the offense and limiting Chow to work in some other capacity. When that occurred, the writing was on the locker room wall. Everyone knew Chow would accept the first good offer to come along.

When it happened, when Chow was named offensive coordinator of the Titans, Carroll was effusive in his praise of Norm in comments to the media, and Chow talked glowingly of how much he enjoyed his time with Carroll and the Trojans. Those who had been close to the situation, however, understood that it had not been an amicable separation, even if no one would talk about it publicly. For weeks afterward, you could still feel the bitterness lingering in Chow's old office on the second floor of Heritage Hall, not to mention the anger from some Trojans alums, many of whom still believe USC never would have lost that BCS title game shoot-out with Texas the following year if Chow had been calling the plays.

Three years later, in a bittersweet twist of irony, Chow, who had been relieved of his duties in Tennessee, accepted the offensive coordinator's job at UCLA, USC's intense crosstown rival. He'll now be working with a fiery new boss, former Bruins quarterback hero Rick Neuheisel, in Westwood, where UCLA fans are quick to remind their Trojan friends that they haven't been to the national championship game since Chow left.

So now the shadow of Chow is hovering even closer, as Carroll and Sarkisian go about picking the quarterback they hope will help them win when they have to play Chow and the Bruins in what is sure to be an emotionally charged game in December. For Sarkisian, maybe more than Carroll, the stakes are huge. He has evolved into one of America's high-profile assistants, and it was clear after he turned down the Raiders' head coaching job, which eventually went to Kiffin, that his goal was to be a head coach at a major university. First, though, he has to prove he can help the Trojans win a national title without Chow, who, interestingly enough, was his original mentor at BYU.

To do it, Sarkisian and Carroll have to make the right choice at quarterback and then make sure whoever they choose plays within their framework. That becomes more and more evident as the practices progress on Howard Jones Field. As the spring days float by, it is almost as if Sanchez, an energized, enthusiastic, gunslinger type in the Brett Favre mold, is being kept under wraps. Equipped with the strongest arm on campus since Palmer's, he is spending much of his time throwing short, safe passes in practice, a quick slant here, a dump off to a running back there. The emphasis is not on making big plays, but on avoiding mistakes. The plan must be working, because the coaches are smiling and patting him on the back and praising him in the media sessions afterward.

In the meantime, a strange thing is happening. Mustain, who senses he is the underdog in the competition, seems to be going out of his way to take chances. He is a pure passer, and he is consistently completing more balls downfield, particularly to Damian Williams, the exciting wideout who transferred from Arkansas with him. It's apparent the two of them already have a strong on-field rapport, but if the duel seems to be heating up, the coaches are quick to tone it down. Both quarterbacks have been carefully counseled to say the right things to reporters.

"I think this is my job now, and I feel things are going well," says Sanchez, whose dark hair and swarthy features have had fans mistake him for Leinart in the past. "I'm just concentrating on making the right decisions." Mustain rubs a hand through his sandy hair and admits Sanchez is the frontrunner. "I'm just out here trying to learn and get better every day," he says. But every once in a while, in his attempt to be politically correct, he slips and lets the competitive fire show through. "I didn't come here to be a backup," he says at one point, then glances around nervously to make sure there aren't any coaches nearby.

Although the quarterback battle is the focal point of the spring, Carroll has plenty of other things on his mind as March turns into April. Thanks to three years of extraordinary recruiting, his overall talent pool is as deep as ever, especially on defense, but he has to find a replacement for Sedrick Ellis, the All-American nose tackle who was his best football player in 2007, and he must address an offensive line that has only one starter returning. Then there is the always intriguing situation at tailback, where no less than six flashy candidates, almost all high school All Americans, will be competing for carries with another highly regarded addition due in the fall.

None of this is anything new. There is always turnover to deal with in college football. Nevertheless, this particular spring has a sense of urgency attached to it, because the USC schedule, for the first time since Carroll arrived, is highlighted by a monumental early-season matchup. Usually, the biggest games Carroll's Trojans play are in November or early December. Not this time, though. This time, Ohio State will come to the L.A. Coliseum on September 13, in an intersectional that will have obvious BCS bowl implications, with the winner likely to be anointed No. 1 in all the early-season polls.

"We won't treat things any different because of that game," Carroll says. "Our routine will stay the same." Maybe, but the Trojans want to be sure they have their best player starting in Ellis's old spot at nose tackle, and they certainly want to identify the starters in the offensive line well before the week of the Buckeyes' game.

If tailback is a problem, it is a nice one to have. Any one of the six Trojans runners would probably start for crosstown rival UCLA and most of the schools in the Pac-10. They are that good. So Carroll is using the spring to get extended looks at some of his less experienced tailbacks, kids such as Allen Bradford, Marc Tyler, and Broderick Green. The likely fall starter, Stafon Johnson, is being used sparingly, while Joe McKnight, the most exciting of all the runners, is forced to miss the final couple weeks of spring practice for academic reasons, although no one expects that to be an issue come fall.

For any of the tailbacks to have success, first the holes must be there. That's where offensive line coach Pat Ruel comes in. A ruddy-faced veteran of thirty-three years coaching in college and the NFL, Ruel is the prototype football lifer, with a thick moustache and a gravelly voice that some of his linemen must still be hearing when they go to sleep at night. With only one starter back from a year ago in All-American candidate Jeff Byers, Ruel's challenge would seem immense, especially at a school where the pressure is as thick as the often smoggy air. But Carroll never goes into a season caught short at any one position, and he and Ruel are comforted by the fact that several of his linemen not only played extensively but extremely well when injuries hit the line like an unsuspected tsunami a year ago. Kristofer O'Dowd, now a sophomore, was stunningly effective early, subbing for the veteran Matt Spanos at center. Quietly, Carroll and Ruel believe he will be a star. At the other spots, kids like Charles Brown, Butch Lewis, Zack Heberer, Alex Parsons, and Nick Howell all have a chance to be solid college players. Then there's Thomas Herring, the 340-pound monster with quick feet who isn't as mature as the others but has more potential than any of them. "If that kid could ever get it together, he could be unbelievable," Carroll says to a couple of cronies on the sideline one day. "Yeah," admits Ruel, when asked about Herring, "his ceiling is pretty much unlimited. But he's got a ways to go yet. He's not as advanced as some of our other guys."

For everything else going on, though, the spring still comes back to the quarterbacks. Two weeks away from the end of practice, in a weekend scrimmage, Sanchez, still playing conservatively, moves the offense but does little to stand out against the first-team defense, while Mustain, working mostly against the second-team defense, throws three touchdown passes. Immediately, the Internet chat rooms come alive with talk that Mustain is about to supplant Sanchez as the starter. The whispers on the practice field after the scrimmage convey the same message.

Carroll senses it, and on the next practice day the following week, he makes the most revealing move of the spring. He orders that Sanchez be given all the snaps with the first team, every single one, limiting Mustain and Corp to working only with the second team. It is as if Carroll is sending a message: It doesn't matter what happened in that weekend scrimmage. Sanchez is our quarterback. Confronted by the media after the Tuesday practice, Sarkisian calmly explains that "nothing has changed." He insists Sanchez always gets the majority of the snaps, but the reporters know otherwise. They begin writing in the next day's newspapers that the quarterback duel is over. Sanchez has won. A week later, Carroll makes it official. He names the junior as his starter going into the fall.

The announcement takes some of the drama out of the "Trojan Huddle," the name that has been given to the old spring game, the final scrimmage that marks the end of spring practice. It doesn't matter in Trojan-mad L.A., though, where some 22,000 people show up at the Coliseum on a cool April Saturday to catch a glimpse of what their beloved Trojans will look like in the fall. The game features lots of offense, with Sanchez making up for an early interception on a rare flea-flicker play to complete 16 of 24 passes for 203 yards and 3 touchdowns, including one on the only long pass the coaches allow him to throw, a beautiful 37-yard spiral that floats gently into the hands of wide receiver Ronald Johnson. Mustain completes 6 of 10 passes for 111 yards and 2 touchdowns in a less-than-impressive showing.

The real surprise of the scrimmage is Corp, the redshirt freshman who wasn't even in the quarterback picture most of the spring. He isn't just good on this day; he is spectacular, completing 13 of 16 passes for 158 yards and 2 touchdowns, including the one in overtime that gives his team the victory. In fact, if you'd just walked into the Coliseum not knowing anything about the team, you'd have thought Corp was the most experienced quarterback of the group. He was that poised and relaxed, and afterward, even Carroll admitted his surprise. "Aaron got into a really nice groove," he says. "He played with a lot of confidence."

Carroll says he was impressed with the team's energy and its overall speed, and talks as if he was pleased with the way the scrimmage went. Still, as much as he wanted to establish the clear frontrunner at quarterback and give him momentum heading into the summer, the last thing he expected, on the final day of the Trojans' spring, was for Sanchez to be overshadowed by a redshirt freshman.

"Oh well," says one prominent USC alum watching from a privileged spot on the sideline, "if nothing else, this should make for a lively first few weeks of practice in the fall."

Maybe a little too lively for Pete Carroll's taste.

Pete Profile

The Quiet Activist

Four weeks to the day before USC's season opener in Virginia, on one of those broiling Los Angeles Saturdays in early August, you'd think Pete Carroll would be sequestered in his air-conditioned office, poring over film or drawing up complex defensive schemes. But he is not.

He is strolling down Martin Luther King Boulevard, just in front of the Trojans' home, the L.A. Coliseum, trailed by several TV cameras, a couple of out-of-breath announcers, a pair of Internet reporters, and me. I'm grasping my notebook and trying not to smile, because it appears I'm in somewhat better shape than the younger TV guys. Directly behind us is an animated crowd that grows to somewhere between 1,500 and 2,000 people who are part of the LA LivePeace March and Rally. It is hosted by the nonprofit foundation that is near and dear to Carroll's heart, A Better LA, and UNITY ONE, two groups dedicated to promoting nonviolence in the streets of Los Angeles and raising public awareness regarding the community efforts toward gang intervention.

Carroll is walking, sometimes by himself up front, sometimes holding hands with his proud wife, Glena, but always smiling and waving to the bystanders and the startled people in their cars heading in the opposite direction on Martin Luther King Boulevard. "No more violence!" chants someone in the crowd behind him with a loudspeaker and microphone. The crowd repeats the chant. "Save our kids!" the gentleman shouts next, and again the crowd repeats his words. "Save our babies!" he screams, and the rhythmic words echo across the warm L.A. pavement.

Carroll is joined by L.A. sheriff Lee Baca, City Councilman Bernard Parks, and San Francisco mayor and magazine cover-boy Gavin Newsome, along with Newsome's new blond bride. But there is no mistaking who the celebrity is on this sun-splashed summer day. Beginning with a brief, premarch press conference emceed by Yogi Roth, Carroll's graduate assistant coach and all-around PR front man, in the shadow of the Coliseum's famous peristyle end, Carroll cannot take two steps in any direction without getting swarmed. People want to shake his hand, or ask for an autograph, or pose him for a picture with somebody's son or daughter or entire family. If you didn't know better, you would think he was the politician running for office in the group. The people, mostly African Americans and Latinos who live in the surrounding area, look at him adoringly, obviously appreciative that this big-time coach, maybe the most famous college football coach in America, would take time out of his busy schedule to do this for a cause they deeply believe in.

"His job is to be a football coach," says Parks, the councilman who was once the city's police chief. "He doesn't need to be out here saving lives. But here he is, helping, trying to get people jobs. I've always believed that the one thing that stops a bullet faster than anything else is a job." Not all the bullets get stopped, though. Only a few weeks earlier, Jasmine Sanders, an innocent eight-year-old playing in the streets of South Los Angeles, was gunned down by a stray bullet from a gang member's gun. Ironically, her funeral is scheduled to be held just a few miles from the rally later in the day.

Another innocent victim, a promising, young high school football player named Jamiel Shaw, was murdered a few months earlier just walking to a store in the same dangerous part of South L.A. His grieving parents are in the middle of the march, holding up a picture of their son in full football uniform. When you glance back at them for a second, you see tears welling in their eyes. Newsome, a politician who is supposed to have a bright future, said that's why he made the four-hundred-mile trip from San Francisco to Los Angeles. "It's inspiring to me, because the Northern California challenges are the same as the Southern California challenges. It seems every week a fifteen-year-old is killed by a sixteen-year-old with a gun. Someone is gunned down all the time in the streets of the inner city. America is the war we really have to win."

So Carroll, the coach who has become successful because he is consumed by winning football games, has quietly turned that same energy and drive into something he considers even more important. "It took somebody like Pete Carroll to say we can do better," says Bo Taylor, who founded UNITY ONE, the violence-prevention nonprofit that works closely with Carroll's A Better LA. "It just shows what can happen if we work together for something positive."

Taylor is the former gang member who became somewhat famous for taking Carroll along on a series of midnight rides through the 'hood in L.A. On this day, he is visibly struggling with his health. Carroll reveals his friend has been diagnosed with inoperable cancer. "He hasn't got much time left," he says. "He's an amazing guy." (Less than two weeks later, Taylor dies from the disease).

As Carroll marches, he notices me walking alongside, notebook in hand, and tries to put into words his goal. "What we want to develop," he says, "is that feeling that you can do it. You can cut down on the violence if you focus on it day by day, week by week, month by month. It's such a long process, but you try to help just by doing the right thing. We're seeing innocent bystanders being victims, where a few people wind up frightening a lot of people. It is a handful of people causing all the problems, and part of that has to do with economics. What's obvious is that everybody is scared, but if you can give them a legitimate way to turn their lives around, they'll listen."

Fifteen minutes later, the march snakes its way down a side street and into the huge Coliseum tunnel. As marchers stroll out into the sunlight again, volunteers are waiting with cold drinks and encouraging shouts. Most of the members find their way to seats at the closed end of the historic old edifice. After everyone drinks and tries to cool off, Carroll steps up to the microphone.

"It's no accident we're here in the Coliseum today," he says. "It's a place with a history of extraordinary championships, and it's no coincidence that we're trying to win and win in a big way. If all of us continue to work at it, we can do this." The subject is not something Carroll has a casual interest in. Listening to him talk a few minutes later, he sounds as emotional as he does the week his team is about to play crosstown rival UCLA. "We're seeing innocent people becoming victims," he says, "and the effect it has on everyone is very much like terrorism. It's a few people who cause the problems, but there are reasons behind that. The thing is, everybody is scared. Many of the gang members are charismatic, high-level-thinking people who run the gangs themselves. Those guys would do anything to change it if they could, but they're just in survival mode. We need to find some way to turn their lives around. If you tell them that's possible, they'll listen. We've talked to a lot of the leaders of the community, and we believe they're going to help. That's exciting to see. This needs to be an emotional movement from the inside out of these communities. If it isn't emotional, we aren't going to get their attention. We need to focus on those who can help us create change."

The midnight rides Carroll has taken through the mean streets of L.A., initiated with the late Taylor and chronicled in newspapers and magazines, as well as on CBS's *60 Minutes,* have become something of an urban legend. "It was crazy; people couldn't believe I would be out there at first," Carroll says. "They were always coming up to me and saying what are *you* doing here? But then we'd laugh and everyone would relax and they'd talk about some of their problems and what we could do to help.

"My goal in doing that is just to let them know someone is thinking about them. They have to know they're not alone. A lot of them think they have only two choices: to go to jail or to die on the streets. Somehow, we have to change that. We have to let them know there are other options they can take with their life. We're trying to get them jobs when we can. We had one kid named Diamond who was a gang member, and we helped find him a job, and now he's turned his life around and he's working and staying out of trouble and even working with our foundation to help others like him."

Carroll got the idea for A Better LA after a conversation with Lou Tice, a longtime friend and founder of the Pacific Institute. They'd always talked about doing something worthwhile for the community, and after one particularly heart-wrenching week of crime and death in the streets, Carroll called Tice. "I told him we need to figure out what to do," Carroll says. "We need to get involved and do something to keep these kids from killing each other." So Carroll and Tice, along with several others, established A Better LA, with the intent to change the gang culture in the area.

Someone once asked Tice if Carroll was as laid-back as he appeared. "Yeah," said Tice, "he's laid-back—laid-back like a ninja ready to strike." Carroll's tireless work for the foundation was recognized in the spring of 2008 at a Summa Children's Foundation gala to honor Carroll. "While Pete Carroll may be best known for his victories on the field," said Brian Werdeshem, the Summa Foundation's cofounder, "his true success lies in his work to end gang-related violence affecting the inner-city communities of South Los Angeles."

In many ways, his work was symbolized by the gala, where half of the proceeds that night went to Carroll's A Better LA. The total donated on that warm spring night? More than $750,000.

This past winter, the USC School of Social Work presented Carroll with the Crystal Heart, the school's highest honor for community service. In an even more moving tribute to the Trojans football coach, it established a scholarship for students persuing graduate study at the USC School of Social Work. Fittingly, it will be called the Pete Carroll Scholarship.

II

Fall Camp: Going into Crisis Mode Early

Here," says Pete Carroll, "catch," as he throws a football at me in the defensive war room on the second floor of USC's Heritage Hall. When I manage to shove my notebook aside in time to catch the ball and toss it softly back to him, the coach grins, tosses the football, an Arena League ball of all things, up in the air a couple more times, then turns his attention to the assistants crowded around the large table before him.

It is early June, and the mood is more kicked back and relaxed, with linebackers coach Ken Norton Jr., the former Pro Bowl linebacker and son of one-time heavyweight champ Ken Norton, resting with his feet on the far end of the table, one foot with just a sock on, the other with just a sneaker. Nick Holt, the intense defensive coordinator, hunches over, the light reflecting on his shaved head. Graduate assistant Kris Richard shuffles papers nearby, while secondary coach Rocky Seto has notebook and pen in hand, as if he is preparing for a major exam.

The head coach has nicknames for some of his assistants. Seto is "Rock," defensive line coach Dave Watson is "Sweaty," for obvious reasons when you watch the way he perspires like a broken faucet during practice, and offensive line coach Pat Ruel is "Golden," his real first name, if you can believe it. But for the most part, this isn't a head coach who works at coming up with colorful sobriquets. On this particular day, Carroll, wearing shorts and sandals, is working on a new defensive formation, flashing the X's and O's on a nearby white greaseboard with a black marking pen, almost lost in his own thoughts. "Come on," he suddenly says, "we have to think of a good name for this," and his assistants all shout out different, colorful adjectives—"smash, crash, rocket," among others—hoping he'll find one he likes. He eventually does, but only after a lot of wisecracks and halfhearted jokes. "Hey," Norton Jr. says, after the meeting breaks up, "it's still the off-season. It's not time to get serious yet."

Seven weeks later, under a hot August sun, it *is* time to get serious, more serious than Carroll ever could have imagined in the first few days of what is called fall camp, even though it's still very much in the middle of summer. Usually, the boss is practically bursting through his white polo shirt with enthusiasm in the opening week, excited to greet his returning players, happy for the chance to practice again after months of inactivity, and eager for the opportunity to check out what his latest batch of blue-chip recruits look like in Trojan colors.

This time, however, there is a somber tone to the proceedings from the very first day. Guard Jeff Byers, the only returning starter in the offensive line and someone who is expected to be one of the team's major leaders, is not participating. Carroll reveals that Byers, probably the most intelligent player on the roster, has been suffering from a mysterious flulike ailment for several weeks—offensive line coach Pat Ruel later describes it as "several months"—and the doctors don't know what it is. The word "parasite" is mentioned, as is the fact that Byers's spleen has been enlarged, two descriptions that do not hint at a quick recovery. Of all the units on the team, this is the one that could least overcome the absence of a gifted, experienced senior who has been mentioned as a possible All-American candidate.

Then there is the depressing news that Maurice Simmons, a

promising linebacker recruit, has been found guilty by a Compton jury of two felonies and a misdemeanor in connection with a street robbery before he even enrolled at school. Reportedly, Simmons and a codefendant were arrested by the Los Angeles County sheriff's deputies after they robbed a man on the street at gunpoint. Though Simmons was not alleged to have handled the gun, authorities said they found the firearm and the victim's belongings in Simmons's car.

Carroll's voice grows uncharacteristically sad as he talks about the Simmons's decision after practice. "I feel really bad for his family," he says. "It is a really difficult situation, the most unfortunate news we could get. We feel sorry for everything he and his family have to go through." Simmons is not likely to be admitted to the university now, so Carroll doesn't have to deal with the situation any further than that. Still, you can tell by the look on his face that he is upset, knowing the young man and those close to him, remembering the joy he saw from all parties when Simmons officially signed his letter of intent to attend USC.

Football-wise, all that pales to what happens on the third day of practice. Mark Sanchez, the strong-armed junior Carroll has been carefully grooming for three years to take over the starting quarterback job, throws a casual predrill pass to teammate Clay Matthews and collapses on the ground. Teammates think he is joking. Some even chuckle and go on about their business, but when they look back, Sanchez is still crumbled on the turf. Team trainers rush over and discover the quarterback has suffered a dislocated left kneecap. They quickly snap it back into place, then cart him from the field for X-rays and an MRI exam. The results show no ligament, cartilage, or bone damage, and a huge sigh of relief can be heard echoing across the large expanse of Howard Jones Field. "We lucked out," says the always optimistic Carroll, but no one is sure what exactly will happen next. Sanchez's left leg is wrapped in a cast to immobilize the knee. He'll wear it at least through the weekend, then slowly begin an undetermined rehab period. "I hope to get back in time for the first game," the quarterback says.

Realistically, however, that won't be easy, and it's entirely possible Carroll will have to open against Virginia with Arkansas transfer Mitch Mustain or redshirt freshman Aaron Corp, neither of whom has started a game at USC.

Typically, Carroll is immediately upbeat about the situation. "This is an extraordinary moment for Mitch and Aaron," he says. "My thought is, we have a guy like Mitch and a guy like Aaron that can jump in and take their shots at this thing until Mark's back in here and battling with them. This is an opportunity, and how we deal with it and how we handle it is important, not the fact that something happened."

Normal people, including most USC fans, have trouble understanding Carroll's reaction. They think he should be dejected, even disconsolate about possibly losing his starting quarterback three weeks away from the season opener. But they don't know this coach and the way he thinks. To him, this is just another challenge. If Sanchez is, indeed, out for at least a few weeks, Carroll considers this is a perfect chance for both him and his players to show how competitive they really are. Suddenly, there will be a practice field duel again at quarterback, and you can almost see the renewed excitement flashing in Carroll's eyes.

"Like we've always said, this is all about competition," he says. The people closest to him will tell you that Carroll lives to compete. "He'll try to beat you at anything, whether it is playing catch with a Wiffle ball or drinking more Mountain Dews than you," says Sports Information Director Tim Tessalone. Everything with him is a competition, and nothing exemplifies that more than the way he coaches his football team. "I think back to my first couple days here," says Ruel, who has worked in both college and the pros. "He has a formula. It's about day-to-day competition in practice. It's about enjoying everything out here. It's a lot different than other places I've worked. There is a plan every day. There is no mixed message. It's about competing every snap."

Carroll says he formulated the philosophy that drives him by reading a John Wooden book in 2000, when he happened to be between coaching jobs. "It was the spark I needed to begin organizing my ideas into a philosophy that would be the basis for what we have here," Carroll says. "When I really soul-searched, I realized it all came down to one thing. I was a competitor. That's me, it's what I've been my whole life. I had to be true to who I was. I didn't want to pretend to be someone or something I'm not."

This is not a manufactured message. This is something Carroll spends long hours thinking deeply about, as proved by the story he tells concerning a recruiting visit he made in San Diego not long ago. "I watched the player and started thinking about all he was going to have to go through to become a high-profile recruit," Carroll says. "Then I was sitting on a plane going back to L.A. from San Diego, and these thoughts just came rushing out of me. So I wrote them down. I realized the message wasn't just for this one kid we were recruiting. It was for everybody I coached." The result is sort of a Carroll version of Wooden's famous "Pyramid of Success." He liked it so much he read it at the team banquet following the 2007 season and printed it on the first inside page of the 2008 USC media guide. It is titled "Always Compete" and reads this way:

If you want to Win Forever . . .
Always Compete.
As you progress through your sporting life . . .
Always Compete.
You're gonna have to make Choices in Life and those Choices
    need to be Conscious Decisions. There's only one person in
    Control here and that person is You . . .
You hold All the cards. You are the Master of You. It's time to
    admit it . . .
You have always known this. So if you're ready, act on it . . .
Always Compete.
Don't you dare try to be too Cool, don't you dare be afraid of
    Life, just "Dare to be Great" and Let it Rip.
Always be Humble, Always be Kind, Always be Respectful . . .
Always Compete!

Everything You do counts and screams who You are . . . there
 is no hiding from You.
Act as if the Whole World will know who you are . . .
Always Compete.
Be True to Yourself and Let Nothing hold you back.
Compete to be the Greatest You and that will Always Be
 enough and that will be a Lifetime!
Always Compete.

The competition resumes on Howard Jones Field, and the quarterbacks who back up Sanchez seem eager and excited. Mustain, the much-hyped, more experienced Arkansas transfer, is widely expected to take over the position in Sanchez's absence. He went 8-0 as the starter at Arkansas as a freshman before controversy flared up with then head coach Houston Nutt, and Mustain eventually felt it was best to leave. The National High School Player of the Year as a senior (much like Sanchez, who is a year younger), Mustain sat out his transfer year by practicing on the Trojans scout team, demonstrating a strong, accurate arm and much promise. Many felt he had an excellent chance to beat out Sanchez in spring practice, but it didn't happen.

Surprisingly, not much happens with this opportunity, either. At least early on, Mustain does not seize control of the position as expected. Corp, the more mobile of the two who had such an outstanding spring game, seems more relaxed and confident, maybe because the expectations for him are not as high. Whatever the reason, after the first two of three scheduled Coliseum scrimmages leading up to opening game week, Corp seems to have earned a narrow advantage. "Everything is still up in the air and we'll just see," says Carroll. "There's no rush yet."

Meanwhile, Sanchez has his cast off and has begun running and throwing some passes. The offense has been so inconsistent in the early scrimmages that there is a growing suspicion it won't be at its best until Sanchez returns. Nevertheless, the early odds are probably still against that happening in time for the Virginia opener.

At least the offensive line has begun to take shape. Byers's affliction is diagnosed as Rocky Mountain spotted fever, something he apparently contracted in a summer visit back home in Colorado. The senior guard is treated with antibiotics and slowly regains his strength in time to return to practice three days before the team's final preseason scrimmage. Not that the one piece of good news completely offsets more of the bad. Joe McKnight, the sophomore tailback who figures to be the team's No. 1 playmaker on offense, is hit by a series of strange mishaps. First, he is sidelined by a serious skin irritation. Then teammate Brice Butler accidentally closes a dormitory door on McKnight's hand, injuring two fingers, slightly fracturing the tip of one. Finally, McKnight suffers a hyperextended elbow in the second scrimmage, forcing him to the sideline for another couple of days, if not longer. The injury list isn't limited to offense, either. Cary Harris, one of the starting cornerbacks, suffers a dislocated shoulder in practice. He could be out a while, too. The only consolation for Carroll is that tailback and cornerback are two of the deepest positions on the team, with terrific football players at both spots who will be eager for the chance at more playing time.

If all the gathering problems are weighing on the head coach, you wouldn't know it on the final Tuesday of fall camp. Carroll pauses before practice to go across the street and give the team band a pep talk. The band members proceed to scream when they see him, like tourists who've just spotted a movie star in a Hollywood department store. "They're so easy," Carroll says later, grinning. "It doesn't matter what you say to them, they love it." At practice that afternoon, still another injured player is added to the list. C.J. Gable, described by the coaches as "the best rounded" of all the tailbacks (that's coachspeak, meaning he's the only one who is an effective pass blocker) goes down after a collision and stays down for several long minutes. Carroll rushes over, takes a quick look, then trots back to practice. The team trainers stay and administer to the well-liked sophomore, who appears to have an injured ankle and hip. Gable is eventually trucked off, MRIs are scheduled, and practice proceeds. When it's over, Carroll follows his usual routine. He pauses afterward, like someone running for political office, to sign autographs and pose for pictures. No one gets turned down, not even an entire youth football team that waits patiently for almost thirty minutes until the coach spots them and comes over. "Where do you want me to stand?" he asks the adults waiting with their digital cameras. They point to the middle, and the young players look up in awe. "How you guys doin'?" Carroll asks. "You gonna root hard for the Trojans this season?" If they weren't before, they are now.

After an extended chat with the L.A. media, next stop, between even more handshakes and autograph seekers, is across the street at the Galen Athletic Center, where Carroll quickly fills up a plastic foam box with food from the players' training table, mixing in rice, some kind of meat, and who knows what else into one large glob, then pauses to fill up a cup with lemonade. "Come on," he says, to me, "now we're going to go look at tape of practice." He enters Heritage Hall, ducks between all the gleaming trophy cases filled with Heismans and whatnot, and practically skips up the stairs to the second-floor football offices.

"I gave the coaches the night off," he says, but he doesn't give himself the same luxury. Later, he and some of the grad assistants will be taking the players to see the movie *Tropic Thunder,* giving them a rare couple of hours away from meetings and camp boredom. For now, he settles into a cushy chair and Pete Dalis, the young administrative assistant in charge of preparing the tapes, snaps to attention and flicks on an iPod to provide Carroll with whatever musical accompaniment he prefers. "He's a lot like me about his music," Dalis says. "He's cross-generational. He likes some modern stuff like Jack Johnson, the Foo Fighters, the Killers, Coldplay, but he also likes the O'Jays and Springsteen and U-2." Carroll begins shoveling in his dinner, like someone who just wants to get some food in him. "Is that a little James Taylor there?" he asks Dalis, who smiles and shakes his head affirmatively.

Up on the giant, wall-sized screen is where Carroll focuses

most of his attention, with a fork in one hand, his trusty remote clicker in the other. He begins by studying the early practice one-on-one sessions that pit wide receiver against cornerback and defensive lineman against offensive lineman in tough, individual drills. It's competition, remember? Carroll loves it.

"Oh, nice grab there," he yelps as up on the screen Jordan Cameron, a promising JC transfer, spears a ball in the end zone with one outstretched hand. Carroll plays it back and runs it again, then a third time. "Wow," he says, "that's a really good catch." Now he watches as Butch Lewis, a projected starter at offensive tackle, stands his ground in the pocket and batters a couple of young pass rushers. "Look at him, look at him," shouts Carroll. "He's making it look easy." Then he turns to me and points to the screen. "See that kid there," he says, nodding toward number 70, freshman offensive tackle Tyron Smith. "He's the best athlete we've ever seen at the position, and it's not even close. He's going to be something."

Carroll asks Dalis if he's heard anything about C.J., meaning Gable. "They say it's a high ankle sprain and some kind of injury to his hip," Dalis says. "They're not sure how bad it is yet." Carroll nods, then, as if his positive nature instantly kicks back in, returns his attention to the screen, looking as eager as a kid being treated to his first action adventure. After more than ninety minutes of watching tape, Carroll gets up from his chair and walks out of the room. "He's about to tell the players they're going to the movie," says Dalis. Ten minutes later, a loud, window-rattling roar can be heard from the floor below. "Guess he just told them," says Dalis, smiling.

Two days later, USC conducts its final full scrimmage of the camp, a game-simulated, afternoon occasion held at the Coliseum in front of a large, midweek crowd of Trojans fans estimated to total more than 10,000. The coach wants the players to learn what their routine will be like when the real games start, so he takes them to their regular midtown hotel to sleep the night before, then buses them to the giant saucer on Figueroa hours early, walking among the crowd, then up and through the famous peristyle end and onto the field, just like they will on September 13 for the first home game against Ohio State.

The scrimmage, with assorted players nicked up and others tired and worn down from a grueling four weeks of practice, is not pretty. The Trojans' offense looks sluggish in the first half, then picks up some in the second, with both Mustain, who has his best scrimmage of the summer, and Corp leading the team on long scoring drives. McKnight, just a week after his hyperextended elbow, runs smoothly and effectively at tailback, and Cameron, the star of Carroll's tape show a few nights earlier, makes a couple of big catches, as does Blake Ayles, a 6'5", 255–pound tight end who could prove to be the most talked-about freshman on the roster. Most of the big names on defense have limited playing time, but others, like junior All-American safety Taylor Mays and promising freshman tackle Armond Armstead, manage to make impressions.

Best of all, though, is the forecast that Sanchez, who definitely appeared questionable for the opener ten days earlier, is making a swift recovery from his dislocated kneecap. He participated in 7-on-7 passing drills earlier in the day and impressed the coaches. "He looked terrific," says Carroll. "He threw like Jonathan Papelbon, a ninety-nine-mile-an-hour fastball," says offensive coordinator Steve Sarkisian. "If he comes back and is ready to practice early next week, he'll likely be the starter in Virginia," says Carroll.

The beads of perspiration gleam under the gray hair that spills down on Carroll's forehead as he strolls, smiling, through an army of cardinal and gold–clad well-wishers on the floor of the Coliseum.

After living through a camp full of early crises, the updated bulletin on Sanchez is, on this warm, slightly humid Los Angeles afternoon, the best news a coach could hear heading into the first game week of a challenging new season.

Pete Profile

Forever Young

It is the one recurring thread that runs through the fabric of Pete Carroll's life. For everything he has done, for all he has accomplished shaking the cobwebs out of USC's football program and bringing it back to the heights of glory and beyond, for every glittering award and trophy that continues to pile up in his home and office, one thing about him has never changed.

He remains an eighteen-year-old kid running around in a fifty-seven-year-old body. He remains the coach who sprints from one end of the practice field to the other like an eager young sophomore who is trying to make the team. He remains the prankster who loves to pull outrageous tricks on his unsuspecting players.

He remains Forever Young.

"You don't get that in coaches today," says Matt Leinart, the Phoenix Cardinal quarterback who was a three-time All American and Heisman Trophy winner for Carroll at USC, "where he's kind of a little kid inside a grown man." Lawrence Jackson, his 2007 All-American defensive end now with the Seattle Seahawks, says, "He does some things that you don't expect him to do, like sing a rap song . . . I don't know how old he is. He's something going on twenty-two." Dallas Sartz, who started at linebacker for him in 2003–2006, adds, "Some of the stuff he does is just goofy. When he's out there, he's one of the guys, play-ing catch with everybody, running around and playing safety. It's fun to play for a coach like that."

At USC, they like to tell the story of the recruit who was taken to the beach with a Trojans assistant coach. They walked onto the pier to get a full view of the surroundings and to breathe in the crisp ocean air. Suddenly, they heard someone shouting at them from down below. Startled, they looked and it was Carroll, boogie-boarding through the water and waving at them with a huge smile on his face. Again, it was an example of the little boy surfacing inside the grown man.

To discover what makes the man, perhaps you first have to look into what he was like in his formative years. For Carroll, it began in his be-loved Bay Area, where he grew up in an upscale tract home in Green-brae, part of affluent Marin County near San Francisco. It was not only home for the Carrolls, it was, apparently, home for the entire neighbor-hood. The kids would all congregate to play out front and swim in the back. "It was a great place," says Skip Corsini, who has known Carroll since they were in junior high together. "We'd play all day, then his mom and dad would have a barbecue and feed you. I still remember that if you stayed long enough to watch Johnny Carson late at night, after it was over, they'd give you a bowl of corn flakes before you went home."

Jim Carroll, Pete's late father, was a liquor salesman by day and the life of the party by night. He was the first one to greet you walking into a room, gregarious and extroverted and, yes, competitive, very com-petitive. He was the kind of man who felt like everyone else's second father. "He'd take us to all the 49ers games at Kezar [Stadium]," Corsini says. "We always had a great time." Rita Carroll, Pete's mom, who has also passed away, provided the kind of warm, sensitive presence that was the perfect complement to her more outgoing husband. "She was Pete's core," says Carroll's friend, Dave Perron. "His soul comes from her."

"Everybody loved going to the Carrolls," says Bob Troppmann, Pete's coach at Redwood High in Marin County. "There were always kids there, sandwiches were always out by the pool, and when they weren't swimming, they were out in the street playing." The word everyone uses about Pete is "energy." If his batteries never seem to run low even now, those who were there say it was even more apparent when he was a kid. "His energy level has always been unbelievable," says Perron, who first met Pete when they played against each other in high school. "There are not many people in the world who are wired like that." Orsini says it didn't matter what game they were playing in the streets of Marin, Pete was always going full speed. "He not only loved to play, he loved to compete," Perron says.

Some things never change. "It didn't matter if we were playing 'dead ball' against the driveway garage, cards, or shuffleboard, Pete always wanted to beat you." Troppmann chuckles when he remembers his favorite protégé growing up. "He was always sort of hyper, just like you see him on the sidelines now," he says. "His mind was always going, even when he was playing Pop Warner and freshman football."

Carroll was, and is, a seemingly happy, secure person. "I always think something good is about to happen," he says, but he admits it wasn't always that way. "I had a dark period there in high school," he says. "I was so small. It killed me. I was only about a hundred and ten pounds-ish. Puberty was a mystery to me. It didn't happen." But the fire that burned in his competitive belly somehow managed to overcome all that. "When he came to Redwood High, he weighed about a hundred and thirteen pounds," Troppmann says. "I think he put some rocks in his pocket or something, but he managed to make the weight to play freshman football." His style was exactly what you would expect. "He hustled nonstop," Troppmann says. "That was just him. He played football all three years, also played basketball and baseball. He was just a gym rat, the kind of kid who was always around. He couldn't get enough of sports."

Carroll was like almost every red-blooded male in America back then. He didn't want to just play sports for fun. He wanted to play them for a living. "There was never any doubt about his ambition," Corsini says. "He wanted to be a pro football player all his life. It drove him then, and I think, in many ways, it still drives him." It's not like Carroll is afraid to admit it. "Yeah, I'm ticked about it," he says. "I think I should be playing. I tell the players all the time, 'You're doing what I always wanted to do.' I went to the World Football League and was cut and tried to get on a team when the NFL players were on strike and couldn't do it. Just one game, and I think I would have been happy. I think it's motivated me in what has happened since. It's driven me. I just wish I could have been bigger. I know I could have played."

Growing up in Marin exposed Carroll to other things, too. "It was the late sixties, and Marin County was ground zero for a lot of stuff," Perron says. "It opened you up to a lot of spiritual things. There is an element he has with the Indian religion, a little schtick he got from Berkeley at the time. They called Bill Clinton the first black president. I always tell Pete, 'You're the first black-white president,' because he identifies so well with the African American community. It's amazing, really. Marin County was predominantly white, but somehow Pete has this thing with the black community. He understands who they are, where they came from. He's been in their homes and knows how to relate. It's pretty remarkable."

Carroll seems to have so many warm memories of his youth, you can't completely shake the Bay Area out of him. Even today, when you walk into his office, his computer is tuned to KFOG, a Bay Area radio station. Maybe all that fun he had growing up helps explain why he continues to act as if he were thirty years younger. Whether it's playing tough, hacking, pickup basketball with his assistants at midday in the off-season or simply dropping back to throw 50-yard spirals to USC's wide receivers in practice, he comes off as someone who never wants to grow up.

"You watch him now, and the energy he exudes is not much different than what he had as a seventeen-year-old," says Perron. "I've gone to his practices at USC," says Troppmann, "and Pete is all over the field. He's always been a hand-on-the-shoulder, pat-on-the-back kind of guy, but at USC, everything is going a mile a minute and everybody gets in the act, but every time you look up, there's Pete in the middle of it. But then, he was always sort of hyper, just as he is now."

He remains the fifty-seven-year-old with the enthusiasm and energy of a teenager. Maybe the story that tells you everything you need to know about Carroll is the one his friends always bring up. It seems there was a player in Minneapolis he was trying to recruit. Bud Grant, the former great coach of the Vikings and one of Carroll's mentors, had a son, Mike, who was coaching in high school. Mike had this highly re-garded athlete Carroll had come to see, and not long after Pete ar-rived, the younger Grant had his star player in tow and wanted to introduce him personally. There was only one problem. He couldn't find the USC coach. He checked the locker room, the field, around the corner, just about everywhere he could think of, but had no luck. Fi-nally, after an extensive search of the entire campus, he located him.

Carroll was in the high school gym, happily shooting jump shots with the tenth graders.

III

Game One: A Healthy Roster
and a Quick Identity Test

Nick Holt listens to the question, then squints into the late afternoon August sun, taking a few moments to ponder his answer three days before the team's 2008 opener at Virginia. USC's defensive coordinator, his shaved head making him look like something straight off a Marine recruiting poster, is in charge of the tough, gifted unit that used to be run by his boss, head coach Pete Carroll. For his first five years at USC, Carroll, the noted defense specialist, was his own defensive coordinator. In 2006, he gave up the title and hired Holt, who'd been the head coach at Idaho. Now, some three seasons later, Holt's defense is the Trojans' most imposing unit, a group that will have to be dominant for USC to live up to its high preseason national ranking. Holt is asked if he feels more pressure knowing his boss is one of the more acclaimed defensive coaches in the business.

"Yeah, there is more pressure," Holt says. "You know you're being scrutinized more. He makes it hard, but he makes it good, too. He does it in a positive way. He finds creative ways for us to become better teachers. He is always looking at our methods, coaching us, correcting us, advising us. Every day, he critiques us as well as our players."

Holt is an interesting study, a forty-six-year-old family man with no hair and intense eyes who regularly listens to National Public Radio instead of the usual sports-talk rants. He swears he doesn't read the newspapers, either, but even he understands this is an unusual year for the Trojans. For the first time in recent memory, there is, at least at the start of the season, no legitimate All-American candidate on offense for USC. The quarterback is new, the tailbacks operate by committee, the search continues for a go-to receiver, and the offensive line has only one returning starter. Ah, but the defense is a different story. It has great players flowing as freely as Rey Maualuga's hair. Regarded as college football's most intimidating player, Maualuga is a unanimous preseason All-American pick at middle linebacker. His buddy, Brian Cushing, the strongside linebacker, joins him on most All-American teams, and Taylor Mays, the 6'3" 230–pound free safety with the kind of prototype NFL body that has the pro scouts drooling all over their stopwatches, is a returning All American.

Carroll already is calling it the fastest defense he's ever had, but for the Trojans to compete for a national title, it might have to be the best one, as well. Holt, with his shaved head showered with perspiration, knows what people are saying. "Honestly, we don't look at it that way," he says. "I know it sounds like BS, but we really don't. Are the expectations high here? Yeah, they should be. It's USC. I expect us to be great. If you don't expect that, how are you ever going to be great?" Despite the loss of Sedrick Ellis, the All-American and two-time Pac-10 Defensive Player of the Year, a nose tackle who might have been among the half-dozen finest players of the Carroll era, Holt thinks this could be a better defense than last season's. "If we can get more turnovers, yeah, I think we can be better," he says. "I think we have more depth than we did a year ago. Some of our young guys, they can really play."

For Carroll's part, he seems in remarkably good humor for a head coach preparing to play a pressurized first game. Part of it is that almost all his injured players are healthy now and ready to perform. Mark Sanchez, the quarterback who dislocated his knee in mid-August, has recovered so quickly it has surprised even the team's medical staff. Jeff Byers, the lone returning starter on the offensive line, is fully over his illness, and even C.J. Gable, the tailback who appeared seriously hurt after one practice, has bounced back and is playing close to full speed again. Sanchez, Byers, Brian Cushing, and safety Kevin Ellison, the four clear leaders of the team, are named captains after an election that almost seemed preordained.

The big talk leading up to game week is an ad that appears in all the L.A. newspapers. It features a picture of Rick Neuheisel, the new coach at crosstown rival UCLA, and proclaims, in large letters, THE FOOTBALL MONOPOLY IN LOS ANGELES IS OFFICIALLY OVER. In an interview with KSPN, the Trojans flagship radio station, someone shows Carroll the ad and asks for a comment. "Who is that?" he asks, smiling. "Joe Torre?"

The coach's relaxed mood carries over to the first Tuesday media luncheon of the season. As usual, the large conference room in Heritage Hall is SRO, encircled by TV cameras from all the local Southern California outlets, as well as a number of dot-com productions. The coach's head table is flanked by two long tables filled with writers hustling to finish their usual fare of pasta and salad before Carroll makes his appearance. When he does, dressed in a white, long-sleeved body shirt with the school's letters emblazoned over his heart, Carroll looks at the writer's plates and kids Tim Tessalone, the sports information director. "Nine, ten months later, and still the same menu?" he asks. Before Tessalone can offer a retort, Carroll sits down and says, "Well, we're ready for some football, here we go. We're really pumped up at this time. We're coming out of camp on a pretty good feeling, particularly in terms of our guys all being available to us."

Most of the key question marks seem to have been answered, too. The biggest was the offensive line, where, early on, the inexperience was more evident than the enlarged bellies you usually see on most offensive linemen. "They're puppies right now," said Pat Ruel, the crusty offensive line coach at one point. "I've got to get a lot of paper to get them trained." Apparently, the training worked. Once Byers recovered from his strange bout with Rocky Mountain spotted fever, the kids seemed to follow his lead and as the season approaches, the blocking appears much more crisp and consistent. Of course, they haven't played a real game yet, either.

The quarterback competition that appeared so up in the air in the spring was clarified, surprisingly, when Sanchez went down with his injury. Mitch Mustain was expected to jump at the opportunity to take over in Sanchez's absence, but he didn't. He was regularly outplayed by Aaron Corp, the thin, redshirt freshman who had starred in the spring game. Neither, however, demonstrated full command of the offense, something Sanchez managed to do as soon as he returned, even if his passing was a little rusty in his first few days. It was as if his absence had erased any previous questions about who was No. 1 at the position, and while Carroll keeps trying to duck the issue of who is No. 2, that is obvious, too. Only Corp has been getting regular reps in practice, alongside Sanchez. Mustain, who has to be regarded as a major disappointment at this point, has been relegated to No. 3. By the end of the week, Carroll even admits as much to reporters.

"What about tailback?" someone asks Carroll after Tuesday's practice. "When will you name a starter?" The coach hesitates for a moment and then says, "We won't. They're all starters to us." Only they're not, really. For regular practice observers, it is clear Joe McKnight and Stafon Johnson are the co–No. 1s with C.J. Gable third and Allen Bradford fourth. Which one will start at Virginia remains to be seen, but it is McKnight, the one with the most big-play ability, who needs to have a breakout season for the Trojans to make a run at the BCS title game. Always before, when USC was successful under Carroll, there was a game-breaking player who would help them pull out pivotal games, especially on the road. If it wasn't Reggie Bush, it was Mike Williams or Dwayne Jarrett. There was no such gamebreaker in 2007, although McKnight offered hints than he could develop into one. Now he will have his chance, with Carroll planning to deploy him a lot like he did Bush, both as a runner and a receiver, hoping to spring him out into space, where he can do his best work.

There is a crowd at wide receiver as well, although by the end of camp, the three that played extensively a year ago—Patrick Turner, Vidal Hazleton, and David Ausberry—were being heavily pressed by Arkansas transfer Damian Williams, 5'10" speedball Travon Patterson, and Ronald Johnson, the deep threat who never could establish much of a rapport with quarterback John David Booty a year ago. Someone in that group needs to become the go-to receiver that was lacking last season. Of the candidates, Williams, who is a bit smaller and thinner, but quicker and more instinctive than last year's threesome, seems to be the early favorite.

Although USC has opened a 19-point choice by the odds-makers, Virginia, coming off a 9-4 season and a trip to the Gator Bowl, should offer an interesting test. Call it a battle of the ex-New York Jets coaches. Both Carroll and Al Groh, the Cavaliers head coach, coached the AFC team in New York. "Only difference is, they didn't want him to leave," says Carroll, grinning. Groh, a disciple of Bill Parcells and Bill Belichick, departed after one season with the Jets to take the job at Virginia, where he has been for seven seasons, two of them as ACC Coach of the Year.

If you have a choice, you don't want to begin a rebuilding season by playing USC, but that seems to be the task facing Groh. He has fourteen starters to replace, including All-American defensive end Chris Long, the son of NFL Hall of Famer Howie Long and the No. 2 overall pick in the draft by the Los Angeles Rams. Then there was quarterback Jameel Sewell, who was suspended for a year for academic problems. It's no wonder Groh seems a bit overwhelmed by what he sees on tape of the Trojans.

"It starts with the talent level," he says. "When you have a higher talent level, the more comfortable you feel with expanding your schemes. There certainly is a very, very high talent level with their players. It is usually pretty easy for those players to get things in a little bit quicker fashion . . ."

Carroll seems to agree. After practice is over on Tuesday, after he is finished signing a zillion autographs and posing for his usual fifty or sixty pictures, he is standing with me in a small corner in front of the Galen Athletic Center before heading in to grab some dinner. For the first time, he talks about the new, aggressive style he hopes to see in this year's team.

"Having Mark at quarterback gives us a chance to do some other things," he says. "I think we'll throw downfield more. John David [Booty] was very conservative. He wouldn't throw it unless he was sure he had a wide-open receiver. That was good in some ways, but I think Mark could be more explosive. He'll use his feet to avoid the rush and give his receivers more time to get open. I'd like to see us get back to the way we were a few years ago, scoring more points on offense."

On defense, too, Carroll might be offering a different look. In practice, the Trojans were blitzing more than anyone could remember. He smiles when that's brought up, as if he had been waiting for someone to mention it. "I think we have the best cover guys we've had in a long time," he says. "If you trust your cover guys, it allows you to do more things defensively." The question is, how much of this new style will Carroll want to showcase in Virginia, knowing the monster game with Ohio State is only two weeks later? I am just about to ask that when Carroll seems to sense it. He turns, ducking into the Galen Athletic Center restaurant, the door closing abruptly behind him. The implication is obvious. We'll all have to wait until Saturday for that answer.

When the team finally leaves L.A. early Thursday afternoon, the trip goes smoothly, until Carroll and his squad arrive at Scott Stadium on the Virginia campus for their walk-through practice on Friday. Virginia officials inform them because of a heavy rain that had soaked the field the previous days, the grass is still being painted. The Trojans won't be able to use the field.

"I'm disappointed," Carroll says, "but we understand, with the elements and all." Sensing a need for privacy, the coach then switches from practicing at a local high school to working out at a small, secluded private school on a field shielded by trees. The only spectators end up being a group of children who emerge from a classroom heading for a nearby playground. Not that there was much to see. The Trojans spend an hour at basically half-speed in shorts and T-shirts.

Game day dawns hot and muggy, featuring the kind of humidity kids from Southern California rarely experience. It doesn't seem to faze anyone, especially Sanchez, who is already emerging as the clear, new leader of this team. Even in warm-ups, his energy is palpable. If the knee he injured less than three weeks earlier is bothering him, you could never tell. He has waited too long for this moment. He arrived at USC with credentials as formidable as any quarterback before him. He was the National High School Player of the Year at Mission Viejo High in Orange County, but Matt Leinart was a senior and the reigning Heisman Trophy winner that first year, so Sanchez redshirted. Then John David Booty, who had waited even longer for his chance, had first shot in 2006. Although there were some who always felt Sanchez had the higher ceiling, Carroll believes in waiting your turn. So Booty started and did well for the next two seasons. No, he was not Leinart, but he lost only three games he started and led the team to two impressive victories in the Rose Bowl.

Now it is Sanchez's time, and above all else, this 2008 opener is about him. USC's defense is widely recognized as one of the best in the land. It is up to the offense and its fiery new quarterback to show that the Trojans can score points as well as prevent them. Both Leinart and Booty, each now playing in the NFL, text message Sanchez during the week, telling him to enjoy the new experience he is about to have. They mention one other thing, Sanchez says, "Don't be nervous. Just prepare." That shouldn't be a problem. Steve Sarkisian appears on ESPN before the game and says that Sanchez prepares harder than any player at any position they've had since Carroll took over at USC. Sanchez is still preparing early Saturday morning, but the excitement he feels is making it difficult. "I don't feel nervous like I did for the three games last year," he says, mentioning the three starts he made, going 2-1 when Booty was injured. "Just more excited. I'm feeling a different kind of nerves." But no one is expecting him to be grimacing or frowning from the pressure. "I can't," he says, smiling. "It's too much fun."

Turns out, the fun is just beginning. With a loud, raucous crowd of 64, 947 jammed into Scott Stadium, USC's most impressive weapon, its vaunted defense, the one Coach Holt said could be this good, turns off the volume early. Virginia's young quarterback Pete Lalich, starting his first collegiate game, looks like someone caught on the train tracks with a speeding locomotive bearing down on him. Maualuga, Cushing, and the rest of the Trojans blurring-fast defense surround him in the first quarter, never allowing the Cavaliers to get a first down, let alone wedge their way from deep in their own territory. The result is that the first fifteen minutes are played entirely on Virginia's half of the field.

Given that luxury, Sanchez and USC's parade of gifted skill players proceed to put on a highlight-reel show, scoring 3 touchdowns in the first eleven minutes, with three different Trojans tailbacks finding their way into the end zone. The game is basically over at that point, although an excessive celebration penalty and an ensuing roughing-the-passer call allow Virginia to mount its lone scoring drive of the day and briefly cut the margin to 21–7. It is 24–7 at the half, but USC quickly regains its momentum after intermission, featuring the offensive line blocking with surprising effectiveness and Sanchez throwing the ball beautifully, even hitting Johnson with the kind of 49-yard bomb that had been missing the previous season.

The final score is 52–7, and if the Trojan coaches had scripted it, the game couldn't have turned out much better. "Everything happened just right," Carroll would say afterward. "Too bad we let them score." Not that Virginia's lone touchdown took anything away from a performance that answered most of the pregame question marks. Pat Ruel's offensive line, with only one returning starter, looks as good, if not better, than the more decorated 2007 bunch. There are plays when Sanchez seems to have enough time to check homework assignments before choosing an open receiver. The protection is that spectacular.

Although he has a few balls batted down and one interception on a tipped pass, Sanchez is almost flawless. He completes 26 of 35 passes for 338 yards and 3 touchdowns, and his leaping, arm-pumping celebration after the 49-yard scoring connection to Johnson only emphasizes the enthusiasm he brings to a team that lacked some a year earlier. "Mark brings energy," says tailback Bradford, in the postgame locker room. You think?

Bradford and the posse of tailbacks are utilized just the way Carroll and Sarkisian wish they could always choreograph it. Gable, Johnson, and Bradford each carry the ball 9 times and all three score touchdowns. McKnight, whose 18-yard punt return set up the first touchdown, carries it 6 times and catches 4 passes. The receivers also put on a show, led by Johnson, or "RoJo," as the players call him, who should be a consistent deep threat with Sanchez throwing, and Williams, who looks like the go-to guy many predicted, finishing with 7 receptions for 91 yards. USC rattles off 558 yards in offense, 208 on the ground. Virginia, meanwhile, manages only 32 yards rushing and 187 yards overall.

Not surprisingly, the Cavaliers are duly impressed afterward. "Their speed was pretty unbelievable," says Lalich, the quarterback who will see better days. "The holes closed awfully fast," says Groh, a coach who can appreciate a good defense when he sees one. "Those two linebackers can really run and close space and the two safeties play like linebackers."

Much to Carroll's delight, the Trojans force four turnovers in the final thirty minutes, and although most of the big names play well on defense, there are other, less-hyped players, like pass-rush specialist Clay Matthews and linebacker Kaluka Maiava, who are even more noticeable. Maybe most important, Carroll's midweek hint of a new, aggressive USC style is showcased. The defense starts blitzing early and never stops, while the offense, with Sanchez's mobility giving him extra time to throw, looks every bit as explosive as the head coach had promised.

The only real question afterward was whether the Trojans were that good, or Virginia was that bad. Probably, it was a little of both, something Carroll and the coaches will undoubtedly mention as the buildup for the Ohio State megagame in two weeks officially begins.

The Buckeyes, ranked No. 2 or 3 in most national polls after the first week, are as experienced and polished as the unranked Cavaliers were young and ragged. But even then, before any alarms can go off in USC's team meetings, there is news out of Ohio that Chris "Beanie" Wells, the Buckeyes All-American tailback and Heisman Trophy candidate, was injured in the team's 43–0 victory over Youngstown State. The early word is that it is a foot injury, and although X-rays are negative, there is understandable concern among Ohio State's ardent supporters.

Carroll, of course, immediately dismisses such talk, saying the Trojans intend to prepare as if Wells will play. "That's how we'll go about it until we know different," he says. The Ohio State game has been the major topic of conversation among USC alumni and boosters for most of the summer, and although Carroll and his coaches kept insisting they were only thinking about Virginia, everyone knew it was in the back of their minds and maybe flickering on more than a few of their summertime tape screens, as well.

Now it can be up-front for everyone to discuss, even if there is a two-week-long wait for the kickoff between these two acknowledged national powerhouses. If anything, that extra time will only increase the Ohio State buildup and add to the anticipation. Sanchez, his eyes already dancing with excitement, looks up at reporters and grins.

"The Coliseum will be rocking," he says. That it will.

Pete Profile

The Accidental Choice

Hardcore USC fans shudder to think about it now, but the truth is Pete Carroll wasn't the No. 1 choice to replace Paul Hackett back in December of 2000. Turns out, he wasn't the No. 2 or even the No. 3 choice, if you can believe it.

Hiring the most successful college football coach of the new millennium was, in shocking retrospect, something of an accident. It wasn't so much a result of Carroll being in the right place at the right time as it was a case of USC almost tripping over itself, only to look up at the end of a crazy, slightly misguided process to find this bright, hyperenergetic candidate more than happy to take the job.

"Really, Pete was my first choice all along," says Athletic Director Mike Garrett now. Sure he was. If that was really the case, why did he and his assistant at the time, Darryl Gross, interview then Oregon State coach Dennis Erickson extensively and remain smugly confident that he would take the job? Why did they come within a last-minute phone call of hiring then San Diego Chargers coach Mike Riley? And what about Mike Bellotti, the highly-successful Oregon coach who had been widely rumored to be listening to overtures from Trojans officials?

Gross, currently the athletics director at Syracuse University, now admits Erickson was USC's first choice. "We thought it was 95 percent sure we had landed Dennis Erickson," Gross says. "We thought it was a done deal. To this day, I'm still shocked Dennis didn't take the job. And when I run into him now, he tells me turning down the USC job was the dumbest thing he ever did in his life. When Dennis fell out of the running, the picture all changed."

That didn't mean Carroll immediately came into focus. Riley was in the midst of a struggling season with the San Diego Chargers, and while his NFL head-coaching credentials had to be questioned, he'd already proven he was a solid college coach. He previously had gone back to his alma mater, Oregon State, and set the foundation for what would become a surprisingly solid program in Corvallis. Earlier, he'd been a former USC assistant under John Robinson, who had the reputation as an excellent offensive coach and someone who had an extraordinary rapport with his players. He was a known quantity to Garrett, and obviously someone who was an attractive candidate—attractive enough, apparently, to bring in for final approval with USC president Steven Sample.

"I was about to get into a car to drive to Los Angeles and meet with Dr. Sample to hopefully seal the deal," Riley says. "That's when my cell phone rang." It was Dean Spanos, president of the Chargers, calling to tell him if he made that trip, he no longer had a job in San Diego. "I had not been told anything firmly yet by Mike Garrett and USC," Riley says, "so I couldn't afford to take the risk. I mean, I had a family and all, so I just couldn't do it."

Many believe Bellotti, who had built a terrific program at Oregon, would be the most exciting candidate of all. His teams were innovative, successful, and fun to watch, and Bellotti even looked the way most USC alums expected a Trojans head coach to look. Garrett would later admit that he interviewed Bellotti, but he insists he never offered him the job.

Carroll's name did come up at some point, along with Sonny Lubick of Colorado State. Garrett swears he had been aware of Carroll since his days as a defensive coordinator for the San Francisco 49ers, but after Hackett (who was hired almost in desperation) was dismissed, angry USC fans wanted someone with some instant recognition.

"That's why Mike went after Erickson first," Gross says. "He'd just won the Fiesta Bowl with Oregon State, and he was the hot coach of the moment."

When Erickson said no and Riley was short-circuited by the Chargers, the field suddenly opened up. Carroll, who had been aware of USC and its potential, was hungry to be a coach again, and eventually he was brought in for an interview. It was at the Marriott Hotel near Los Angeles International Airport, and Gross, who helped in the process, said Carroll, dressed in an expensive pinstripe suit, looked the part as soon as he stepped into the room. "He knocked it out of the park," Gross says of the interview. "He was so prepared. He knew what style he would play, how he'd hire a staff, what he'd do about recruiting. He had it all covered."

It was no coincidence. "I was ready for the challenge," Carroll says. "I thought it was an extraordinary opportunity." He had checked USC out among those in the coaching community, and although some felt that parity had come to the Pac-10, others whom he respected told him USC, with tremendous tradition and resources, was a program just waiting to explode back to prominence. It just needed the right coach to ignite the fuse.

When USC officially announced the hiring of Carroll, the Southern California media were not enthused. Those of us who were working newspaper people at the time studied his resume and saw what looked like a recycled Paul Hackett. Most of his success, like Hackett's, had been as a coordinator, not as a head coach, although he'd been the head man for both the New York Jets and the New England Patriots, leading the Pats to the playoffs on two different occasions. Still, he had no background in the Pac-10, no experience as a college head coach, no knowledge of recruiting in the area and, in a wild, offense-minded conference, he was known more as a defensive specialist.

His experiences as a head coach in the NFL, where he was fired twice, left him with a reputation as a coach who wasn't tough enough to lead professionals. He was too rah-rah, they said. "Peter Prep School," is what some called him. "I don't think they understood me very well," Carroll says. "They couldn't believe a head coach would ride a bike to and from practice. They thought I was a freak. I actually enjoyed the games. I loved it, loved competing at that level. I didn't look all tormented like those other guys."

You don't think he's specifically referring to that current New England coach in the gray hoodie, do you? Anyway, there were others who always thought Carroll got a bad rap in the pros. Boomer Esiason, the CBS broadcaster who was Carroll's first pro quarterback with the Jets in 1994, is one. "My experience with Pete is that I thought he was one of the most innovative, smartest head coaches I'd ever played for," says Esiason. "My only regret is that I was thirty-four at the time. I wish I could have given him what I had at twenty-six through twenty-eight." Esiason saw Carroll in his first year as a head coach at any level. "Going from coordinator to head coach is a big difference," he says. "He had a lot to learn. He had a lot of different methods that were awkward for older players. He was big on psychology and things like that. Some older vets didn't want to go down that road, but I thought the way he ran practice and approached games was brilliant. He ran some of the best practices I've ever been around. If Pete had a fault, it was that he never understood the political games you had to play. He could have ingratiated himself with [owner] Leon Hess a little more."

Maybe that's why Carroll only lasted one year with the Jets. His next NFL head coaching job was three years later, in New England, where he followed Bill Parcells and preceded Bill Belichick. In three years, he took the Patriots to the playoffs twice before going 8-8 his final season. "When he first came in, I know [owner Bob] Kraft saw him as the anti-Parcells," says *The Boston Globe* columnist Bob Ryan. "He and all of us felt how refreshing it was to have someone who could be cordial and nice off the field. We all rooted for him to succeed. It was kind of like rooting for a Labrador retriever. Every year it got worse. I know there were people who told me he was too rah-rah for the NFL, but it would be disingenuous for me to say that I saw that. I think Pete was handicapped some by [Drew] Bledsoe at quarterback. Would history be kinder to him if he could have had [Tom] Brady at that position? We'll never know. I'm not saying categorically that he can't coach in the league, but I do think he's found his perfect niche at USC."

Carroll's admirers and friends always felt his high-energy style would be an ideal fit at the collegiate level. "No question about it," says Dave Perron, who has known him since high school. "When he started at SC, he told me, 'Dave, this has so much potential!' He *knew* he was going to kill it. He just *knew*." That's what Carroll tried to tell the skeptical media back on that December day USC introduced him at a press conference in Heritage Hall. In what would come to be typical Carroll style, the Trojans' new head coach was enthusiastic enough to appear almost manic in front of the media. He refused to stand still, moving around the room the way Chris Rock moves around the stage. "This is a golden opportunity for me," he said, with a steely look in his eyes. "I don't think I could be more prepared for this."

Eight years later, Garrett, Gross, and every USC fan on the planet looks back and grimaces at how close the university came to hiring someone else. If landing the most successful college coach of his generation proved to be a strange combination of fortunate timing and dumb luck, one thing loyal Trojans everywhere are quick to agree on today:

They're extremely happy it turned out the way it did.

IV

Game Two: Finally, It's Time
to Play the Buckeyes

I s Pete more intense for this game? Well, let me put it this
way," says Ken Norton Jr. "Usually we stay working until ten
or so every night. This week we've been staying past twelve."

Pete Carroll probably has been staying even longer. It is not
uncommon for him to sleep in his office on the second floor of
Heritage Hall a couple of times a week, although he doesn't try to
make a big thing of it like so many pro football coaches have in the
past. This week, you guess, he and his staff have been putting in
more hours than ever before. The game with Ohio State is that big.

It is a game that's been talked about for more than a year, the
kind of juicy intersectional matchup you don't see much in college
football anymore, especially this early in the season. USC vs. Ohio
State is usually reserved for a January 1 date in the Rose Bowl, or a
BCS championship bowl in Miami or New Orleans. But here we
are, in the middle of September, and, finally, here it comes, the
newly anointed, No. 1–ranked Trojans, who moved up after their
impressive victory over Virginia, against the No. 5–rated Buckeyes,
two teams that began the season ranked among the top three in
everybody's poll. It is a Saturday-night, nationally-televised game at
the Los Angeles Coliseum with national championship implications

that has the whole town worked up, even in the middle of baseball pennant races that find both the Dodgers and Angels atop their respective divisions. ESPN has assigned what seems like half its national staff to cover the game, and KSPN, the local ESPN radio affiliate, will start broadcasting early in the morning and continue all day long, through the five o'clock PDT kickoff and for two hours after the game, allowing for more than twelve consecutive hours on the air.

How crazy has everyone gone over this game? Well, Stub Hub.com, the popular online ticket agency, is offering two premium, 50-yard-line seats for—are you ready?—five thousand dollars . . . *each!* So, yes, it might not be an exaggeration to call it college football's early-season Super Bowl, even if Ohio State did take a little of the edge off the game with a less than scintillating performance against lowly Ohio University the week before, scrambling in the fourth quarter to come back and win, 26–14, at home and dropping a couple of pegs in the national rankings. The Buckeyes were without tailback Beanie Wells, the Heisman Trophy candidate who was being held out after injuring his foot the week before, and were clearly looking ahead to the Trojans the following week. Early on, both Wells and Ohio State's usual high intensity are expected to return for the game that will draw a national TV audience that could rival the recent political conventions.

For the Trojans, it's been a two-week buildup, with a bye coming after their resounding 52–7 victory at Virginia. By Tuesday of the second week, Carroll seems so amped he could run through the wooden doors leading to Howard Jones Field. He doesn't, of course. He pauses, as he always does, to rub the bronze plaque that dedicates the entrance as Goux's gate. The late Marv Goux is the most famous assistant coach in USC football history, a fiery top lieutenant under John McKay who epitomized Trojan tradition and gave some of the more rousing pregame speeches known to man. Ask anyone who was lucky enough to hear them, and he'll tell you that Goux's emotional, profanity-laced talks in the tiny, crowded catacombs of the old P.E. building before home games with Notre

Dame were unlike anything preached before or since. "I've been in this game a long time," former USC coach John Robinson says, "and I've never heard anything like that." Carroll, knowing of Goux's reputation, spent hours talking to him and being counseled by him after accepting the USC job. Taking both hands and rubbing the bronzed replica of Goux's face has become a daily practice ritual for the head coach, as if to make sure he'll carry some of Goux's indomitable spirit with him.

Once inside the practice field, Carroll spots another legendary old Trojan, eighty-five-year-old Jim Hardy, who quarterbacked the team to victories in two Rose Bowls and was player of the game in one of them in the early 1940s. The head coach puts his arm around Hardy and says, "You live for these games, don't you?" Hardy, who regularly drives in from his retirement home in Palm Desert to watch practice once a week, smiles and shakes his head, appreciative that the coach, with so many other things on his mind, still takes time to talk to him. "It's going to be big man on big man, Coach," Hardy says. "You know I love it."

Carroll loves it, too. You can see it in his eyes. You can sense it in his body language. When his team lines up to practice kickoffs, the head coach lines up with it and sprints downfield with the players, the whistle around his neck bouncing off his back. When the loud horn sounds and the offense and defense have to return to the smaller patch of lawn behind the goal posts, it's the flat-bellied coach who is out in front, racing to beat the players who are almost forty years younger.

Among other things, the coaching matchup in this game is one everyone will be watching. Heading into this season, Carroll and Jim Tressel are widely regarded as the two preeminent coaches in college football. Carroll was 76-14 coming into 2008 with two national championships and a third BCS title game appearance. Tressel was 73-16, having captured one national title with appearances in both of the last two BCS championship games. If their records are alike, their personas couldn't be less similar. Carroll epitomizes everything California, from his tan complexion and tousled hair to the celebrities like Will Ferrell and Snoop Dogg he allows to prowl his sidelines. Tressel reeks of everything that is small-town Midwest, with his perfectly parted hair and his straight-laced tie and sweater vest on game days. Carroll's practices are open to the public. Tressel's are guarded like they're secret CIA operations. At $4.4 million a year, Carroll is the highest paid private university employee in the United States. Tressel recently signed an extension that will pay him $3.5 million a year.

As different as they are, though, they seem to share a common respect for each other. "I don't know Tressel," Carroll says. "He's from Akron, and I'm from San Francisco. I respect him and his program, though. It's an incredible team. They have great history, great players, and extraordinary ability. They're really, really talented, and they're as athletic as anyone we've played." Carroll knows all about the aura of Ohio State. He worked there one season as a defensive secondary coach under Earle Bruce in 1979. "We had a great year, we won every game," he says. "It was a historic year, except for the last four minutes of the Rose Bowl when [USC's] Charlie White kicked our butt." Carroll's favorite moment, though, came one night when he was watching a basketball game in Columbus. He happened to glance out the window of the arena and down below saw Woody Hayes. "He was teaching a class there," Carroll says, "and as soon as I saw him, I raced out of the arena and ran as fast as I could. I caught up to him and introduced myself and got to chat with him for about ten minutes. He actually knew who I was. I was thrilled about that. It remains one of my great memories."

Tressel is not Hayes, who was famous for winning Big Ten and national titles with his three-yards-and-a-cloud-of-dust approach. He plays it more modern and wide open on offense, even, heavens to Woody, lining up in a lone-back formation at times. Tressel is, however, a Ohio native whose father, Lee, was a longtime coach at prep-power Massillon before moving to Baldwin-Wallace College, where he coached twenty-three years and won a Division III title in 1978. Jim was an all-conference quarterback for his dad at Baldwin-Wallace before deciding to become a coach himself. He worked at the University of Akron and Miami, Ohio, then took over at Youngstown State, where he coached fifteen years, winning four national championships and qualifying for the Division I-AA play-offs *ten* times. He and his dad are the only father and son to both coach teams to national championships. Tressel accepted the job at Ohio State in January of 2001, almost exactly when Carroll took over at USC. Like Pete, he was not bashful about his goals. Later, in that first year as the new head coach, he addressed a crowd at a Buckeye basketball game. "I can assure you," he said, "that you'll be proud of our young people in the classroom, in the community, and especially in thirty days in Ann Arbor, Michigan."

It didn't take long for Tressel to start winning games (he was 6-1 against Michigan heading into 2008) and winning over fans. It is not uncommon to see signs on campus that read IN TRESSEL WE TRUST or GOD WEARS SWEATER VESTS. Not surprisingly, in public, Tressel plays it close to his famous vest. Unlike Carroll, you will not see him on any national TV commercials, and, as intensely as he appears on game day, it is doubtful if he knows, or cares, who might happen to be on the opposing sideline. Many of the current USC players were recruited by Ohio State and Tressel. "He is a great coach and a great person," says Trojans quarterback Mark Sanchez. "He was tough to say no to." Tressel, for his part, has spent the greater part of this week raving about USC and its athletes. "Gosh, all those guys were on our wish list when we were back in the re-cruiting days. Some of those guys we had a chance to really get to know, like Jeff Byers, who was a quality kid and great player. Kristofer O'Dowd, who was out here at our summer youth camp . . . Blake Ayles we got to know and Ronald Johnson. Mark Sanchez spent time out here, and on and on. They have great talent, but what I love about them is the discipline. They play the game the way it's supposed to be played. They play it fast and they play it tough. They play it clean and they have fun . . . I just enjoy watch-ing them on film. I enjoyed it more, I think, when I was just trying to study them than when I'm trying to play them."

At USC, meanwhile, the excitement seems to be building

along with the tension leading up to this game. "You can't help but be excited," says senior wide receiver Patrick Turner. "This is why you come to a school like this, to play in these kinds of games." It's almost as if the athletes are relieved they're finally allowed to talk about Ohio State. "We were told to only talk about Virginia," Turner says, "but you know we were all thinking about Ohio State a little bit over the summer." A little bit? "Let's just say it's been in our conversations for a while," says Kyle Moore, the talkative senior defensive end. "Oh yeah, it came up a couple of times over the summer." Sophomore tailback Joe McKnight grins when someone asks him if that was the case. "You approach it like any other game, but you know you're going to be more excited," McKnight says. "You come to SC, you're going to play in front of the world. That's why you come here."

The personal matchups in this game are getting lots of attention, both locally and nationally. The one everyone wants to focus on is the battle between All-American middle linebackers James Laurinaitis of Ohio State and Rey Maualuga of USC. Laurinaitis is a two-time All American and Butkus Award winner who is a prototype "Mike," as football people call middle linebackers. He is a great leader and a sure tackler with wonderful instincts. Maualuga, a returning All American and defensive player of the game in the last Rose Bowl, is bigger and faster and ultra-aggressive, sometimes to a fault. If Laurinaitis has been the more consistent college player, Maualuga is probably more coveted by pro scouts because of his size and speed. He admitted to playing at an astonishing 273 pounds in the Rose Bowl but has now trimmed down to a svelte, for him, 250-plus pounds.

"The thing about these guys," says USC assistant Norton Jr., "is that they're aware of each other. They've been to the same All-American banquets and gotten to know each other. They even text each other. Rey is aware of Laurinaitis, and he's aware of Rey. They have this built-in competition, and that's great, because you just don't have these type of athletes come along all the time."

By Thursday of game week, there is an almost electric current of anticipation and anxiety that you can feel running through Heritage Hall, where the players gather. In a special teams meeting that afternoon, Dennis Watson, the defensive line coach who also coaches some of the special teams (Carroll doesn't have a coach whose job is to solely be in charge of special teams) tries his best to be heard among the players' shouting and whooping in the corner meeting room that could pass for a mini-cineplex theater on the first floor. Somehow, you don't picture Jim Tressel's meetings being this loose and relaxed, but then, these programs are as different as their head coaches. "You're lucky it's happy Thursday," Watson says to the gathering of about twenty players. "I'm in a good mood today."

Watson is in a good mood most days, pleased to be back working after undergoing treatment for a dependency on painkillers. In June, following an arrest on suspicion of driving under the influence of prescription drugs, Watson was urged by Carroll to seek help. He took a leave of absence in July, returning to work a month later, apparently no longer dependent on drugs such as Vicodin or various muscle relaxants he used after five surgeries for back and neck injuries he incurred playing football. Watson, thirty-two, acknowledged in a story in the *Los Angeles Times* that his recovery is ongoing. "The only thing that's changed," he told a *Times* reporter, "is that I'm going to be a better father, a better husband, and a better coach." On this day, he's just trying to be someone who can relate to his players.

A large, white movie screen drops down, and highlights of Ohio State's kickoff team in its previous game with Ohio University are shown, with Watson using a bright red pointer to pick out players. "C.J.," he says to tailback C.J. Gable, "we want you to seal the backside. We don't want our lead blocker against these guys." Now it's time to plot USC's kickoff returns. "We're gonna run Jet Left until the bleeping sun goes down," says Watson. "You gotta make that kick-out block, Garrett Green. You gotta kick him out. That's what I want to see. *Bam!* I want to see that chinstrap knocked out. *Bam!*" John Madden would love this. "We want to get a hat on a hat, guys, a hat on a hat," Watson says.

Now it's defensive line coach Nick Holt's turn. He's in charge of punt returns and coverages, and the intensity in the room rises with the decibel levels of Holt's voice. "Pay attention," he screams at one freshman, "and quit smiling. There is nothing f—ing funny about this." With a large pencil positioned on the left side of his ear, Holt continues to shout out directions as the players watch the screen. "Usually, they like directional punts," he says, "trying to keep them toward the short hash [mark]. You can't lag, guys. They have solid personnel. These are good football players we're dealing with."

The focus switches to punt returns. "We're going Cat Right here, guys, and Taylor," he says to Taylor Mays, the All-American safety, "the biggest thing here is your block. You have to make that block for this to work." They watch plays, then rewind them and watch again, and the longer they go, the more Holt starts screaming, "No penalties, guys, we've got to be sure about that; we don't want any penalties." At that point, in the back of the room, Carroll slips in and stands in the middle of the second-to-last row. "That's right," he says, "no penalties. We've got to be good about that."

The room finally clears for fifteen minutes, but then the entire squad shows up for a full team meeting, amid loud chatter and shout-outs. "OK, OK," says Dennis Slutak, the Trojans' chunky director of football operations, "listen up." Slutak proceeds to give the itinerary for the next couple of days, especially important to the freshmen who are experiencing their first home game. He explains where the buses will be, who can and can't come to the team hotel the night before the game, what happens immediately after the game, then mentions the NCAA's generous $15 per diem, amid much hooting from the players who know that hardly pays for a decent lunch at most L.A. restaurants.

Slutak leaves, and the noise level in the room cranks up immediately and continues until Carroll walks in, strolls to the front, and slaps his hands twice. The place suddenly grows so quiet you could hear a jock strap drop. He shows tape of the Turnover of the Day from Wednesday's practice, and when Maualuga is seen ripping a football from the hands of a scout team's running back, the place explodes. The lights go back on, and Carroll is smiling. "All right," he says, turning serious, "this is No Repeat Thursday. It's our last full practice and we want to be precise out there. We want to do stuff exactly right. If you want to do it on Saturday, you have to do it today. You black shirts (members of the scout team), don't let up out there. Don't give in. I want you to compete your asses off.

"We had seven penalties in our [first] game. They had seven penalties in their first two games. You have to think about what you're doing out there. Do you really want to be the guy who messes up this weekend? Do you? Do you really want to be the one?" Now Carroll switches to the matter of free time on Thursday night. This is something coaches can't control, so it worries them even more. "You've got to watch yourself," he says. "It's Thursday night, a lot of guys out, a lot of young guys will be out for the first time. We've got to take care of each other. You older guys have to watch out for the young guys. Protect the team, that's what is important. You can't fight. No yelling, no pushing, no defending your honor or anything like that. You're football players, and you do any of that and you're going to get nailed. The eyes of America are on you. Have you guys been watching *SportsCenter* this week? This is a huge game, and everyone is watching. You have to be careful. You have to take care of yourselves. All right, let's make it a great weekend."

When Saturday dawns, it is gray and overcast, but it seems even gloomier for Ohio State fans. Tressel has announced that Wells, his Heisman candidate at tailback and the one player who dictates everything the Buckeyes do on offense, is out with a sore foot that hasn't healed in time for him to be ready. "Beanie probably won't talk to me for the next year, but that's my decision," the coach says. If anything, the news makes USC fans feel even giddier, so much so they start arriving at the Coliseum as early as 7:00 in the morning, ten hours before kickoff. ESPN's Game Day crew is on hand, and most of Fraternity Row, along with the cheerleaders and almost everyone else on campus, arrive to shove their way in front of the huge set to watch and shout at Chris Fowler, Kirk Herbstreit, Lee Corso, and the guys. To prove this is more than just an average game, long rows of corporate tents are lined up between the Coliseum's peristyle end and Figueroa, the main street that runs adjacent to the stadium, making it look like a mini-Super Bowl Sunday. In the pre-Carroll days, there was none of this pregame buzz and activity, but since he's taken over, the area in front of the peristyle end has become a meeting place for fans and alumni to linger amid the local ESPN radio affiliate, KSPN, and its own stage filled with talk show hosts. There are smaller booths for giveaways and others filled with authors signing their latest USC books. This continues for hours and lasts until just before kickoff. At about 2:30, the team buses arrive and the players and coaches get off and take "the walk" that has now become a Trojan tradition. With Carroll, dressed in his latest dark designer suit and tie, leading the way, he and the players, wearing their cardinal colored USC sweatsuits, and the assistant coaches slowly walk through a lane created by howling, cheering fans on both sides. When they get to the Coliseum gate, they continue to walk down through the seats at the peristyle end, where the already seated USC students spot them and register their first decibel-busting reaction of the day. The contingent continues down the stairs and onto the Coliseum's manicured lawn where they gather at midfield, with Carroll wedged somewhere in the middle. He addresses them for a few moments, they listen, then break up and slowly head to the locker room.

By the time the 5:25 P.M. kickoff finally arrives, it almost seems anticlimactic, especially after USC and Ohio State, like two wise, old heavyweights trying to feel each other out, both sputter offensively and are forced to punt on their first possessions. On the Buckeyes' second possession, though, Tressel makes the first serious move in this coaching chess match. Knowing he has to find some kind of gamebreaker with Wells out, he inserts Terrelle Pryor, the wildly hyped 6'6" 235–pound freshman at quarterback, alternating him with Todd Boeckman, his fifth-year senior at the position. Pryor was the nation's most sought-after recruit who eventually narrowed his choices down to Ohio State and the Buckeyes' fiercest rival, Michigan. When he finally opted to go to school in Columbus, the town reacted as if it were some kind of national holiday. Pryor is a thoroughbred of an athlete who runs like a wide receiver. He has commonly been compared to Vince Young when he played at Texas, but, like Young, his passing skills are not yet refined. So Tressel, again ignoring the old Woody Hayes conservatism, shifts into a spread offense whenever Pryor comes in, positioning the quarterback deep with one running back. On each snap, Pryor slips the ball into the running back's stomach and either leaves it there, or takes it out and runs or passes himself. Early on, it seems to be working, with Ohio State moving the ball downfield for the first time. Pryor runs for some key yardage and even completes a pass to Dane Sanzenbacher for 15 yards and a first down at the USC 40. The Trojans oblige with a pivotal penalty, Boeckman comes back in to throw for 12 yards and a first and goal at the USC 5. Nevertheless, the Trojans' defense and an Ohio State false-start penalty force the Buckeyes to settle for a 29-yard field goal from Ryan Pretorius. It's not what they wanted, but they take a 3–0 lead and seem to be feeling pretty good about themselves.

The feeling doesn't last long. Sanchez takes over at his own 26, and he and McKnight immediately kick the USC offense into gear. Sanchez's crisp passes and McKnight's wiggly runs get the Trojans down to the Ohio State 35. That's when athletic fullback Stanley Havili circles out of the backfield and slips behind linebacker Marcus Freeman. Racing alone along the far sideline, Havili reaches up for a looping Sanchez pass that is thrown a little high. He strains to catch it on his fingertips and then acrobatically pulls it down, somehow managing to keep his balance the rest of the way until he lunges facemask-first into the end zone. It is 7–3 Trojans, and the crowd of 93,607, the largest in fifteen years, is going nuts.

The emotion seems to rev up the defense, and they quickly force Boeckman and friends to go three and out. When USC gets the ball back, it's still in the same, smooth offensive flow. Sanchez completes a couple of passes, then McKnight, running behind an inexperienced but surprisingly effective offensive line, bursts into the secondary for 24 yards and a first down at the OSU 26. Then it's Havili again, catching a pass for an 11-yard gain, followed by a Buckeyes' roughing the passer penalty. Eventually, USC has a first and goal at the 1, where it's Carroll's turn for a chess move. Sanchez takes the ball, makes a pretty play fake, then softly throws a ball to the back of the end zone where a wide open Blake Ayles, the tall, freshman tight end, makes the catch. Now, with a P.A.T. made by kicker David Buehler, it's 14–3, and amid the growing noise cascading all around them, the Buckeyes are starting to feel the pressure.

They react well, though. With Boeckman and Pryor continuing to alternate at quarterback, they put together an impressive drive, highlighted by Pryor's 13-yard run to the USC 19. But, that's where USC's defense takes over, with Matthews, Fili Moala, Kyle Moore, and Brian Cushing exerting huge pressure on Boeckman, who doesn't have time to find any receivers. The drive stalls and Pretorius's ensuing 46-yard field goal attempt is wide right.

Now it's Ohio State's defense that rises up, forcing Sanchez and Co. to go three and out. Unfortunately, though, that brings the Trojans' most intimidating unit back on the field. With the Buckeyes backed up in their own end and a little desperate to get some points before halftime, Boeckman tries to throw a short spiral into the flat. Only Maualuga, all 250-plus pounds of him, is there, lurking. He intercepts the pass and takes off down the sideline like a 180-pound scatback. The pro scouts in the press box must be swooning. "That was like the dream of my life right there," Maualuga says later. He isn't about to let anyone interfere with his dream, running over one defender, then tiptoeing to avoid the chalk along the sideline for a 48-yard touchdown return. It is the play that breaks the game open and gives USC a 21–3 lead at the half.

In the second half, it becomes apparent that Carroll, the noted defensive guru, has adjusted to Pryor and the spread. It also seems clear that without the threat of Wells and his powerful bursts between the tackles, the Ohio State offense is severely limited. The Trojans' offense, meanwhile, keeps on rocking. After a Moala sack stuffs the Buckeyes inside their 5, they punt out and give USC the ball on the Ohio State 36. It takes Sanchez only six plays to direct the next touchdown drive from there, with one of his lasers finding Damian Williams on a slant for a 24-yard score to make it 28–3 with another successful P.A.T. by Buehler. Two minutes later, the revved-up Trojans start another drive from their own 35. A pass and a C.J. Gable run are followed by a Marcus Freeman roughing the passer penalty that gets the ball down to the 17. Then Sanchez, showing the mobility that his predecessor John David Booty lacked, avoids the rush, steps off to one side, and finds Williams again, and this time he's so alone it appears he is about to receive a punt in the corner of the end zone. The wide receiver from Arkansas allows the pass to fall softly into his hands and it's 35–3 heading into the fourth quarter. From there, Carroll takes his foot off the accelerator. He begins substituting liberally, allowing both his backup quarterbacks, Aaron Corp and Mitch Mustain, to get some playing time. It doesn't matter. Tressel's frustrated team gains a total of only 28 yards in the final fifteen minutes and trudges off the Coliseum floor with the giant scoreboard lights blinking the 35–3 final.

USC fans, ecstatic that their No. 1–ranked team played up to its lofty perch, rush joyously onto the field afterward. Sanchez, who has become a particular favorite of Los Angeles's large Hispanic community, does his version of the Lambeau Leap, jumping into the stands near the Coliseum tunnel to receive hugs and back slaps, not far from the sign that reads VIVA SANCHEZ. Maualuga, his large tattooed arms bulging out from his uniform, trots off smiling and waving to the fans, while Carroll shakes hands with Tressel, then remains near midfield to do the early TV interviews for stations battling 11:00 deadlines.

Afterward, Carroll can't hide his happiness, even pausing for a few moments to gush like that teenager who grew up in Marin County. "To come out and play like this is really, really cool," he says, thankfully leaving out the word "dude" at the end of the sentence. "We practiced so well, an outcome like this, I thought it could happen. Tonight, it didn't matter who we were playing. This is the essence of what we're trying to do here. . . . When we prepare this well and have all our guys, we're tough to beat. That's the standard we live by."

Carroll is talking about the general philosophy of his program, which is to collect all the five- and four-star recruits you can, practice like hell, then let them go play against teams that don't have nearly the same talent. It is the reason his offensive line, so young and raw early in camp, has matured fast enough to blow open huge holes in an Ohio State defense regarded among the finest in America. It faces better players in practice than it does in games.

The head coach is also talking about Sanchez, the new poster child for this 2008 team, who has waited his turn, studied and learned, and now that the opportunity has come, has jumped in cleats-first. He has thrown seven touchdown passes in the first two games, and his name is appearing regularly on all the early Heisman Trophy lists.

"It's fun to watch him," says Carroll. "I'm sure its fun for you, too. He played great. He audibled a couple of big plays. That time he hit Damien in the corner, he used his feet to avoid the rush. He's a great football player . . . and a brilliant, kid, just a brilliant kid. You can tell. He's pretty savvy with you guys, too."

Someone asks Maualuga who the team's No. 1 Heisman candidate is. "You're looking at him," he says. He is kidding. He knows linebackers don't win Heismans. They do win the Butkus Award, though, and the man, himself, Dick Butkus, was at the game and paused afterward to chat a moment with Carroll. Pete probably asked him, "What do you think of number 58?" Sanchez certainly thinks highly of him. "I want to get Rey on offense," he says, smiling. "No, I'm just glad he came back to play this season. He could easily be playing on Sundays."

Rocky Seto, the defensive backfield coach, strolls by and says the boss is happy with this victory. "Pete is pleased," he says. "He knows we beat a really good team. That pass we had intercepted right before the half probably ticked him off, though. Turnover ratio to him is everything. He goes crazy over that. Tonight, we won that battle three to one, so he should be happy."

There are no significant injuries to speak of, although Mc-Knight, who had a great night rushing for 105 yards and averaging 8.8 per carry, had to leave the game with migraines. "Joe's OK, he's had migraines before," says Carroll. "Joe is a great competitor. There's nothing he can't take on. Last year, we overloaded him. We were so excited about what he could do. This year we've simplified things a bit for him and it's paying off."

Everything paid off in this game. At the end, after the locker room had finally cleared out of recruits, media, and most players, Carroll could be found in the back with offensive coordinator Steve Sarkisian, already in suit and tie, carrying his briefcase, and Sanchez, naked except for the towel wrapped around his waist and another draped over his shoulder.

The three of them stood there for a while, talking and smiling. They had earned that much. On this memorable night in L.A., there was plenty to smile about.

Pete Profile

The Facebook Coach

Pete Carroll would never say it, but he loves being described as a new kind of football coach, the cool, hip, fifty-seven-year-old who is miles ahead of most of his stodgy contemporaries when it comes to having his own page on Facebook, his own personal blog on the Internet, refining the art of text messaging, and twittering his heart out to recruits, players, alums, fans, and friends.

"He's told me, 'I'm going to do whatever is happening today. I don't want to be stuck in the past,'" says Ben Malcolmson, the twenty-three-year-old who has a new, full-time position as director of online media for Carroll and the USC football program. Clearly, this is a revolutionary idea. How many other college football coaches have a director of online media?

"Pete's up on the times," says Malcolmson. "He's amazing that way. I compare him to my dad, who's about the same age and can barely type out an e-mail. I think it is Pete's way of having a connection with the kids. He doesn't use it as a blatant recruiting tool, but the cachet that comes with it definitely helps. It's just who he is. It's genuine, and this is just another vehicle to help portray that side of him.

"The Facebook thing started in February of '08," Malcolmson says. "It was my idea. I'm on it, so I figured why not get Coach on it? It's been really cool. Coach loves it. The maximum number of friends you can have on the site is five thousand, and he maxed out on that real fast. Everyone wants to be Pete Carroll's friend. You can't contact people through Facebook, because of recruiting rules and so on, but Coach has a lot of fun with the site. He'll give little mini-movie reviews, things like that."

Malcolmson is a story in and of himself. He was a staff member of the school newspaper, the *Daily Trojan*, a senior sports columnist from Dallas, Texas, who found he was getting bored writing the usual opinion pieces. "I was looking for some cool ideas, so I ran with the women's cross-country team, I spent a day as football manager, things like that. Then one day I saw an ad for walk-on tryouts for the football team. I talked to Coach Carroll about it, explaining I wasn't coming to make the team, I just wanted to experience what it was like and write a story. So I did, even though I hadn't played football since the fifth grade and hated the physicality of it."

So Malcolmson, all 6' 165 pounds of him, tried out as a wide receiver and went home to write his story that night. The next day he received a phone call from a friend. "Dude, you made the team," the friend told him. Malcolmson thought his buddy was putting him on. "Then I thought Coach Carroll was pulling a prank," Malcolmson says. "So I went to see him, and he says, 'No, you made the team. You're quick and you can catch the ball. We want you.'"

Malcolmson thought he was dreaming. He couldn't believe it. Until he ventured out to his first college spring practice as a player. "It was rough," he says. "I was getting hammered. I'd get home at night and I was hurting. I learned a lot about Advil and ice. It was also hard learning the plays. I didn't realize how difficult it is mentally." Three weeks into spring practice, the hard-knocking fact of reality hit him. He dislocated his shoulder. "That was heartbreaking," he says. "I had gained fifteen to twenty pounds because they feed you so well, and I was actually starting to dream that maybe this could happen. I had surgery and they told me I'd be out nine months. I had enrolled in grad school in communications management, so it looked like my brief football career was over, but something inside me couldn't quit. Four months later, I was back on the field. The doctors were amazed."

Malcolmson suited up and made it through the season. "There was no way I was going to get into a game," he says. "I was the twelfth receiver on the list, on a team that had Dwayne Jarrett and Steve Smith. And we had a lot of close games that season, so it wasn't like Coach could flood the field with walk-ons at the end." Malcolmson had written about his exploits in the *Daily Trojan*, however, and he began to have a cult following around campus. T-shirts were printed that read GET BEN IN. Posters were made. Chants began to be heard in the final minutes of games at the Coliseum to let Malcolmson play. Finally, it happened. On Senior Night, in the final home game against Notre Dame, Carroll put Ben in on the final play.

"It was just a quarterback-kneel play, but it was still amazing," Malcolmson says. "It was an out-of-body experience. The people were cheering for me. It was really cool. By the time I got back to the locker room, I must have had fifty text messages. All the pain I'd gone through getting hammered and enduring the injury, it was all worth it. It was a great experience overall."

Malcolmson was concentrating on his graduate work the following spring, but he found himself missing his football connection. "I talked to Coach and asked if I could contribute in any way. He said, 'I've got an idea. We're starting a Web site about the team. I'm glad you came to me. I can't think of a better person to run it.'"

So USCripsit.com was born. "When we started, we didn't have any real direction," Malcolmson says. "Coach told me to do what I want. I started a blog, trying to add to it hourly. I'd have fifteen to twenty posts on an average day. I had great access, so I was writing about stuff inside the meeting rooms, what the coaches had for lunch that day—some silly things, some personal—but it was a big hit. Trojan fans loved it. Halfway through that year, Coach and his agent thought it would be best to combine my blog with the Web site, and the new address is PeteCarroll.com."

For his part, Carroll is thrilled with this new project. "Ben has demonstrated he is an extraordinary guy with a great work ethic and he has tremendous perseverance," the coach says. "I like him. He's one of a kind. He's done a great job with the Web page. He's absolutely the perfect one to run it."

So now Malcolmson is fully engrossed in the USC football program. "I'm probably around Coach more than anyone in the office," he says. "I've gotten to know him really well. The thing about him is he is always so positive. Even when he's mad, he transitions to what positive we can take from that. We lose to Oregon State, and he asks what we can do to turn that positive. We can win all the rest of our games and go to the Rose Bowl. OK, we'll concentrate on that. It becomes infectious.

"The coolest thing is that it applies to more than football. It applies to life in general. His three rules are no whining, no complaining, no excuses. I don't think he understands how big his philosophy is. I try to tell him, but he says, 'No, no, it's just football.'"

Malcolmson's next logical step would seem to be a position as a graduate assistant coach, but he swears it will never happen. "I don't want to be a coach," he says. "Coach sleeps here two or three nights a week during the season. His assistants, they all work so hard. Those guys are crazy."

Journalism isn't his thing, either, he has decided. "No, I don't see myself doing that," he says. For now he is comfortable in his new full-time position, blogging away, finding new vehicles to allow people to peek into the many facets of USC football and maintaining Carroll's popular profile on Facebook.

College football's first director of online media is only too happy to keep his New Age coach flowing smoothly in the complex, but always growing world of cyberspace.

V

Game Three: Always Be Wary
of an Old Nemesis

The inevitable emotional letdown after Ohio State is tempered, at least for some at USC, by the arrival of the conference season. Don't laugh. The Pac-10 has been tougher on Pete Carroll than the paparazzi have been on Brad Pitt and Angelina Jolie.

Of the 14 losses in his first seven years with the Trojans, 9 have come in the conference, most of them against weak, outmanned teams that didn't appear to have a chance. Take away two of them, an unthinkable defeat at the hands of punchless, crosstown rival UCLA in the Rose Bowl in 2006 and an even more surreal stumble against a 41-point underdog Stanford team at home in 2007, and Carroll might have had four national championship trophies instead of two, gleaming at him every time he walked into Heritage Hall early this fall.

Lots of theories have been forwarded as to why the UCLAs, Stanfords, Oregons, and Oregon States give the Trojans more problems than the Ohio States, Auburns, and Oklahomas. Part of it is that Pac-10 opponents occasionally have caught USC emotionally flat, maybe between big games. Another part is that by playing the Trojans year in and year out, they are more familiar with their schemes and how they can best be blunted.

Let's face it, at this point, USC, unanimously ranked No. 1 nationally after the Ohio State romp, has enough talent to stock three or four Pac-10 schools with blue-chip athletes. When it comes to raw ability, athleticism, and depth, no other school in the conference comes within mailing distance of the Trojans. So if a stumble happens here and there, maybe it can be excused. Not if it happens every year, however, and especially not if it happens *this* year, when all the planets seem properly aligned and Carroll's club has sprinted out of the blocks like Usain Bolt in the 100 meters at Beijing.

There are ten days between the thundering victory over Ohio State and a Thursday night national TV date against Oregon State in Corvallis, and for Carroll much of it is occupied with an uncomfortable off-the-field matter. Shareece Wright, a starting senior cornerback, is charged with a felony for resisting an officer on September 7, the open Saturday between the Virginia game and the home opener with the Buckeyes. Apparently, Wright was at a friend's party in Colton in Southern California's Inland Empire, forty miles or so from L.A. The party grew too loud, the police arrived after complaints from neighbors, and what occurred after that depends on whose version you believe. Carroll knows about all this before the Ohio State game and allows Wright to play, anyway, saying he didn't have enough information to make an informed decision on his cornerback's status. Not everyone agrees with a move that some see as self-serving, but this is Pete Carroll, so few in the media criticize him for it. Now Wright and three codefendants are scheduled to appear in court for a settlement conference on October 29, and instead of dwelling on his future, Carroll talks to the team, trying to use it as a "teachable moment." There is another open weekend between games, the last of the regular season, and the coach doesn't want any of his kids to get into similar trouble. "It's a tremendous challenge for everybody to stay in line, to keep track of what's going on and do the right thing," says Carroll. In the meantime, the media is now questioning the coach about Wright's future. Will he play at Corvallis, or not? "I don't have all the stuff that I need to make that decision," Carroll says at first. Later, the coach announces he is disciplining Wright but declines to specify how. He does say, however, that if Wright's slight neck injury allows, he will play in Corvallis.

Turns out, the neck injury is more than "slight." A further MRI finds a hairline fracture of the vertebra, and suddenly it's no longer a case of whether Wright will play in the next game. It's a matter of whether he will be out longer than the early six-week estimate by doctors. "We're all surprised," says Carroll. "We didn't know it was that serious. Neither did he. We all thought it was a stiff neck." It is a measure of the depth Carroll has built that this injury is considered disappointing but it is not cause for a crisis. Not as long as senior Josh Pinkard, a cornerback Carroll described two years ago as the finest athlete on the team, is healthy again and ready to step in as Wright's replacement.

Meanwhile, Oregon State and Mike Riley lurk in the background. Although the Beavers were beaten by Stanford and walloped by Penn State in their first two games, they came back to batter a bad Hawaii team, and history shows Riley's clubs always improve as the season progresses. On paper, this should be a major mismatch, but the site and the coach should combine to make it interesting. Carroll and the Trojans don't have fond memories of Corvallis. Four years earlier, on the kind of foggy night you used to read about in Edgar Allan Poe stories, Oregon State raced out to a 13–0 lead on a struggling, disinterested Trojans team and appeared on the verge of springing a huge upset. But USC rallied in the second half, and then, clinging to a 14–13 lead, Reggie Bush fielded a punt on his own 35-yard line, seemingly pinned against the sideline. With one of his trademark jukes, Reggie left one onrushing tackler groping for air before cutting back sharply and swiveling through a crowd of Oregon State players like some kind of ghostly apparition to race 65 yards through the fog for the touchdown that helped the Trojans prevail, 28–20.

Then, in 2006, another Riley-coached team pulled off a stunning upset of undefeated, No. 3–ranked USC, streaking to a 33–17 lead over the mistake-prone Trojans, then holding off a furious John David Booty–led rally in the fourth quarter. With 2:39 to play,

Booty went 80 yards in ten plays, finding Steve Smith with a 2-yard pass for the touchdown that brought the visitors from California to within 2 points. But an ensuing 2-point conversion pass attempted by Booty was batted down, and the Trojans' hope for an undefeated season evaporated in the cool, Northwest air, 33–31.

So no, Riley isn't intimidated by USC. He was, in fact, so close to becoming the Trojans head coach before Carroll got the job, he could almost smell the food cooking at those tailgate parties outside the Coliseum. In a private one-on-one interview, the Oregon State coach relives some of those tumultuous days. It was late in 2000, and Riley, who had been a popular USC assistant under John Robinson years earlier, was now the head coach of the San Diego Chargers in the midst of a lousy season. Nevertheless, USC Athletics Director Mike Garrett, remembering how well Riley was regarded as the Trojans offensive coordinator, had interviewed Riley in the aftermath of the Paul Hackett firing, been duly impressed, and now had arranged for him to meet with Steven Sample, the school president, to apparently seal the deal. That's when Riley got the call from Chargers president Dean Spanos, telling him if he made the trip to L.A. for the interview, he no longer had a job in San Diego. The coach had a family and couldn't take the risk. So Riley stayed with the Chargers, Carroll eventually accepted the Trojans job, and fate continued to bounce like a crazy punt inside the 20-yard line for the current Oregon State coach.

A few weeks later, Stanford called. Riley was told he was a finalist for the job that eventually went to Buddy Teevens. Then, it was Indiana's turn. Finally, Alabama, his alma mater, slipped into the picture. Riley played for Bear Bryant in Tuscaloosa and was intrigued, but at the same time the UCLA job came open. "I turned down Indiana waiting for Stanford, then I turned down Alabama waiting for UCLA," he says. When the Bruins' job went to Karl Dorrell, Riley says he felt "like I'd been kicked in the stomach." Later, he said, "I don't want to sound too dramatic about lost faith and all that, but I have to admit to thinking, 'Whoa, what's going on here?'"

All eventually turned out well for the personable coach who grew up in Oregon, played at Corvallis High, and had his son, Matt, accepted at the university only weeks before he took the job. "In the big picture, I couldn't be happier," says Riley, an uncommonly genuine, self-effacing sort who understands the odds he faces trying to recruit in a town you can miss if you doze off for a few minutes while driving through it. "Here, you've got to uncover rocks," he says, "but it's working out well. I like recruiting, and I like the direction the university is going."

Hardly anyone seems to remember, but Oregon State has been the second-best team in the Pac-10 the past two seasons, finishing at a robust 9-4 and outpointing Maryland, 21–14, in the Emerald Bowl in December. At USC, some of the older players, the ones who still recall the pain of that 33–31 upset that cost them a shot at a national title on their last trip to Corvallis, are trying their best to tell the freshmen and sophomores on the team to be wary. "I remember Corvallis," says senior defensive end Kyle Moore, after a long midweek practice. "I remember it's cold and it's loud. I keep trying to tell the younger guys. I keep trying to tell them what the plane ride back felt like after we lost. I tell them it was a quiet plane ride. I'm telling them we've got to try everything we can to not let that happen again."

In the middle of adjusting to a short second week after the bye in preparation for the rare Thursday-night game in Oregon, Carroll makes a somewhat shocking move. He announces that Garrett Green, a longtime senior emergency backup, is the new No. 2 quarterback behind starter Mark Sanchez. The news catches everyone, including members of the media, by surprise. Carroll says he's doing it because of Green's "experience in the system," but the suspicion is he is doing it more to light a fire under Mitch Mustain and Aaron Corp, the two highly regarded quarterbacks who were heavily recruited national high school prospects. Green was not. Because Sanchez has taken such total control of the position, advancing from a new, unproven starter to a sudden Heisman Trophy candidate in a matter of a few weeks, some of the motivation has ebbed away for Mustain and Corp, who realize any playing time will be limited as long as Sanchez remains healthy. Psychologically, they're probably feeling a bit depressed, but at this level of college football, players still have to perform in practice. If they aren't, something has to be done. That's what seems to have happened here.

For his part, Green comes off both surprised and excited about the opportunity. "You're always trying to climb as high on the depth chart as you can," he says. Carroll had moved Green, a high school quarterback, to receiver earlier and employed him as a prominent part of his special teams. A kid who clearly loves to play, Green says he'll miss running down the field covering kicks. "I would still like to play special teams," he says, smiling. "That's a tough one to swallow." It has to be tougher for Mustain and Corp, both of whom have stronger arms and better all-around skill sets. "You never want to get demoted," says Corp, "but you just have to go out and work harder." Carroll has indicated this is a situation still in flux, so it will be interesting to see what happens in the next month.

In the meantime, both coaches are eager to talk about the Thursday national TV match. Riley is not without some weapons on offense. Sammie Stroughter, the senior who was granted a medical hardship year by the Pac-10, is one of the more explosive receivers in the nation, and the tiny Rodgers brothers, tailback Jacquizz and wide receiver James, are both talented kids who play a lot bigger than they look. Then there is junior quarterback Lyle Moevao (pronounced *Moy*-vow), who Riley thinks is just starting to come into his own. "Our perimeter, talentwise, is as good as we have had for a while," says the coach. "The best way to describe us right now is that we are growing as a program." USC, he knows, is already fully grown. "They are impressive," he says. "They do a tremendous job of utilizing personnel and fitting guys in. They have a true identity of what they have done and built up through the years on both sides of the ball . . . I think they have really good personnel and they coach them well. That's a tough combination."

Off by himself, before his afternoon meetings with assistants,

Carroll pauses to tell me he understands what he is going up against in Riley. "Mike does a great job . . . they're really well-schemed," he says. "This is one of my favorite defenses in the conference year in and year out, the style they play, the manner in which they play their secondary. . . . This is a team that can make it really hard on you. Their offense is real high-tech, NFL-style, too. They do the same things year after year. That's scheme, coaching, all that other stuff, as well as good players." Like all others in his profession, Carroll regularly compliments opponents, but when discussing Riley, there is a level of admiration in his voice you don't hear very often.

Much of the conversation heading into this game centers on the early slump of Pac-10 schools. After three weeks, USC is the only unbeaten team in the conference. Oregon has lost to Boise State. Cal has lost at Maryland. UCLA was pummeled by BYU. Washington was blown out by Oklahoma. If the conference continues to struggle this way, the speculation is that it will hurt the Trojans in the computer-based BCS system. Already, they're saying if an SEC team like Georgia and a Big Twelve school like Oklahoma finish undefeated, USC would be the odd team out because the weak Pac-10 competition would knock it out of the BCS title game. Unfortunatetly, there is more discussion about this on campus and in the locker room than there is about Oregon State.

Typically, unlike the media and maybe some of his players, Carroll doesn't want to talk about any of that. "We can't control that, so we don't worry about it," he says. "All we can control is how we play every week. If we go out and play hard and play up to our capability, everything else will fall into place." It's a nice thought, but even he knows it doesn't always work out that way. One year, USC finished first in the final AP poll and didn't get to play in the BCS championship game. The same thing happened to an unbeaten Auburn team one year. The fallibility of the BCS system is always there, hanging over the proceedings like the thick smog on a bad air day in L.A.

Happily, there is nothing wrong with the air on a typically crisp, Northwest game day in Corvallis. It is cloudy and cool for much of the afternoon, but the sun makes its way out just before kickoff. The atmosphere around Reser Stadium is even more electric than predicted. Because the university is on the quarter system, classes haven't even started yet, but that hasn't prevented students from stampeding through the premises as if they were sprinting to a free Coldplay concert. The lines for student tickets wind halfway around the stadium, and the arrival of the nation's No. 1 team, as well as ESPN's national TV cameras, only enlivens an already revved up home crowd, with many of the fans tailgating, chowing down on burgers and hot dogs and chugging cold beverages, since early in the morning.

By the time the six o'clock kickoff nears, the overwhelming noise drowns out everything else. Then the game starts, and the place really goes bonkers. The 25-point underdog Beavers win the toss and defer to the second half. So USC gets the ball first, promptly going three and out, much to the unmitigated joy of the home folks. That's when Moore and the Trojan seniors start to get that old, uncomfortable, queasy feeling. Oregon State takes over on its own 40 and immediately begins giving the ball to Jacquizz Rodgers, the little hummingbird of a freshman tailback at 5'6" and 193 pounds. The former Texas Prep star, who scored a mind-boggling 136 touchdowns in high school, proceeds to run through the middle of the Trojans' massive line, squirting out the other end like a slippery bar of soap. It is almost funny at first, but USC, surprisingly playing more of a 3-4 defensive alignment than its usual 4-3, fails to see the humor in it as Jacquizz goes for 7 yards, then 8, followed by 8 more. A few more plays and the Beavers are deep in Trojan territory, where Moevao finds Jacquizz's equally small brother, James, on an 8-yard touchdown pass. Sixty yards in eight plays in less than six minutes, and now Reser Stadium is generating so much noise the grandstands are shaking.

On USC's next possession, Sanchez and Co. again go three and out, and it's almost as if Riley knows exactly what the Trojans want to do on every play. They throw a quick hitch to a wide receiver, and an Oregon State tackler is waiting. They try Joe McKnight on a gimmick direct snap, and the Beaver tacklers are there to hit him. It's like that for most of the first half, with USC not manufacturing a first down until deep into the second period. Meanwhile, The Jacquizz Show continues. When he isn't darting up the middle, he is scooting to the outside. Wherever he is, the Trojans can't seem to tackle him. After another long, 62-yard drive, the little guy caps it off with a 2-yard power burst for a 14–0 lead midway through the second quarter. Now, if you look closely, you can almost see the beads of perspiration forming on the foreheads of Carroll and his frantic USC assistants. Ken Norton Jr. is shouting. Nick Holt is furiously waving his arms. Steve Sarkisian grimaces in deep thought.

A few minutes later, McKnight, who is having a horrible night, gets the ball again on another gimmicky direct snap, then fumbles it away. Oregon State recovers and—guess who?—tiny Jacquizz rips off yet a new assortment of big runs to highlight another impressive Beavers drive. USC's frustration hits a new high when first Averell Spicer's personal foul penalty gives OSU another chance, instead of having to settle for a field goal. Then, on a Moevao pass, the Trojans' Kevin Thomas seems in position in the end zone for an interception, only to have the ball go through his hands into the waiting arms of James Rogers for a touchdown. It is 21–0 Oregon State, and mercifully for the visitors, the half ends.

By any account, it is the worst thirty minutes of the Pete Carroll Era at USC. The listless Trojans are getting manhandled on both sides of the line of scrimmage, finishing with just three first downs to the Beavers' 16 and being outgained 220 yards to 75. If you hadn't known any better, you'd have thought the kids in orange were the No. 1 team in America, not the limp-tackling, mistake-prone bunch in white. This is not the first time a Carroll-coached team has fallen behind at intermission, but it is the first time one of his Trojans teams has looked completely overwhelmed.

As is his custom, Carroll makes some adjustments in the locker room, switching back to his base 4-3 defensive set, and on Oregon State's opening possession of the third quarter, USC finally stops

Jacquizz and the Beavers, forcing a punt. USC takes over on its own 38, and tailback Stafon Johnson, who has hardly been utilized enough in the first few weeks of this new season, busts off an 11-yard run. Then Sanchez finds some rhythm, hitting Patrick Turner on completions for 10 and 12 yards before finding Damian Williams for 14 more on a courageous fourth and 9 call by Carroll. On a first down at the OSU 26, the USC quarterback lofts a beautiful touch pass into the arms of Ronald Johnson and the score is cut to 21-7.

Now the Trojans have a bit of momentum, and before the quarter is over, they strike again, going 70 yards in seven plays, climaxed by a pass to Williams, who tiptoes along the sideline and goes in for a 30-yard touchdown. With 2:55 left in the period, it's 21–14, and the sense is the No. 1–rated team in America is about to blow by the plucky underdogs.

Only it doesn't work out that way. Oregon State controls the field position, wedging USC deep in its own territory. A flicker of life comes on a Stafon Johnson 10-yard run for a first down to open one drive, but another of those damaging USC holding penalties nullifies the play, and the Trojans are forced to punt three plays later. After that, Jacquizz keeps running and the clock keeps ticking. USC can't seem to do much about either.

With 3:15 to play, driving to climb out of a hole on his own 2-yard line, a frantic Sanchez completes one pass to get out to the 14. But throwing into triple coverage on the next play, his spiral sails over Damian Williams's head and into the arms of Greg Layborn, who returns it 28 yards to the Trojan 2. Moments later, Jacquizz burrows his way into the end zone and it is 27–14 after the P.A.T. fails. USC could give up at this point, but Ronald Johnson returns the kickoff 48 yards, and Sanchez completes four consecutive passes, the final one a 14-yarder that Turner plucks away from a defender in the end zone. That makes it 27–21, and it comes down to an onside kick attempt. When Oregon State recovers it, running out the clock is easy; not getting swallowed up in the sea of delirious orange-clad fans who rush the field afterward is not.

It takes a few moments for everyone, in Oregon and across the nation, to realize what has transpired. For the second time in a row in Corvallis, a Riley-coached team upsets Carroll and puts USC's BCS title hopes in major jeopardy. It also leaves some serious questions lingering in the cool Northwest air. Did Riley really outcoach Carroll again? Were the Trojans just flat, or are they seriously overrated? How could they look so good against Ohio State and so bad against Oregon State? And what happened to that defense that was giving up only 5.5 points per game going in?

In the hollow silence of the USC locker room, Carroll looks as stunned as anyone. He shakes his head when someone asks about his team's inability to stop Jacquizz Rodgers, who finishes with 186 yards on a staggering 37 carries. "I am just beside myself," he says. "We couldn't tackle him." Stanley Havili, the talented fullback who surprisingly never touched the ball in the game, looks up and says, "They just beat us up, plain and simple." Taylor Mays, the All-American safety who suffered a chest injury that had him coughing up blood at one point, is duly impressed with Mr. Rodgers, the tiny OSU tailback. "He ran the ball hard, he ran the ball with a lot of heart," Mays says. "He was not intimidated, not scared at all."

Later, Carroll admits he knew something was wrong on the hour bus ride over from the hotel in Eugene to Corvallis in the afternoon. At one point, he stood up and noticed all the players were sleeping. Turns out, they slept through the first half as well, and it could be the thirty minutes that ruin USC's national title hopes.

An hour after the game, Carroll is talking about reality, how the Pac-10 is a lot tougher than everyone else in the country thinks. "This is the way it is," he says. Back home, in Trojan Nation, they don't want to hear that. This is the third consecutive year USC has suffered a hiccup in the Pac-10, and although this one is still early enough to overcome, the alumni and boosters can't be happy losing to a 25-point underdog a year after being embarrassed by a 41-point 'dog in Stanford. The next day, the perpetually energized Carroll is already off, flying to Hawaii on a recruiting visit. Clearly, he has had time to view tape and reflect on what exactly happened. "It's about carrying the focus of practice to the game, and I didn't do a good enough job," he says, in a phone call with L.A. reporters. "It has to start with me."

He is right about that. All of a sudden, the rest of a potentially shaky 2008 season most definitely starts with him.

Pete Profile

Sparring with the Media

It isn't that the Los Angeles sports media is soft and laid-back. It's just that it isn't as hard-boiled and cynical as the sports media in New York or Philadelphia, or even Boston, for that matter.

There are no large, sarcastic tabloid headlines, no gossipy columns that follow the athletes' exploits off the field, and no regular second-guessing of seemingly every in-game decision. There certainly is none of the rabid coverage that fanatical college fans demand from the football-crazed Southeast Conference publications. Instead, the tone and the subject matter in Southern California is more reflective of a readership that, as a whole, isn't as intense and diehard as readers in other parts of the country.

But that isn't to say L.A. writers and columnists can't be critical, or they're hesitant to take their shots when they feel it is necessary, like immediately after this season's shocking early-season loss to 25-point underdog Oregon State. More than a few L.A. writers, as well as the many bloggers and new Internet columnists, reminded readers that this annual problem Carroll has with far less talented Pac-10 rivals has become a disturbing trend. In New York, or Philly, or Boston, however that criticism from columnists would have come down like a hard-driving wrecking ball. In L.A., it was more like a gentle bump by a car that lurched out from behind you on the 110 Freeway.

When Pete Carroll was first announced as the new head coach at USC in December of 2000, there was a large group of critics (including this one) who wrote that he was a curious choice, that he seemed more a clone of the failed and just fired Paul Hackett than the next coming of John McKay. Since then, of course, Carroll has proved all of us wrong, winning over the media the same way he has won over Trojan fans, producing six consecutive conference championships (going into this season), six top-four finishes in the national polls, a thirty-four-game winning streak, two national championships, and a steady stream of impressive bowl wins to go along with his even-tempered, fun-loving personality.

Carroll has become a master of dealing with L.A. writers and sports-casters. "Pete gets it, whatever it is," says Tim Tessalone, USC's sports information director, who has dealt with six different football head coaches in his thirty-one years on the job. "He understands the media. He's a master at it. He isn't calculated about it. He is genuine. Other coaches are tight and limited with the media. We're just the opposite. We embrace having the media here. I have to think we're way different than any other school in the country in how accessible we are with our players and coaches to the media."

Does Carroll read the newspapers? Maybe not all of them at once, but don't be fooled. He is aware of almost everything that is written about him. When I was a columnist for the *Orange County Register* and he was near the end of his team's thirty-four-game winning streak, I wrote that the pressure seemed to be taking a toll on him physically, that I had never remembered seeing him appear as worn down. Next time I saw him, he looked up and smiled. "So you think I look tired, huh?" he asked.

Every year, visiting writers from around the country come to USC and are stunned that the practices are open, not only to the media but to most of the general public. "When you compare Carroll to the peo-ple in the SEC and the Big Ten, he comes off as the most accessible coach in America," says Dan Weber, a former Trojans beat writer for the *Riverside-Press Enterprise*, one of the many large suburban news-papers that cover the team. "You not only can talk to him every day, you can watch what his team is doing every day. That's almost unheard of at most schools. This is one of the few programs in America that doesn't have a state trooper always walking alongside the head coach. Tommy Tubberville of Auburn had one taking him to practice every day. That's not Pete. He wouldn't want one. I think Pete wants us [the media] here. I think he understands that every kid he's recruiting can follow USC football on the Internet, reading blogs or newspaper Web sites. I think he figured that out before anyone. He is just the perfect personality for this team and this town."

Gary Klein has been the USC beat writer for the *Los Angeles Times*, by far the biggest circulation newspaper in the area, for seven years. He agrees that the daily access is terrific. "But I think he [Carroll] does it as much to monitor the media as the media is monitoring him," Klein says. "Has he complained to me about something I've written? Oh, sure. Any beat reporter has issues that come up over the years, but when he indicates he isn't thrilled about a particular story, my stance is that it's kind of too bad. I have to do what I do. He gets over it. He may not al-ways like what the media does, but he understands the media's job. He is open to talk about it. He won't always agree even after we talk, but he understands my side of it. It's a healthy thing. Sometimes, when you're working on a story, he doesn't like the fact you're digging, but at the same time, he respects the fact you are."

The *Times* has two main columnists. Bill Plaschke is the prize-winning lead columnist who, more often than not, writes off the news of the day. T. J. Simers is the acerbic, controversial Page Two columnist who regularly inserts himself into his columns.

"To me, Pete is among the best I've dealt with," says Plaschke. "He's totally transparent. You can go to any practice, you can call him anytime, and he always returns your call within two hours. He is always available. Once, when a lot of things were happening with [Reggie] Bush and [Matt] Leinart, I remember calling him and asking him if his program was falling apart. He answered right away. He's great about that. I remember going to the Rose Bowl practice here one time, just walking in, then going across the street to the Coliseum, and there were armed guards at the gate, preventing anyone from going in to the Michigan practice. Another thing I like about Carroll. He doesn't talk like a coach. He talks like a forty-five-year-old Redondo Beach surfer dude who just happens to coach the football team. If you rip him for something, he never gets mad. He'll still talk to you, and at the end of the day, you wonder why you ripped him. I think overall, he understands our role better than anyone."

Simers is the prickly member of the L.A. media. His shtick, as some like to call it, is an attempt to rattle coaches, managers or athletes, particularly when they're being interviewed in a large group. "Rattling isn't the right word," Simers says. "I try to challenge them. I find him [Carroll] to be one of my greatest challenges. He likes it. At his Tuesday media lunches, he doesn't want me to ask the first question. As competitive as he is, he wants to be competitive in the interviews. He does it with humor, with intimidation, and a kind of aw-shucks attitude. I went to him once after a player of his got into a fight. I challenged him on it. His first reaction was to get in my face. I told him to knock it off. You can't do that if you're the No. 1 coach in the country. Then he backed off and he was thoughtful and respectful. He's got it together. The way he handles the media is the way he handles the BCS controversies. You just go out and have fun. He is one of the best at not answering a question.

"I like the fact he takes people at face value," Simers says. "My attitude is, you want to play and spar, let's play and spar. I like to push his button on the NFL. I do it to tweak him. He's absolutely convinced he was a successful NFL coach. I tell him, 'You don't want to go there.' But then, it's all in fun. There are not many coaches you can find who have such a great concept of fun."

After the *L.A. Times*, the two most influential newspapers in the immediate area are the *Orange County Register* and the *L.A. Daily News*. Scott Wolf, who covers USC for the *Daily News*, also writes a popular blog on the paper's Web site. On his blog, he playfully refers to Carroll as "Caesar," hinting at the coach's all-consuming power. "I've found him [Carroll] to be very accommodating and easygoing," says Wolf. "He doesn't restrict you, but I don't think he reads that much, either. The only time the Caesar thing came up between us, he laughed about it."

Mark Whicker is the smooth, well-regarded lead columnist for the *Register*, someone who has traveled the country more than most writers. "There is no question Carroll is the most available coach at that level," Whicker says. "He gets the whole process. I was doing a piece once and needed to talk to him after a Friday night practice, and he stood there and talked to me for a full half hour, from 6:30 to 7:00. That was on a Friday night. You're not going to get that from most guys. I remember Arkansas writers coming here, and they were astounded to see how open the practices were. I tell a lot of my friends around the country, 'Yeah, it's really tough here. You have to park your car, walk to the field, grab the door, and open it.' They can't believe it."

Carroll isn't one of those coaches who makes it a habit to know every writer's name, "but I think he has a vague idea who we are," Whicker says. "He is always cordial about it. I think he likes working with people at the college level. He's told me that the NFL was like working on a mountaintop. There was no communication. I think he enjoys that part of the college experience."

Carroll also goes out of his way to make national sports writers and sportscasters comfortable, but with them, as with local writers, the trick is to keep the coach's attention. It's almost unanimous among those who have been around him. Maintaining attention span is not one of his strengths. "He's unique in that regard," says Tessalone. "He jokes that he's got ADD [attention deficit disorder]. He has an incredible gift to be able to concentrate on many things at once, but you have a real small window in your time with him before his mind motors off onto something else."

"I never worry about the reception I'm going to get at USC," says Ivan Maisel, who covers college football for ESPN.com. "What I worry about is whether Carroll is always focusing on what I'm asking him. The batting average there is decent, but not great. Yet, when dealing with him, I understand why he is so good in the living room. Because he likes people. As far as the media is concerned, he understands that usually we're going to help him."

Carroll's own reaction to dealing with the media is that it is part of his job. "Bud [Grant, his former boss with the Minnesota Vikings] was a big influence on me when it came to the media," he says. "I've learned to respect the fact you guys have a job to do. I think I have a responsibility to help you do it accurately. So I try to be accessible and honest."

As for the more eclectic members of the L.A. media, Carroll just smiles. "I don't mind guys like T. J. [Simers]," he says. "I try to have fun with it. I don't take him too seriously because we talk privately at other times and I understand what he's about." As for Wolf, the beat writer who refers to him as Caesar in his blog, Carroll says, "I know that it's out there, but I don't worry about it. Really, the bottom line for me when it comes to the media is that I try to deal with it the way I deal with everything else."

VI

Game Four: Setting the Tone
for the Rest of the Season

Rocky Seto, the young secondary coach, is sitting at a desk in the offices on the second floor of Heritage Hall on the Tuesday morning after the Oregon State game, shaking his head, marveling at the disposition of his boss.

Pete Carroll had just suffered one of the biggest upset losses of his eight-year run at USC, watching his team get wildly outplayed on both sides of the line of scrimmage by the 25-point underdog Beavers and having the whole, embarrassing thing televised nationwide by ESPN. Most college head coaches, in a similar situation, would have arrived back at work screaming and shouting and rattling off four-letter epithets.

"But he wasn't angry," says Seto, with an amazed look on his face. "He just said we have to do things right. Not different, just right. I've seen this before. This is when Coach is at his best. He is a master at focusing on what's ahead, instead of what's happened in the past." Steve Sarkisian, the offensive coordinator, is quick to agree. "The great thing about Pete is that his energy level is so high," says Sarkisian. "Everyone's energy escalates after a loss, but Pete is a very upbeat guy. With him, it's all about moving on to the next one."

Maybe, but the 27–21 upset in Corvallis left some serious questions that are still hanging there, in the broiling, 95-degree air on the Howard Jones practice field on Tuesday. Like, what exactly happened to the offensive and defensive lines? Were they just flat, or did they suddenly regress? And what about the running game? Will Carroll and Sarkisian ever sort out a tailback rotation that produced only 86 yards rushing against the Beavers? Maybe most important, what's the condition of middle linebacker Rey Maualuga, who suffered a strained right knee in the game? With a 4-1 Oregon team coming to town that has averaged 300 yards-per-game rushing, it's no time to be without your All-American middle 'backer.

Even Carroll is still trying to sort out what transpired in that Northwest shocker, although ensuing upset loses by No. 3 Georgia and No. 4 Florida on the weekend buffered some of the heat USC was taking, even after dropping from No. 1 to No. 9 in the polls. "I don't think we had the same edge," Carroll says. "I think it's normal to be like that after a big game [against Ohio State], but we gave Oregon State a tremendous boost, letting them score on their first drive and letting them stop us on our first three drives. It is something I take great pride in not allowing. I didn't get it done."

Now there is a new challenge in a game that suddenly has become much more pivotal than anyone expected. If USC, the six-time defending Pac-10 champion, loses, it goes to 0-2 in the conference and Oregon would go to 3-0, virtually guaranteeing the end of the Trojans' Pac-10 title run. Instead of the Rose Bowl or the Orange Bowl, Carroll and his players would be staring at the strong possibility of the Holiday Bowl. The new, growing tension around the football offices is escalated when, in a team meeting early on Tuesday, Carroll calls out Chris Galippo, a redshirt freshman middle linebacker. "It's your time to step up," he says in front of the whole team. "This is why you come here, to play in situations like these." Except this isn't the way USC wants it. Galippo, at 6'2" and 255 pounds, is a five-star recruit and high school All-

American from nearby Orange County who was the best defensive player on the field in the spring game. He has a promising future, but he has had two back surgeries in the past year, the last one only thirteen weeks ago, and it would be a stretch to believe he is anywhere near full game shape. Twenty-four hours later, Carroll seems to accept that fact and moves Brian Cushing, his other All-American linebacker, from the outside into the middle, relegating Galippo to backup status, although it's likely he'll play some and, if effective, perhaps go as long as he can.

Carroll's biggest move of the week is an obvious attempt to send a message to the team. He demotes Averell Spicer, the defensive tackle who was guilty of not just one, but two personal foul calls against Oregon State, one of them a game-changer. He calls in Spicer and tells him he won't be starting against Oregon Saturday night in the Coliseum. "Coach had a talk with me and said that they can't start me having two personal fouls in a game," Spicer says. "They told me I was supposed to be a better leader, to lead by example, and I definitely wasn't doing it. I understand that."

So sophomore Christian Tupou becomes the third new starter for the game against No. 23-ranked Oregon. Untested sophomore linebacker Michael Morgan moves in at Cushing's outside line-backer spot, and Alex Parsons, a semiexperienced junior, steps in for Zack Herberer, who is out with an injured toe at right guard. This is not the way the Trojans would prefer it against a team that seems far more dangerous than the 17-point underdog status provided by the oddsmakers. People forget Oregon was the hottest team in the country a year ago, sprinting off to nine consecutive victories, averaging more than 40 points a game, to become the favorite for the BCS championship. Quarterback Dennis Dixon, who had become the deft director of Coach Mike Bellotti's spread offense, seemed on his way to the Heisman Trophy. Then, two weeks after Dixon and the Ducks had outpointed USC, 24–17, Dixon blew out his knee against Arizona, losing the game and all the momentum they had built up. They proceeded to drop their next two games, against UCLA and Oregon State, before regaining their composure and dispatching South Florida, 56–21, in the Sun Bowl.

Yet another one of the coaches USC considered before hiring Carroll, Bellotti has turned Oregon into a consistent national power, with the help of an eager alumni, noted Nike owner, and devoted Ducks fan and donor, Phil Knight. Bellotti guided Oregon to a No. 2 ranking and a Fiesta Bowl victory in 2001 and has led the university to eleven bowl appearances in thirteen seasons. He has done it with a wildly entertaining style, demonstrating the ability to win with a straight drop-back quarterback like Joey Harrington and the flexibility to change, with a more athletic, gifted running quarterback such as Dixon. Unfortunately, the Dixon injury kick-started a tidal wave of problems at quarterback, with no less than seven players knocked out of action at that position in less than a year. Nate Costa, who had won the job heading into 2008, was injured in camp and ruled out for the season. Justin Roper, his backup, also has a bum knee, but Bellotti has hopes he will be ready to contribute against USC, although he is saying third-stringer Jeremiah Masoli, who is back from a concussion, is the likely starter, with a pair of freshmen also available. For all their chaos at quarterback, the Ducks have opened up 4-1, losing only to a ranked Boise State team. "I think we are playing all right," Bellotti says in a phone interview during the week. "I think we are struggling a little bit with turnovers, and it's probably a result of the youth and inexperience at quarterback. We are making the turn in that regard and getting better each week."

It is Oregon's running, not its passing, that has Carroll concerned, especially after the way his team was pushed around against the run in Corvallis. In the USC coaches' offices, they're still frantically trying to figure out why the defense broke down so drastically against Oregon State and its tiny tailback. For most of the horribly ineffective first half, the Trojans went with what appeared to be a 3-4 alignment that clearly wasn't working. At his Tuesday media lunch, Caroll says he didn't use the three-down set that much. "We just shifted some," he says. Later, Kyle Moore, the senior defensive end who, like most of his teammates, didn't have a good game, seems to disagree. "We played a 3-4 in the first half, and that didn't help," Moore says. "We went back to our base [4-3] in the second half and we got better. They ran 45 times on us with two basic plays and we still couldn't stop it."

Bellotti admits he took notice. "Oregon State had a great game plan and executed that game plan well," he says. "We are trying to find ways to take that game plan and implement it ourselves. I don't know if that's going to work." If anything, Oregon's offense is much more explosive than its cross-state neighbor's. In five games, the Ducks have scored 237 points, including the 63 it hung on Pac-10 punching bag Washington State the previous week. The Ducks finished the game ranked fourth in the nation and first in the conference, with a 308.6–yard rushing average. "They just ripped in that game," Carroll says. "They have a very wide-open attack. It is really kind of the epitome of the spread offense with the quarterback being featured as part of the running attack, but it's their running backs that are the biggest threats. Jeremiah Johnson always has been a good player, and the new kid, [LeGarrette] Blount, has really given them another element. Jonathan Stewart was a heck of a football player, but this guy runs maybe more physical, in a more physical nature about him. Jonathan, you know, he played on the edges maybe more effectively. But Blount really comes at you and breaks tackles and makes you miss. He has an attitude about him. They really recruited well in getting him."

In a game that could develop into a wide-open shoot-out, USC is hinting that the best way to control Oregon's volatile offense is to keep it off the field. For that to happen, the Trojans will have to run the ball better than they did at Oregon State, averaging a meager 3.9 yards a carry. "We have to find a way to get more than 22 carries," Sarkisian says. They also have to find the identity of their best running back.

This has been an issue since Reggie Bush and LenDale White left after the 2005 season. Carroll recruits running backs the way politicians recruit voters. He can never seem to have enough. Two years ago, he had ten on the roster, most of them four- and five-star recruits out of high school. This year the list has been cut down to six, with four apparently in the regular rotation heading into the opener at Virginia. Since then, the carries have been few and far between for everyone but Joe McKnight, the sophomore from Louisiana who had a good game against Ohio State (105 yards in 12 carries) but a terrible night at Oregon State. McKnight gained only 10 yards in 7 carries in Corvallis. Stafon Johnson gained 48 in the same 7 carries and had two runs of 10 and 13 yards called back because of penalties.

So it would seem natural that Johnson, who is clearly the bigger, more effective runner between the tackles, get more opportunities, maybe even take over as the primary ball carrier, with McKnight, who is smaller but flashier, becoming the change-of-pace, hybrid back who will run and catch passes out in space. Except in Carroll's mind, it is never that easy. For whatever reason, McKnight seems to be his favorite, maybe because he reminds him of Bush. Or maybe it is because he tries to go out of his way to give high-profile, out-of-state recruits as much playing time as possible, as a signal for future prospects. At one point this week, Carroll praises Johnson, noting that "he was very effective, moved the pile well, made some space for himself." But at another point, the coach says the first three weeks he has "still been searching a little bit, trying to get the best combination." Maybe in his most revealing comment, though, he says he'd like to have a Bush-White kind of combination, adding "you have Joe and the other factor." It is always "Joe" and someone else. That's just the way it seems to go with Carroll. "This is not a problem," he says. "It is going to work itself out in my mind."

Not in everyone's mind, though. Early in the week, Allen Bradford, the junior who has been running fourth in the so-called four-man rotation, admits his frustration in a story in the *L.A.*

Times. He had no carries and dropped the only pass thrown to him in Corvallis. "Even with as many tailbacks as we have, I shouldn't be going through this," he tells the *Times.* "I just want to play. I came here to play . . . I'm a junior. I shouldn't have to talk to them about getting the ball." Those who cover the Trojans regularly understand Bradford's frustration. He might be the team's most effective practice player, consistently breaking off more big runs than any other tailback on the team in workouts for the past two years. Yet for whatever reason, the coaches have never seemed overly enthusiastic about him, whether it's his failure to pass block as well as others or just that he isn't exactly the kind of tailback Carroll and Sarkisian envision.

Remarkably up to now, Carroll has been careful to avoid any full-blown controversy at tailback, but when you're winning it is easier for everyone to buy in. When you lose, even if it's just one game, then the second-guessing begins. Each of the top four candidates has an excellent case. McKnight is the best breakaway type. Johnson is the purest runner. C.J. Gable, the top pass blocker, also might be the most well-rounded, while Bradford, with his 5'11" 230–pound frame, is the most powerful.

Sarkisian, sensing this is becoming a hot-button issue, says the Oregon game will be different. "We're going to give some guys the chance to run the ball," he says. "We're going to do some things to help us. Schematically, we're going to create some opportunities." At one point, I ask Carroll how often he'd like his team to run. "I don't know," he says, sounding a little irritated. "How many times do we want to run it? We want to run it 40 times in a game. I like rushing for 200 yards and 40 carries. Those kinds of numbers, when we play well, that's what happens. You know, so there's plenty of runs for everybody. We're not concerned when that happens."

USC's fan base seems concerned. There is an uneasy feeling heading into the weekend, knowing what happened on both sides of the line of scrimmage in Corvallis and understanding the kind of prolific offense Oregon and Bellotti will bring to town. The only soothing factor, perhaps, is that the game will be played in the Coliseum, where Carroll is 38-1 in his last seven and a half years.

Game day dawns cool and cloudy in Los Angeles, with a light morning rain pelting the ground around the Coliseum. "Great," mumbles one early-arriving fan clad in USC colors, "it's Ducks weather. Feels more like Oregon than L.A." Before kickoff, there is a press box announcement that Bradford would not be suited up for the game because "of a sore hip." Remembering his complaints about lack of carries in the newspaper earlier in the week, you can't help but wonder if the tailback is really out with a sore lip. Coaches never appreciate players who air their differences in the media.

Once the game begins, the weather is not the only thing remindful of USC's last visit to Oregon. The visiting Ducks take the opening kickoff and proceed to move effortlessly down the field, mostly behind Masoli, the third-string quarterback who is gaining most of his yards with quick fakes and darting runs off the spread formation. The ground game the Trojans couldn't stop in Corvallis seems to be haunting them again, and after a 14-play, 70-yard drive, the Ducks are ahead, 7–0. Mark Sanchez leads USC back on its first possession, but his crisp passes only get them to the Oregon 4, where the Ducks hold and David Buehler kicks a 21-yard field goal to make it 7–3. Oregon takes off again, with Masoli running and passing for good chunks of yards, but this time it is the Trojans' turn to hold, limiting the Ducks to a Matt Evensen 24-yard field goal. Still, it's 10–3, Oregon, and more than a few boosters and alumni are squirming uncomfortably in their expensive Coliseum seats.

Happily for them, the evening, and maybe the rest of USC's season, takes a sharp turn in the next few minutes. The Trojans piece together a sort of chugging kind of drive that leaves them with a fourth and 2 on the Ducks' 34-yard line. Carroll looks at the yard marker, glances up at the scoreboard, and orders Sarkisian to call a play. He is gambling and going for it. Sarkisian, to his credit, selects a beauty. USC's receivers run a little crisscross pattern on a "pick" play, as the coaches call it, and Damon Williams glides down the sideline wide open. Sanchez finds him with a floating spiral for touchdown that ties the score at 10, sending the crowd of 82,765 into a frenzy and the momentum swinging to the Trojans' side. Less than three minutes later, after USC forces the visitors to punt, Sanchez drops back, once again using his athleticism to avoid a diving tackle attempt near his ankles. He steps up into the pocket and delivers a rocket 50 yards downfield to Ronald Johnson, who is five yards behind the nearest Ducks defender. It goes for a 63-yard touchdown, and just like that, it's 17–10, USC. Another Buehler field goal stretches the lead to 20–10, and then with only slightly more than a minute to play in the half, Oregon's Bellotti makes a decision that blows the game open.

With a first and 10 on his own 20, instead of running the clock out, he orders Masoli to throw the ball. His pass is complete to Jaison Williams, but Josh Pinkard, the defensive back who had waited two years to start again, strips him of the ball and falls on it at the Ducks' 21. A personal foul penalty gives USC the ball at the 10, and with 18 seconds to play in the half, Sanchez finds Turner in the corner of the end zone for an 11-yard touchdown and a seemingly insurmountable 27–10 lead as the teams go in for halftime.

The second half begins with a 22-yard touchdown run by the Trojans' Stafon Johnson that features the kind of dazzling cutback move even Reggie Bush would have admired, but almost before the buzz from that play is over, a loud gasp emanates from the crowd. Sanchez is horse-collared and sacked by Nick Reed, an old high school teammate of his from Mission Viejo, no less, and the quarterback, whose left knee seems to buckle under him, is collapsed on the floor of the Coliseum and not moving. Trainers and Carroll sprint toward him from the USC sideline, and the giant saucer is immediately reduced to one collective hush. Minutes go by, with doctors and trainers rubbing and examining the same knee that had suffered a patella displacement a few weeks before the season. Sanchez not only gets up and limps off, however, he eventually comes back into the game, to the amazement of practically everyone. Why would you let him back in to have that knee exposed to further injury? No one really explains it later, but clearly, the injury must not be too serious.

The game, itself, ends up 44–10, and except for Carroll allowing backup quarterback Mitch Mustain to throw a 59-yard touchdown bomb to David Ausberry in the final minutes, seemingly rubbing it in a bit on Bellotti and the overmatched Ducks, the final thirty minutes were distinguished by USC's domination on defense, shutting off that supposedly lethal Oregon running game. The visitors, who had been averaging over 300 yards on the ground, finish with only 60 this time on 39 carries, a 1.5-yard average. Blount, the large, physical tailback Carroll had been gushing over, is limited to a net zero yards in 9 carries.

The Coliseum mood is understandably festive as the teams trot off the field. So it comes as a surprise when Carroll, as he races by me in the large tunnel heading to the locker room, turns and loudly shouts "S——t!" I think he is kidding at first, but then I notice the look on the coach's face. He is definitely not kidding. When I ask him about it later in the locker room, Carroll says, "I'm just still mad about what happened last week. I loved this win tonight, but I'll be forever frustrated and bitter about my effort [in Corvallis]. I'm still pissed. I had a sense six months ago [that] that game could be a problem. In all ways I tried to avert it, and it still frigging happened. I don't want to take anything away from Oregon State, but look at the difference [in our play]. I don't think I could own up to that until we came back to win. The thing is, the wins kind of get washed out. The losses stick forever."

Sanchez's health is naturally a main topic of discussion in the locker room. Nick Sanchez, the quarterback's father, who is at all games and almost every practice, stands quietly to the side as his son is interviewed. "Yes, my heart dropped there for a couple of minutes," he says. "I waited until the next series to go down [on the field] and then he gave me the thumbs-up. The knee is sore, but I think he's going to be OK." His son tries his best to soothe any concerns. "I just aggravated it [the knee] a little," he says. "It was scary for a moment. It just kind of bent a little funny, but nothing popped. It is a good thing I had a brace and a patella brace."

Sanchez and the receivers are getting most of the attention, but it was the defense, especially the run defense, that was the key to this game. Cushing, the senior who might be the best pure football player on the team, stood in front of his cubicle staring down at the wrap around his broken right hand. Playing middle linebacker for the first time in place of Maualuga, he was all over the field, more active than ever, even knocking down two passes in coverage that he might have intercepted had his hand not been broken. "Yeah," he says, shaking his head, "I think I could have had those, but it was good going out there and playing like we're capable of playing." As for the new position, well, Cushing acts like he wouldn't mind another game or two at middle linebacker. "It was fun," he says. "You're in on a lot of the action."

After most of the locker room has cleared out, Carroll is still there, lingering at the far end of the room, talking about his speech to the players the night before. "I reminded them about our record in the Coliseum [a stretch of 38-1 going into this game], and asked them how many teams in any sport, baseball, pro football, anything, go six or seven years losing only one game at home. I told them they have to respect that. They have a responsibility to carry that on. It was a big, teachable moment last night. You could tell the guys got it." The coach reiterates how important it is to bounce back like this. "It's something we need to grow on," he says. "This was a big moment for us. It reminded us we have to do things properly each week."

At that moment, he interrupts the interview session. "Hey Rock, good game," he shouts. "Really, Rock, great game . . . great game." Rocky Seto, the secondary coach, looks over, smiles, and shakes his head in affirmation. After Carroll turns his attention back to the writers, Seto glances back one more time, and you can almost read his mind.

The young assistant was right a few days earlier in his office. The head coach is at his best when focusing on what's ahead.

Pete Profile

The Rock Star Recruiter

Bud Grant, the legendary Hall of Fame coach for the Minnesota Vikings, remembers when a young assistant on his staff named Pete Carroll asked what it took to be a great coach. "I said, 'Pete, your No. 1 job as a coach is acquiring the best players.' Later, after he was fired by the Jets and Patriots, I called him and told him that the only thing that caught up with him in the NFL is that he didn't have enough good players. He said he'll remind me of that one day. Not long ago, he called me from USC and he said, 'You know where I am now? Well, we have the best players.'"

Nobody argues that fact anymore. When it comes to the fine art of recruiting quality high school athletes, no one in college football does it better than Pete Carroll.

He has become a recruiting rock star, the guy who knocks out No. 1 national classes the way some guys knock down beers after work. From 2004–2007, Rivals.com rated USC's recruiting class first in the nation three times. The other year they had it ranked second. When the Trojans haven't been one or two, they've almost always been in the top five. Many think this recent class that just officially committed in February, led by All-Everything quarterback Matt Barkley, could be among his best yet.

Competing against other Pac-10 schools, Carroll's advantage is even greater. In the three-year period from 2005 to 2008, the Trojans signed twenty-nine players ranked among the top fifty in America. The rest of the Pac-10 combined to sign four. "They are in a different stratosphere than everybody else when it comes to recruiting," says Oregon State coach Mike Riley.

Other coaches come and go, but when USC's charismatic coach shows up at the front door, whether it's in a smoggy L.A. suburb or a tiny town in Kentucky, everything stops. It is like George Clooney just drove up. Even at high school games in Southern California, it ceases being just another evening and turns into an event when Carroll appears. "Pete's amazing," says Ed Orgeron, the new University of Tennessee assistant coach who worked for Carroll as an assistant and recruiting coordinator from 1998 to 2004 before leaving to become a head coach at Mississippi. "It's like he's got a magic pill, or something. As soon as he walks into a room, everybody is his friend. Nobody is better than Pete with parents."

Nobody is more competitive when it comes to going after five-star athletes, either. "He goes beyond competiveness from anyone I ever saw," says Orgeron. "Other guys regularly get doors shut on them. He always finds another door open. He has a knack for finding another way. He sometimes goes to thirteen, fourteen, fifteen schools in a day. He'd show up at some practices at 6:00 A.M. After a few years with him, we had completely captured Southern California. We were getting all the top recruits locally and going after the best ones nationwide. It was incredible. His energy never ends."

When a new NCAA rule prohibited head coaches from going on the road to recruit in May, nobody was angrier than Carroll. "That's a rule for lazy guys who don't want to work hard," he says. "Those of us who do shouldn't be penalized."

Carroll's best ally is the cell phone. Spend any time with him, day or night, and you'll look over and he is suddenly chatting to a recruit on his cell. "So how's everything, are you working hard?" he'll ask. "You keeping up on your grades?" Sometimes, in the middle of a coaches' meeting, he'll be talking, then hand the phone over to an assistant. "Here," he'll say, "Sark wants to say hello." After USC's most important victory in the Carroll era, the 55–19 national-title clincher over Oklahoma in the 2005 Orange Bowl, they say Carroll was already on the phone with recruits on the bus ride back from the stadium to the hotel in Miami. Local prep coaches often are stunned to look over at the sideline at practice during an average week and see the coach of the often No. 1–ranked Trojans. "Other coaches don't do that," says Long Beach Poly coach Raul Lary. "If you're a player and the head coach of the No. 1 team is there watching you at a practice or at a game, that can be pretty impressive to a young man."

Carroll takes it beyond that. You can be standing with him in the middle of a postgame press conference in the USC locker room when he'll suddenly stop and look over at a teenager lingering nearby. "Hey, 28," he'll say, "heard you got three last night. Keep it up and you'll wind up dressing in here one day." The young man, startled that the nation's most famous college coach not only realizes who he is but knows his number and how many touchdowns he scored the night before, proceeds to light up like the Coliseum scoreboard.

Number-one draft picks, that's what Carroll calls the best players he recruits every season. "In the NFL, you only get one No. 1 pick a year," he says. "In college, I can go out and sign fifteen No. 1 picks every year if I'm doing my job right." Most of the time, he is.

"Other schools can razzle and dazzle you with their facilities, but not Coach Carroll," says Mark Sanchez, his current star quarterback. "He doesn't promise anything. If a coach promises something, you know he's promising someone else. Here's what he said to me, 'We have great quarterbacks here. We think you're great. You can compete with those guys. I'm not going to tell you that you can start here. But I think you're good enough to play here.'"

Taylor Mays, his current All-American safety, says it was the same with him. "Coach Carroll never promised I was going to play like some other coaches. He never went out of his way to overrecruit me. He just told me they wanted me and if I wanted to compete to be a great player, I should come to this school." Jeff Byers, the senior guard and captain of the 2008 team who played his high school football in Colorado, says he was blown away by Carroll's personality. "He wows everybody," says Byers. "He just has a personality people naturally gravitate to. You can see he genuinely cares about you and that he is a passionate person. My folks were really impressed. Heck, I was really impressed."

The actual recruiting is preceded by evaluating. "Pete is so good at that part of it, too," says Orgeron. "There were thirteen million people in our surrounding area (Southern California), and he had to pick the select few guys we'd go after. Over the years, there were very few times when he wasn't correct." Like most coaches, Carroll gives each of his assistants specific areas in the country to oversee. "You have an area, you go on the road and gather a list of athletes, then you trim it down and present it to the staff," says Rocky Seto, who started this season as the defensive backfield coach at USC. "But there is no question who has the last word. Say one of us really likes a receiver, and the coach doesn't like him. We're not going to take him."

On out-of-state recruits, especially, Carroll is very discriminating. "He tells us he only wants kids who are capable of being first-round NFL draft picks," says Seto. It is that mind-set that has helped the Trojans become such a consistent national power. It is how they landed a Mike Williams from Florida, an Everson Griffen from Arizona, a Byers from Colorado, and a Joe McKnight from Louisiana.

"We don't really recruit against other schools in the Pac-10," says Carroll. "We get eight of the top ten kids from California, and something like fourteen of the top twenty. Over the years, the Pac-10 has taken a hundred kids a year out of the state of California. If we can get the top ten of those hundred, that means nobody else in our conference is getting them."

Carroll admits he is very selective when it comes to picking athletes. "Especially with the out-of-state kids, we look at the makeup," he says. "Is he a California-type guy? We find fifteen or twenty we really like. If we can get five or six of those, we're in pretty good shape. But they have to be kids talented enough to project as NFL first-round picks. If they aren't, we don't want them."

The intense recruiting began immediately for Carroll at USC. His very first class was small, only sixteen recruits in all. Nevertheless, it included two future NFL players, linemen Shaun Cody and Mike Patterson, and a future Heisman Trophy quarterback, Matt Leinart. Cody, widely regarded as the best defensive lineman in the country his senior year in high school, was a particularly impressive "get" because Notre Dame was a strong favorite of his parents, with the Irish in it all the way to the end. When Cody did sign with the Trojans, it was a signal that the recruiting landscape had changed. USC was a big-time player again for the first time since the John McKay–John Robinson glory years.

From there, it has only grown to a point where almost every top-ranked national recruit lists USC among his possibilies heading into his senior season in high school. As for in-state recruits, well, the Trojans' goal is to visit each of the 1,053 football-playing high schools in California every year. If the numbers have changed over the years, Carroll's style hasn't.

Brice Butler, a young wide receiver from Norcross, Georgia, matriculated to USC, probably because his mother, Cyrillyn, was even more impressed than her son. "Coach Carroll is so funny," says Mrs. Butler, "because when you see him on TV, he's usually very calm on the sideline. He might get excited every now and then, but his personality on TV is pretty much the same when you meet him in person. He played basketball with my youngest two sons out in the yard when he was back here for a visit. If my neighbors would have known they were on their court, they would have died. They missed an opportunity because they weren't home that day. That's what is really neat about him. When we came out there, we went to Manhattan Beach, and he talked to Bobby [her husband] and me for a little while, but he kind of gravitated to my youngest sons. He talked about the beach, the guys out there with boogie boards and surfing. He can get down to anybody's level. That was real impressive to me."

John Sanders, the head coach at Saguaro High School in Arizona, talks about how often Carroll, who recruited one of his players, Corey Adams (who eventually signed with Arizona State), shows up on his campus. "Coach Carroll has been here three times, and that says a lot," says Sanders, who added that some other local Arizona coaches hadn't been around much. "But Pete Carroll has been here three times. After we won our second consecutive state championship, Pete was at the school the following Monday. You should have seen the reaction when he walked into our weight room. One of our kids asked if he could take a picture of the two greatest coaches in the country. When Pete agreed to put his arm around me, there were about seventy cell phones pointed at us. It was crazy. Coach Carroll is like a rock star with the kids."

Since he's been at USC, Pete Carroll not only goes after the best high school football players in America, he signs more than anyone else.

Bud Grant must be very proud.

VII

Game Five: A New Star Grapples
with a Wounded Knee

How are you gentlemen doing on this beautiful, fall afternoon?" says a smiling Nick Sanchez, addressing a group of writers at the start of USC's Monday practice. Mark Sanchez's father seems in a surprisingly good mood, considering his son, the team's starting quarterback, is sitting in an equipment cart, his injured left knee still heavily wrapped, watching instead of participating, as his teammates begin getting ready for the next game with Arizona State.

"Maybe he knows something we don't know," says one writer. Or maybe not. Either way, one thing is clear about this 2008 Trojans team under Pete Carroll. Sanchez, the gifted redshirt junior, has become the focus of everything that is going on, whether he is on the field throwing those blurring spirals of his, or on the sideline watching with a knee that has been battered two different times now. Two weeks before the opener, it was a dislocated kneecap that looked like it might keep him out for an extended period, but to almost everyone's surprise, including Carroll's, Sanchez recovered quickly enough to start and play a terrific game at Virginia. In the last game, he twisted that same knee in what appeared to be another serious injury. Now here he is, wearing his yellow number 6 jersey, but relaxing in the equipment cart on the sideline, observing while Mitch Mustain, the new No. 2 quarterback, takes the majority of the reps.

Sanchez's injury is officially labeled "a deep bone bruise," and while his lack of activity on Monday causes a minifrenzy among reporters, no one else seems too concerned, including Carroll. "I don't know," he says about Sanchez's condition, in a quick postpractice interview. "I don't think anybody knows. The swelling is the issue." Still, if you've been around Carroll long enough, you can sense when he is worried and when he is not. This does not seem to be one of those times when he is. "I'm going to follow my usual Monday routine," he says, grinning, on the steps leading to his office. "I'm going to make some recruiting calls and then break down film of Arizona State."

For his part, Sanchez seems the most upbeat of all. "I feel good," he says. "It feels a lot better than I thought. I'm walking around good. I want to practice as soon as I can. In the meantime, I just have to elevate the knee and ice it. Do I think I'll start on Saturday? I think I'll have a shot."

It is a measure of Sanchez's growing stature that everything he does, or doesn't do, now becomes news. He has emerged as the clear new star of this team after only four games. Much of the early Heisman Trophy hype generated after that rousing blowout of Ohio State faded in the dark shadows of the startling upset loss to Oregon State. Nevertheless, Sanchez and the Trojans both reemerged with a big game in the 44–10 mugging of No. 23–ranked Oregon. It isn't just his impressive numbers so far, the 1,069 yards and 13 touchdown passes. It is the way he has established his own identity at what has become USC's clear glamour position. John David Booty, his immediate predecessor, was a solid, winning quarterback who was extremely accurate and effective, losing only three games in two seasons as a starter, one of them when forced to play the second half with a broken finger on his passing hand. There was no flair to Booty's game, however. He was a straight, drop-back passer with little mobility who rarely took chances. He came across as semi-robotic at times. Almost immediately, it became obvious that Sanchez is his polar opposite. More athletic and able to roll out as well as drop straight back, he is more apt to throw the ball deep and much more likely to gamble on gunning the ball between defenders. The defining play of the young USC season is a typical example. Sanchez had dropped back and was about to be sacked by an Oregon lineman when he made a quick, almost jukelike move up in the pocket, leaving the potential tackler sprawled in his wake. Buying an extra two or three seconds, he looked up to spot Ronald Johnson running free in the Ducks' secondary and found him with a beautiful, arcing, 63-yard strike for a touchdown. "That's a dimension we didn't have before," Carroll notes, which is a nice way of saying Booty couldn't have made that play.

Sanchez is playing the part of a star off the field, as well. Booty wasn't a charismatic personality. Sanchez is. Tall and swarthy, he is handsome enough to have been confused for Matt Leinart, the Hollywood-loving bachelor, when Mark was a redshirt freshman. "Matt, Matt, would you sign my football?" the tiny Trojan fans would scream. Sanchez would smile and explain he wasn't Matt, he was Mark. Sanchez was smart enough to learn from Leinart, though. He watched the way he dealt with fans and media and modeled himself after the smooth Heisman Trophy winner. If anything, Sanchez is even more gracious with the media, pausing after interviews to personally shake every reporter's hand and thank him or her. On sports talk radio or TV shows, he is careful to refer to the hosts as "Mr. [Colin] Cowherd" or "Mr. [Kirk] Herbstreit."

He has come a long way from the young player who found himself arrested on suspicion of sexual assault on campus a couple years earlier. No one could believe it at the time because nobody seemed to have a more clean-cut image than the former high school All-American from Mission Viejo, California, and after a thorough investigation no charges were filed. Still, the incident seemed to make Sanchez realize that he is not just another student on campus. He is a football player who has to be extra diligent in everything he does, on and off the field.

These days, that incident seems long forgotten, and the cover-boy smile is flashed easily by the quarterback who appears to be having the time of his life. "I can't tell you how much fun it is to go out there with my teammates every week and try to win games," he says. The same teammates he helped win over with summer barbecues at his house named him one of the team's cocaptains, and there is no doubt he has assumed a strong role of leadership.

By Thursday of Arizona State week, the talk of Sanchez possibly sitting out has dissipated. He is back on the practice field, taking the majority of the snaps and moving around without any discernible discomfort. "He's a quick healer, I guess," says a grinning Carroll after practice. "I thought he looked good," says Steve Sarkisian. "but we'll have to wait until tomorrow to really know."

What is known already is that USC, with Sanchez, has become more of a pass-first, run-later offense. After four games, the Trojans have rushed for 613 yards and thrown for 1,204, almost a 2-1 ratio favoring passing. Carroll keeps saying he'd ideally like to run for 200 yards a game, but so far he has failed to establish a featured tailback. Joe McKnight, the one he seems to prefer, hasn't performed as consistently as hoped, and Stafon Johnson, seemingly the favorite of most fans and boosters, as well as many writers, hasn't carried the ball enough to establish a full-blown presence. The result is that this team, unlike Carroll's most recent national championship group of Reggie Bush and LenDale White, sets up the run with the pass, a system that seems a little precarious given the state of Sanchez's knee.

The daily health bulletins concerning the USC quarterback this week have taken away some of the hype surrounding Arizona State, the team most expected to challenge the Trojans for the Pac-10 title before the season. The Sun Devils have stumbled, though, losing their last three games after a 2-0 start, one of them to relative lightweight UNLV, and, like Carroll's team, come into Saturday's game unsure of the condition of their quarterback, Rudy Carpenter, the conference's most experienced passer. Carpenter suffered a severe ankle sprain during last week's game with Cal, left the stadium on crutches and has been pronounced as "very doubt-ful" most of the week, although he was back on the field practicing lightly by Thursday.

With or without Carpenter, one thing you know about Arizona State is that Dennis Erickson figures to have them ready for USC. A sixty-one-year-old coaching vagabond, Erickson is sort of the Larry Brown of football. He has coached six different college programs, three of them in the Pac-10, and two different NFL teams. In 2000, when USC originally began its head coaching search, it was Erick-son, not Mike Riley or Mike Bellotti or Pete Carroll, whom Athlet-ics Director Mike Garrett first contacted about the position. "He was the name coach we thought we needed," says then assistant AD Darryl Gross, now the athletics director at Syracuse. Reportedly, Erickson was offered a five-year deal for $7.2 million and turned it down to stay at Oregon State. Later, Erickson would be quoted pub-licly that it was "the worst decision I ever made."

But it's not like he needed the Trojans to boost his coaching resume. He's done quite well as it is. Although he started as the head coach at Idaho, he first gained notoriety by going to Washing-ton State and turning that dismal program around, going 9-3, up-setting highly ranked UCLA and Troy Aikman and taking the Cougars to the Aloha Bowl, the first bowl game the school partici-pated in since 1931. That earned him an offer from Miami, where he replaced the legendary Jimmy Johnson and proceeded to direct the Hurricanes to two national championships, earning an overall .875 winning percentage in six seasons, highest in the history of the school. He didn't do it without his share of controversy, however. The Hurricanes became known as something of a renegade program at the time, and when some internal rules were found to be broken, Erickson eventually left for what was called "lack of institutional controls." Shortly after his departure, the NCAA put Miami on three years' probation.

From Miami, he jumped to the NFL, coaching the Seattle Sea-hawks for four relatively uneventful seasons, then accepted the posi-tion at Oregon State, where Riley, in his first go-around in Corvallis, had preceded him and upgraded the program's talent. In his first year, Erickson went 7-5 with the Beavers, their first winning record in 29 seasons. The next year, in maybe his greatest coaching feat, he directed Oregon State to an 11-1 record, the best in the school's 150-year history, snapped USC's 33-game winning streak vs. the Beavers, and stunned Notre Dame in the Fiesta Bowl, 41–9.

Like basketball's Brown, Erickson never seemed happy in one place, though. His next stop was the San Francisco 49ers for two seasons, then back to Idaho, where he first started. The Vandals were thrilled, at least for all ten months Erickson hung around. In 2007, he jumped to Arizona State, where he worked his magic again, directing the Sun Devils to a 10-3 record and a spot in the Holiday Bowl.

Now he is getting ready for a game that could catapult him and his team back onto the national radar, but he understands what he'll be facing in the Trojans. "They've got great players, and they do a helluva job coaching them," he says. "Pete's been in the NFL, so he knows what he is doing. He is getting the right guys and fitting them in. You've got to get great players at their level. It's all about evaluation." Asked what it will take for another Pac-10 team to approach USC's consistency, Erickson smiles. "They're always going to be good," he says of the Trojans. "I think some other teams will have to step up to that level. I think we're one that is capable of doing it in time, but it takes time. It took Pete time."

Actually, it took him all of about a season and a half, but you get the idea. Erickson understands the ground rules. So when Carroll talks this week about Arizona State's gifted athletes and their well-designed offense, he is not blowing smoke. This is one of the better coaches in college football he will be facing on Saturday, and he will certainly be up for the challenge. The question, much like it was against Oregon State after a big, emotional victory, is whether his players will be equally enthusiastic.

So on the first fall day that actually feels like fall in Los Angeles, with the winds billowing and temperatures dipping into the 60s, these two teams with their unsteady quarterbacks finally take

Enthusiasm plus: Pete Carroll, in full flight, racing onto the field for a USC game. *(Courtesy of the USC Athletic Department)*

In the good old days: Pete with Norm Chow (left) working the same sideline. *(Courtesy of the USC Athletic Department)*

Throwing the football is one of Pete Carroll's favorite things to do, either before games or during regular Trojan practice sessions. *(Courtesy of the USC Athletic Department)*

ESPN's Chris Fowler interviews Pete after another Rose Bowl victory.
(Courtesy of the USC Athletic Department)

Sometimes the concentration gets intense, as this expression shows.
(Courtesy of the USC Athletic Department)

The Pinnacle: Pete holds up the BCS Championship Trophy after a victory over Oklahoma in the 2005 Orange Bowl. *(Courtesy of the USC Athletic Department)*

Happy days: Heisman Trophy winner Matt Leinart and Pete celebrate after one of their many victories. Leinart was 37-2 in his three years as a USC quarterback. *(Courtesy of the USC Athletic Department)*

In full practice gear, Pete carefully observes all that's going on at Howard Jones Field. *(Courtesy of the USC Athletic Department)*

Media time: Pete takes his turn at Pac-10 Media Day in downtown Los Angeles. *(Courtesy of the USC Athletic Department)*

Like father, like son: Pete and Brennan, his son and assistant coach, strike a similar pose while studying the action of a USC game. *(Courtesy of the USC Athletic Department)*

Pete holds up the Rose Bowl Trophy after a victory over Michigan in 2006. *(Courtesy of the USC Athletic Department)*

First impressions: Pete speaks at his introductory press conference after being hired as the new USC football coach in December of 2000. *(Courtesy of the USC Athletic Department)*

Touchdown! Pete exults as the Trojans score on another big play at the Coliseum. *(Courtesy of the USC Athletic Department)*

Good times: Pete and former quarterback John David Booty whoop it up after a big Trojan victory in 2007. *(Courtesy of the USC Athletic Department)*

Leader of the band: Pete, waving a Trojan sword, leads the USC Marching Band as it plays after the 55–19 romp over Oklahoma in the 2005 BCS title game in the Orange Bowl. *(Courtesy of the USC Athletic Department)*

Happy talk: Pete smiles at something one of his assistants in the press box has to say after another successful USC scoring drive. *(Courtesy of the USC Athletic Department)*

Gatorade bath: His players douse Pete with the usual postgame liquid to acknowledge yet another Trojans victory. *(Courtesy of the USC Athletic Department)*

His favorite cause: Pete speaks at the LA LivePeace Rally at the Coliseum with the late Bo Taylor (left), founder of UNITY ONE, at his side. Pete helped organize A Better LA to fight gang violence in Los Angeles. *(Courtesy of Adam Maya)*

Final days: The late Bo Taylor (left) speaks at the LA LivePeace Rally with Pete listening intently. Taylor, who was instrumental in working with Carroll in helping battle gang violence, died shortly after the rally from cancer. *(Courtesy of Adam Maya)*

the field. Early on, Sanchez is showing no signs of his injury, whipping a 34-yard, first-quarter strike to Ronald Johnson, then zipping a 19-yard pass into the belly of Damien Williams that takes the Trojans to the Arizona State 2. Three plays later, Sanchez, shaky knee and all, bullies his way one yard for the touchdown. Less than four minutes have passed at the Coliseum, and USC is ahead 7–0. As often happens with Carroll teams, the Trojans tend to relax after jumping out to a quick lead. Joe McKnight breaks away 41 yards on a pretty draw play, but it isn't until midway through the second quarter that things get interesting. Sanchez finds Patrick Turner for 22 yards, then, with Arizona State bringing pressure and starting to knock him around some, fires an incompletion. Two plays later, with tacklers draped on and around him, he finds Johnson for 29 yards and a first down at the Sun Devils' 20. Williams sprints 16 yards on an end-around reverse, then Sanchez drills a ball into the wide receiver's chest for a 4-yard touchdown.

Arizona State's Carpenter, meanwhile, is not coping quite as well. USC's defense, once again reaffirming its status as the team's strongest unit, is all over him. He begins to look less like a quarterback and more like a prizefighter getting pummeled in a corner. Not surprisingly, with Rey Maualuga and friends bearing down on him, Carpenter makes his first big mistake, underthrowing a pass that Trojans cornerback Kevin Thomas picks off and returns 46 yards down the sideline for the touchdown that basically puts the game away, 21–0.

If it seems as though the rest of the sun-splashed afternoon will be a breeze for Carroll's team, it is not. It is anything but. Sanchez isn't getting beat up as badly as Carpenter, but he is not enjoying a walk through nearby Exposition Park, either. The Sun Devils' aggressive defense is slowly getting to him and by late in the second quarter, he seems to have lost much of his rhythm.

In the third quarter, it gets worse, much worse. It evolves into the worst fifteen minutes of Sanchez's young football career. Physically, something appears wrong. His knee looks unstable and besides cutting down on his mobility, it seems to be causing him to throw off the wrong foot. He personally is responsible for four turnovers in the quarter, fumbling once and suffering three interceptions, as many as he had totaled in the previous four games. The final one isn't his fault. Williams, his favorite receiver so far in 2008, uncharacteristically bobbles a throw that hits him right on the numbers, with the ball bouncing high into the air and then into the arms of ASU safety Troy Nolan. USC's determined defense, though, doesn't let the Sun Devils take advantage, with the wobbly Carpenter finally getting knocked out of the game in the third period. After another Maualuga body slam, the Arizona State quarterback staggers to the sideline and gives way to young, inexperienced Danny Sullivan.

The turnovers are only part of the ugly story for USC. Personal fouls and penalties, in general, a recurring theme these past couple of years, continue to plague the Trojans. This time they are nailed on ten occasions for 86 yards, with senior Kyle Moore's inexplicable decision to wait until a play is over to grab a Sun Devil player by the jersey and toss him five yards downfield ranking as the clear lowlight. Mercifully, the third quarter comes to an end, and the final period is saved, somewhat, by McKnight's fresh legs. Looking more frisky than everyone else on the field, the sophomore tailback cruises his way along on an old-fashioned, run-dominated USC drive, gaining 68 of the 92 yards that culminates in a 2-yard Stafon Johnson touchdown plunge to provide the final score in the 28–0 victory. It is a game that belongs, mainly, to the Trojans' defense, especially to Maualuga, Brian Cushing, safety Kevin Ellison, Thomas, and tackle Fili Moala, who personally blocks two ASU field goal attempts in that sloppy third period.

If the game doesn't rank high on the aesthetic meter, it doesn't seem to matter in the crazy world of college football. The 28-point shutout should look good on the BCS's wild, weekly dance card, particularly after No. 1 Oklahoma, No. 3 Missouri, and No. 4 LSU all get knocked off. There is a good chance the No. 9 Trojans will move up a few notches in the polls, not that Carroll is impressed with any of that. "They're not all going to be pretty," he says afterward, referring to the victory. "I can't look at this without talking about the defense. Time after time we were making all those mistakes on offense, handing the ball back, the defense wouldn't hear of it. They played great." Everyone else? Well, they were not so great. "It was clear Mark was struggling," Carroll says of Sanchez. "It's incredible that he played, to tell you the truth. It was rough getting through it. He is a hero in my mind. I know he's not happy with it, but I'm proud of the game he had."

Neither Carroll nor Sanchez will admit the knee injury affected his play, although the coach does say the quarterback "wasn't clear on stuff and he was hesitant. There wasn't anything wrong physically. He just wasn't as sharp as he could have been. He didn't practice at all Tuesday and only a little Wednesday. I think that took its toll." Sanchez holds his briefest postgame interview of the season. Reporters try to be tactful, but he won't hear of it. "You can say interceptions, I'm not embarrassed," the quarterback says. "Just a tough outing for me. I wasn't making bad reads. I just made bad plays." He suggests his errors can be cleaned up with a full week of practice. "That's all I've got," he says. "Sorry, guys."

Carroll seems almost demoralized by the large collection of penalties his team continues to pile up. "We got sloppy, really sloppy," he says. "The penalty situation is just horrible. We talked about it all week, but we still had five or six huge penalties. We're going to have extra officials at our practices this week. We've got to do something. Until we solve it, we'll continue to be vulnerable. It could cost us a game down the road."

Meanwhile, the Pac-10 race is beginning to take shape. California is on top with a 2-0 record in the conference and 4-1 overall, but it travels to 2-1 Arizona next Saturday, while 2-1 USC gets 0-4 Washington State, the worst team in the Pac-10 and one of the worst in the country. Stanford, clearly improving under second-year coach Jim Harbaugh and coming off a 24–23 upset of Arizona, is 3-1 in the Pac-10 and 4-3 overall. After the Trojans go to Spokane, they travel to Arizona the following week. Cal doesn't come to the Coliseum until November 8 in what could be a showdown for first place.

None of that seems as important at the moment as the condition of Sanchez's knee. Is it sore enough to give the quarterback a week off? Certainly, the Trojans, who could be as much as 40-point favorites against the Cougars, could win that game with backup Mitch Mustain at quarterback. Would it be worth the gamble to allow the Trojans' new star an extra week of rest before the next siege of big games arrives?

Carroll won't even admit to giving that any serious consideration, but you know the topic will be discussed in the coaches' closed meetings early in the coming week. Having Washington State on your schedule is the closest thing to a bye. Maybe Carroll should take advantage of it.

His history suggests he won't. He prefers not to mess with the flow, and, if anything, he waited too long to get Sanchez off the field late against Arizona State. This is high-stakes stuff he is dealing with here, however, and the long-range goal, an eventual berth in the BCS title game, something that has eluded him the past few seasons, is still out there, blinking at him from off in the distance.

He doesn't want to do anything that could damage Sanchez's confidence, but he doesn't want to see his national title chances buried by a wounded knee, either.

Pete Profile

No, He's Not Perfect

This just in: Contrary to what a large segment of USC's most fervent fans and alumni believe, Pete Carroll is human. He makes mistakes. He has frailties, just like the rest of us. It's just that when you go 12-1 or 11-2 every year, grinding out a steady stream of BCS victories, All-American players, and Heisman Trophy winners, then mixing all that in with a national championship every four seasons or so, well, some people tend to overlook the blemishes.

They like to think Carroll is perfect. He is not.

To his credit, he is the first to admit as much. When he screws up, he tells you. To this day, when you bring up that infamous upset—some call it the biggest upset in college football history—by 41-point underdog Stanford at the Coliseum in 2007, he says he messed up. "I never should have left [quarterback] John David [Booty] in with that broken finger in the second half," he admits. "That was my fault." Every loss in the past few seasons has caused him enormous pain. "I can't begin to tell you how much they hurt," he says. Don't even bring up that 41–38 last-second defeat suffered at the hands of Texas and Vince Young in the 2006 BCS title game in the Rose Bowl. "That one will always bother me," he says.

Not everything bothers him, though. Carroll has developed a thick skin. Part of it is what he went through in his brief NFL head-coaching career, where heavy criticism had to be endured in both New England and New York. "If I can handle that, I can handle anything," he likes to say. The other part is just the reality of coaching in the sports fishbowl that can be Southern California, where, in the fall, the entire sporting focus is centered on him and his Trojans. Without a professional team in the area since 1994, USC football is now the primary topic of conversation on L.A. sports talk radio and television, not to mention everyone's favorite blogging and Internet subject.

The result is that everything from Carroll's tactics and strategy to his hairstyle and choice of clothes remains under constant scrutiny. Despite the fact he is the winningest coach in college football for the past eight years, he has had more than his share of critics along the way. Some of the criticism is a stretch, but some of it is valid. This book wouldn't be complete, or balanced, if some of those issues weren't brought up and examined. Here, then, are some of the more popular knocks against him:

He Can't Win the "Little Ones"

This one is hard to argue. The only thing keeping Carroll and USC from capturing four, or even five, national championships has been the disturbing proclivity to lose games to overwhelming underdogs. It happened in 2006, when first Oregon State pulled off an upset, then a lightly regarded UCLA team dispensed a 13–9 stunner. It happened in 2007, when the Trojans somehow got beat in that aforementioned Stanford game, 24–23. Then it happened for the third consecutive season this fall when Mike Riley and Oregon State conspired to win their second straight game in Corvallis against heavily favored USC, 27–21. Each time, the loss prevented the Trojans from a likely spot in the BCS Championship Game. In his eight years with the Trojans, Carroll is 14-2 against teams ranked in the Top 10. Yet 10 of his 15 defeats in that span have come against teams that weren't ranked. How do you explain it? Carroll can't, and that frustrates him even more. He is a control freak. It is the major reason he is coaching in college, where he has full authority over what goes on, rather than the NFL, where much of that decision-making rests elsewhere. Yet he has been unable to control the annual hiccups his team has suffered the past three seasons. "I knew this was a dangerous game," he said, after the loss to Oregon State this year. "I felt it all along, but I couldn't seem to do anything about it. Things get you sometimes. It's not always something you can control. I can't tell you how frustrating that is." This is a team that annually has as strong a collection of athletes as any school in America. The oddsmakers know. They have the Trojans favored in just about every game they play now. As long as that's the case, losing the "little ones" will continue to haunt Carroll and his fan base until the coach is able to solve the problem.

He Should Have Kept Norm Chow

This might be the most popular criticism of all, and it, too, is difficult to defend from Carroll's side. Some would contend offensive coordinator Chow was the sole designer of the offense that, with Matt Leinart and Reggie Bush both in the backfield, might have been the most prolific in college football history in 2004–05. That is hardly the case. Carroll re-tooled the offense after his first season on the job, scrapping some of the short dink-and-dunk passes Chow preferred for a stronger running game and a more vertical passing attack. Once that was done, Chow proved a master at play calling, developing quarterbacks Carson Palmer and Leinart into Heisman Trophy winners and creatively taking advantage of mismatches opposing defenses would afford. USC was never better balanced on game days than it was when Carroll was running the defense and Chow was directing the offense from high in the press box. It is no coincidence that the rhythm and flow of the Trojans' offense has gradually diminished each year since Chow's departure. Carroll would argue otherwise, but as bright and promising as young coaches Lane Kiffin and Steve Sarkisian were, they weren't Chow. The media critics aren't the only ones who have noticed, either. Some of USC's donors, including some who are considered the most important and influential, reportedly have brought this up in meetings with Athletic Director Mike Garrett.

They have been told that, in lieu of the record, it is no big deal. Still, the bottom line is difficult to ignore. The Trojans haven't won a national title since Norm Chow left.

The Reggie Bush Controversy

The ongoing NCAA investigation involving former USC All-American and Heisman Trophy winner Reggie Bush is hardly ever mentioned around campus these days, but at times it feels like the elephant in the sparkling Heritage Hall trophy room, right next to the Heisman with Reggie's name on it. The allegation is that Bush and his parents received extra benefits during his playing career from a pair of agents who were attempting to launch an agency called New Era Sports and Entertainment. Bush was to be their first client. USC has no official comment on the matter, pending investigations by both the NCAA and the Pac-10 Conference. The question is, if the allegations are true, what, if anything, could Carroll have done about it? "I am held responsible," Carroll says. "What difference is it if it's fair, or not? It would be bad if I didn't recognize what my responsibility is. It's my job to educate the players, their families, and extended family. I have to make them aware of the seriousness of the situation." But can any coach have full control over what goes on away from the football field, especially when it comes to family members? Is it a coach's fault if some players or their relatives aren't strong enough to resist temptation? It is a question that, even now, doesn't appear to have a clear answer.

The Tailback Shuttle

This is a relatively new one that is a result of Carroll's overwhelming success as a recruiter. He has landed so many blue-chip tailbacks, he doesn't know what to do with all of them. So he tries to play as many as he can, alternating them in some sort of semi-chaotic tailback shuttle that rarely provides any fluidity to the running game. This was never a problem when he had LenDale White and Bush at the position, shrewdly utilizing both of them in a style so effective they were nicknamed "Thunder and

Lightning." Once they were gone, though, the weather forecast changed. Now there is a steady stream of swift, gifted, and often stylish runners, none of whom has emerged as anything close to a featured back. In 2007, Carroll began with no less than ten talented tailbacks on the roster. This season, the total had been trimmed to six at the start of fall practice. It is not surprising that, along the way, there have been defections. Dissatisfied, disillusioned kids have left to find greener pastures and more carries somewhere else. Carroll, who can be stubborn about these things, argues that you can never have enough players at a position that lends itself to injuries. But the rare times when the running game has operated smoothly in the past couple of seasons, such as Chauncey Washington rummaging through the mud at Cal in 2007, or Stafon Johnson or Joe McKnight slashing their way to a big night a couple times this year, came when one tailback was left in for more than a few plays in a row, gaining rhythm and confidence as he went along. Many fans, especially old-time admirers of the John McKay–Tailback U. years, would like to see Carroll pick one or two tailbacks and stay with them exclusively. But the more you talk to the coach, the more you sense he has no plan to go away from his tailback-by-committee approach.

His Teams Lack Discipline

Carroll's admirers say his team's aggressive, emotional style is one of the keys to his success. His detractors claim his players tend to be sloppy and undisciplined, leading to an abundance of penalties that often kill drives and sometimes lead to surprising losses. The numbers don't lie. His teams consistently rank near the bottom of the Pac-10 in penalty yardage, and yes, some of the penalties can be grievous, such as the one by defensive lineman Averell Spicer that wiped out an Oregon State field goal, allowing the Beavers another shot at a first half touchdown this past season at Corvallis. Instead of being down 17–0 at halftime, the dozing Trojans found themselves behind 21–0. That proved to be a huge difference when their second half comeback fell short in a game that eventually cost them a shot at the national title. "We work on cutting down on penalties all the time," says Carroll, who regularly employs a cadre of officials at practice, trying to spot any disturbing trends, "but at the same time, I hate to take away from the aggressiveness of our defense. It's part of what makes us who we are." USC's players are also sometimes criticized for congregating on the sidelines to celebrate late in games they are about to win handily. "Our kids are just having fun," says the head coach, and that's one criticism he will accept gladly. Like his team, Pete Carroll is regularly guilty of having fun on the job.

VIII

Game Six: Penalties-R-Us?
Say It Ain't So, Yogi

He is the youngest, least experienced coach on the staff, appearing more like one of the players, or maybe a team manager, instead of a graduate assistant in charge of the quarterbacks. In many ways, he is also the most interesting of Pete Carroll's current protégés, and he certainly has the most colorful name.

Yogi Roth, at age twenty-seven, looks less like a football coach and more like a television sports announcer, which he happened to be for a couple of years in Pittsburgh. Of course, that was after he interned in the mayor's office in that same blue-collar city, and several years before he took off for Australia and Bali and spent time as a 100 percent, certified surfing dude.

"There is nothing Yogi can't do when he puts his mind to it," says Carroll. "He is a treasure, a smart, creative, hard worker. He can do anything he wants in the future, absolutely anything."

Roth seems to be proving that at USC. He started as a video and Web assistant but quickly moved his way onto the coaching staff, where he helps tutor quarterbacks by day, flashing sideline signals to them during games, and often serves as a kind of quasi-public relations man for Carroll by night. When Carroll speaks at a public function, he is usually introduced by Roth, who, with his well-coiffed, stylish appearance, could pass for one of those young reps at the William Morris Agency. There is a slickness about Yogi, a confidence bordering just on the edge of arrogance, that makes you feel this is a young man with big plans for himself. Much of those plans, it would appear, are tied directly to Carroll.

"Yogi is really an extension of the family in some ways," says Dave Perron, who is one of Carroll's best friends and a major business adviser for the coach. "He is a friend of Pete's son and daughter and part of a group, a core of five or six of us who are involved in all things we are doing for Pete [outside of football]." The group is unofficially called "Team Pete." Besides Perron, who works on charitable projects for financier Michael Milken, and Roth, that group includes Carroll's agent, Gary Uberstine. "Yogi is really integral to the group," Perron says. "He's really a special young man. He is a very candid kid who has great skills, and he has this connection to Pete because they like to do some of the same things, like surf at the beach and climb mountains. Most of all, I think Yogi wants to be part of this kind of comet that Pete is."

As this warm October afternoon spills into dusk on Howard Jones Field, Roth is spending time after practice, personally working with backup quarterback Mitch Mustain on his footwork on the pitch play. A former wide receiver at Pitt and an All-State high school star in Dalton, Pennsylvania, Roth steps over center himself and visually shows Mustain how the play should be executed, first with a pitch right, then with a pitch left. The quarterback studies the coach's footwork, then tries it himself, looking a little clumsy at first but gradually catching on. Some twenty minutes later, they finish, Roth pats Mustain on the back, and they head off the field.

"If you asked me what my dream job would be, I'd say to be a head coach someday," Roth says. "I'd love to do that and be able to influence kids and society. But you have to understand, it wasn't too long ago that I went to Bali and Australia, planning to go all around the world and surf for the rest of my life. Then I got that TV job in Pittsburgh, and I decided my goal was to be the next Kirk Herbstreit."

Turns out, Roth, whose mother is an Israeli immigrant and whose maternal grandparents were Holocaust survivors, has called more audibles in his young life than most of his quarterbacks. He grew up and became close friends with Brennan Carroll, Pete's son and USC's current tight ends coach who also went to Pittsburgh, and soon Brennan was inviting him to L.A. to spend some time together. "I came out here and got to know Coach [Carroll] and after a while, he asked me if I'd like to have this administrative job on his staff. I already had the TV job in Pittsburgh, but here I was, at age twenty-two, with an offer to come and learn at the best college football program in the world, maybe the best program of all time. I figured I could always go back to TV. So I came out here, got my Masters in communications management, and started working as a video assistant. I won't lie to you. That job came with a lot of grunt work."

Roth didn't seem to mind, though. Having the opportunity to work near Carroll made it worthwhile. "The first time I met him I had this terrific conversation," Roth says. "He told me if you want to be great, you've got to do one thing and be great at it, not ten things and be average." Roth must have been doing enough to impress people in his job, because when Lane Kiffin, the offensive coordinator at the time, left to become the head coach of the Los Angeles Raiders, he offered Yogi a job as the NFL team's receivers coach. "It sounded amazing," Roth says, "and I was ready to go. Then Coach [Carroll] called. He said, 'What do you think of becoming a quarterback assistant on our staff?' Well, I was living in Hermosa Beach, about a block away from the water. It was pretty nice. Anyway, I went over to see Sark [Steve Sarkisian, the current offensive coordinator], then Coach took me out to breakfast the next morning. It all came down to where my heart is. The chance to work with the quarterbacks at USC, well, that was an unbelievable honor. I couldn't walk away from that."

The decision seems to have worked out well for both parties. "Yogi has done a great job for us," Carroll says. "He and Brennan helped create our Web site and he's worked on A Better LA. Moreover, he's a natural coach. He loves the game and he has a lot of character and leadership qualities. Can he be a head coach some-day? Absolutely."

For his part, Roth seems determined to be involved in as many things as Carroll will allow. "Yeah, I've been the MC at some of his functions," he says. "My idea is to keep creating value for myself. I work a lot of hours, and there are a lot of nights I stay up late with Coach. He is an amazing guy. I really think we have a lot in common, especially some spiritual stuff. We kind of connect on that. I think he's like most of the successful leaders in the world. He makes himself accessible. He is always willing to teach and he is willing to learn, too. I've gone out on his trips to the L.A. streets, and the thing I'm most impressed with is how he listens. He doesn't preach. He listens. He is that way with everyone. He listens to you and asks your opinion."

As for Team Pete, the core group of Carroll advisers Perron mentioned, Roth shakes his head and smiles when it is brought up. "I don't even know what it is," he says. "It's just a bunch of close friends who get together and brainstorm some." Even so, the suspicion is that Roth definitely knows what it is and is well aware of what he and the group are doing. Ask him about his own future and he shrugs. "I don't know," he says, "whatever the universe wants me to do. In the meantime, I've got my Masters from USC, have a job I love, I'm single, live across the street from the water, and drive to work every day with Brennan, who's my best friend. I'm having a blast."

Roth's dream scenario, much like the one USC continues to harbor for the 2008 season, has been temporarily interrupted by the Trojans' frustrating penchant for penalties. If this team and coaching staff want to finish 11-1 and still have a shot at a berth in the BCS title game, they have to figure out a way to stop accruing the mountain of penalty yardage that has them last in the Pac-10 in that egregious category. Carroll is aware of the situation and has tried to address it, but so far nothing has helped. "We've been a little bit sloppy and a little bit unlucky," he says. "We've been getting a lot of illegal hits on quarterbacks, but some of that is we get a lot of shots on those guys." In other words, the defense is so good at getting to the quarterback, a few late hits are unavoidable. They are also costly. All the penalties are. It was a damaging penalty, right before the half at Oregon State, that probably cost the Trojans their chance at a comeback victory. If it hadn't happened, USC's mindset, as well as its whole BCS position three and a half weeks later, might have been strikingly different.

Some think the lack of discipline is a direct result of the makeup of Carroll's current staff. There are too many young, affable coaches like Roth, while there is no one with the intimidating presence of Ed Orgeron, the loud, ultraemotional defensive line coach who left the program four years ago to become head coach at Mississippi. He is currently the defensive line coach for the New Orleans Saints. Not all of USC's players were fans of "Coach O," as they called him at the time, but almost all of them feared him and respected him. "Coach O was definitely a special person," says senior guard Jeff Byers. "There is not one person in the whole country who could replace Coach O. I think now our coaches discipline us more as a group. I don't think this rash of penalties will continue. I don't think Coach Carroll will let it continue." Maybe, but there is no one on this staff who reacts the way Orgeron did. They still tell the story of the 2005 BCS Championship Game in Miami. USC had long since put overmatched Oklahoma away in a game the Trojans eventually won 55–19, but the Sooners managed to score what seemed like a late, meaningless touchdown. Only Orgeron didn't think it was meaningless. Orgeron thought a Trojan player was loafing on the TD play, and as the team came off the field, the assistant accosted the player and engaged in a face-to-facemask confrontation that everyone saw. It was Orgeron's way of showing that players never should stop playing hard, no matter what the situation. Another story, perhaps apocryphal, had Oregeron calling a player into his office, shutting the door, and physically challenging him. "Come on," an angry Orgeron reputedly said, taking off his shirt, "let's see what you've got." Whatever he'd been doing wrong, the shaken player supposedly corrected it.

USC has had a history of strong, discipline-minded assistants, from the legendary Marv Goux back in the John McKay and John Robinson eras to Orergon. On most staffs, they are described as the "butt-kicker," the coach who takes it upon himself to make sure these young, often impressionable kids have their full attention. There is no one on Carroll's staff like that now. Ken Norton Jr., the loud, chirping linebackers coach, comes close, and defensive coordinator Nick Holt can be heard raising the decibel level. Nevertheless, based on the way the team has played the past couple seasons and early in this one, including last week's penalty-scarred game with Arizona State, none of the present voices seem to be getting through the way Goux and Orgeron did.

If the problem isn't fixed, it could be costly as the 4-1 Trojans head into the sixth Saturday of their twelve-game, regular-season schedule. But it is not expected to be a major factor in Pullman, Washington, where, on this particular weekend, Carroll's team is a 42½-point favorite over 1-6 Washington State. No one has to remind the Trojans of the pitfalls of Pac-10 road games. Their upset loss to 25-point underdog Oregon State in Corvallis remains too fresh in their minds. So does the fact that 10 of Carroll's 15 losses in eight years have come at the hands of conference opponents.

But Washington State should prove to be an entirely different matter. In a difficult transition year under new coach Paul Wulff, the Cougars have become the Pac-10's newest fall guys. Cal scored 66 points on them, Oregon hit them for 63, and even Oregon State dropped 66 against them. They are last in the conference in total offense and, just to keep things consistent, last in total defense, as well. They've given up 316 points in seven games and rank 117th in the nation against the run. "It's been tough," Wulff says in a phone interview. "You never want to go through a season like this, but I believe all things are possible. If we play a great game, we can be in the ballgame. I believe that, and I have to get them [his players] to believe that."

Carroll will be trying to get his players to believe the same thing. Some of what is beginning to look like a rash of injuries might help him be more convincing. Tailback Joe McKnight, coming off his best game of the season, injured his toe late against Arizona State and will not play this weekend. Neither will starting offensive tackle Butch Lewis and defensive end Everson Griffen, who've both been ill all week. Linebackers Brian Cushing and Kaluka Maiava are both struggling with injuries but are expected to start, and it has been abundantly clear for the past two weeks that Sanchez, the quarterback who is the team's most important player, is operating at less than 100 percent.

All this could give some of USC's younger players a chance to make an impression, especially Broderick Green, a young bull of a redshirt freshman who is expected to move into the tailback rotation in place of McKnight against the Cougars. At 6'2" and 240 pounds, Green has had flashes of eye-opening power running in practice, and if nothing else, he could give USC the much-needed effective short-yardage tailback the team has been lacking of late. If this game plays out as the oddsmakers think it will, Carroll should be able to flood the field with young, eager backups for much of the final quarter, if not most of the second half.

On a cold, cloudy Saturday in the Northwest, the game proceeds precisely the way everyone figured. For one fleeting instant, when USC's Ronald Johnson fumbles the opening kickoff, the plucky Cougars seem to be in it. But Johnson scrambles to recover his own fumble, and exactly at that point, the mismatch begins. Washington State is completely outmanned, especially up front, and the Trojans seem able to do whatever they want whenever they want. If you didn't know any better, you would have sworn this was USC's first string against the scout team in practice. It begins with Sanchez, looking almost frisky and little like the sore-kneed quarterback who'd been limited a week earlier, hitting Patrick Turner with two touchdown passes in the first seven minutes.

The Cougars, meanwhile, with unsteady Kevin Lopina at quarterback, appear reluctant to throw the ball and content to play it safe and somehow run minutes off the clock. First downs seem almost out of the question for the home team, while the Trojans continue to pile up yardage effortlessly. Another Sanchez touchdown pass, this time to Ronald Johnson, is framed around tailbacks Stafon Johnson and C.J. Gable racing off for huge chunks of yardage. Gable scores 1 touchdown on a 17-yard scoot, followed by another Sanchez TD pass to Johnson and even 1 more to tight end Anthony McCoy. By late in the second quarter, the score reaches a staggering 41–0, and with USC driving yet again in the final minutes, Carroll mercifully allows the clock to run out, rather than piling it on.

In the second half, the Trojans coach practically empties his roster onto the field, allowing everyone and anyone who made the trip to get some playing time. Sanchez comes out after the team's first possession in the third quarter, and eventually, all three of his backups, Mitch Mustain, Aaron Corp, and Garrett Green, get into the game, albeit mostly to hand off. Johnson and Gable, both of whom have rushed for more than 100 yards, also get to rest while redshirt freshman tailback Broderick Green seizes the opportunity to show his stuff. The 240-pound kid with the quick feet from Little Rock, Arkansas, rumbles unapologetically through the poor, shredded Cougars, amassing 121 yards and 2 touchdowns before he is finished. Washington State can do little to stop the onslaught because its own offense is stuffed by a USC defense that hasn't given up any points now since late in the Oregon game, some 10 quarters ago. The final score is 69–0, and it marks the first shutout of the Cougars in 280 games. USC finishes the game with 28 first downs to WSU's 4, outrushing the Cougars 362 to 88 and outgaining them overall, 625 yards to 116. Sanchez's 5 touchdown passes, all in the first half, ties the school record.

Significantly, the Trojans accomplish it all without any turnovers and, more important, with only two penalties for a meager 15 yards. It is close to a flawless performance that can only be diminished by the fact Washington State might be the worst Division 1A team in America. Still, as kind of a midseason prep race for the stirring stretch run of a second half that awaits, this was a runaway success. "We have a chance to really make this turn here with a lot of things going in our favor," says Carroll afterward. "They're having a hard time up here getting things together, and I feel bad for them. But we are going to go after every single game that we've got and just keep on roaring ahead into this schedule."

Sanchez, who was clearly depressed over his 3-interception, 4-turnover performance against Arizona State, seems excited about both his mini-comeback and the team's new attitude. "We're on the up-and-up and ready to peak at the right time," he says. "It wasn't like I was trying extra hard to get it [the Arizona State game] past me, but I just wanted to focus like I normally do, get back to my routine and play like I know how."

Johnson, Gable, and Green are the first three backs to rush for 100 yards in the same game since 1977 at USC, when an eventual Heisman Trophy winner named Charles White joined Dwight Ford and Mosi Tatupu in accomplishing that feat. If McKnight, who was resting with his sore toe, had been available, the Trojans might have made it four backs. "It felt like a high school game when you get all the carries," says Gable, knowing that at USC, you have to take your carries when you get them. Carroll seems especially pleased with Green, the new power back who could bring an extra dimension to the offense. "It's an exciting style to add with the other guys that we have," the coach says. "He brings it, and he's good in the open field as well."

For all the dazzling offensive numbers, it is USC's defense that continues to be the team's most impressive unit. Washington State converts only 1 of 13 third-down attempts and never does make it across midfield at any point in the game. The back-to-back shutouts are the first for the Trojans since 1971, and the 69-point victory margin is the largest at the school in some 77 years. "Oregon State is still fresh in our minds," says Cushing, the linebacker who had another excellent game. "We go into every game now remembering what it felt like and that's why we've continued to do what we've done."

Almost before Carroll and his players are finished savoring the victory, they look up to find what now appears to be the Pac-10

Game of the Year approaching the following Saturday at Arizona. The Wildcats improved to 3-1 in conference play with an impressive 42–27 victory over Cal in Tucson. The Bears had been unbeaten in conference play and were slight favorites going into the game, but Arizona came from behind with the help of freshman tailback Keola Antolin, who ran for 149 yards, to set up a showdown with USC that will have the whole state of Arizona in a frenzy all week.

Carroll doesn't have to be reminded of the challenge of facing a rising Pac-10 opponent in a hostile environment. He's been there before and knows it will be an imposing task. But this is a coach who has a long history of having his teams show dramatic improvement in the second half of the season, and the look on his face and the sound of his voice make you think he feels this could be more of the same.

"We are going to go after every single game that we've got and just keep on roaring into this schedule," he says, "and we'll see what we can get done."

Pete Profile

A Special Bond Between a Coach, a Team, and a Stricken Teen

Sometimes a story comes along that makes a coach and a team forget all about the pressures of a season or the current ranking in the BCS computer polls. This one began four years ago when an eleven-year-old boy from Prairie View, Wisconsin, with brown hair, blue eyes, and a smile as warm as a winter fireplace, quietly adopted the USC Trojans as his favorite football team.

If anyone needed a diversion at the time, it was Ryan Davidson, who originally had been diagnosed with a brain tumor at age six. The cancer was in remission for five years, but then in April of 2004, it reappeared. The chemotherapy treatments and the endless digesting of pills and various experimental methods made it tough, but Ryan hung in there. Jim Phillips, a family friend living in California who was impressed with Ryan's courage, sprinted into action. He arranged for Ryan and his dad, Kirby, to fly West and have choice seats for the USC-Cal game.

"We got there and the first thing we did was go to Heritage Hall," says Kirby Davidson. "Ryan wanted to pose by the Heisman trophies. Next thing I know, someone says, 'Let's go up to the athletics offices.' So we do, and Pete Carroll walks out, looks over and says, 'You must be Ryan. We've been expecting you.' Well, Ryan is grinning from ear to ear by now, so we take a picture of him with the coach. Then Carroll says, 'Ryan, come into my room.' He takes him into his office and spends a few minutes before we [his dad and Phillips] go in. When we get there, Ryan is looking at game film with the coach and has the clicker in his hand, and they're talking like they're best of friends."

After that came a flurry of activity that included meeting Heisman winner Matt Leinart, assistant coaches, and an assortment of players. From there, the Davidsons and Phillips were escorted to Howard Jones Field, where the team practices. "The kids just all took Ryan under their wing," says Kirby. "They went out of their way to make him feel like one of the team." When practice was over, the Davidsons were startled to find the best was yet to come. "The players all got into a group and they started whooping and calling Ryan's name," Kirby says. "They packed him into the center, and they raised him on their shoulders and they're all chanting, 'Ry-an! Ry-an! Ry-an!' At that point, I have to tell you, Dad was forced to wipe a few tears from his eyes."

After the game, a close USC victory, Ryan was escorted to the locker room. "As soon as Coach Carroll saw him, he shouted, 'There he is,' and came over and gave Ryan a big hug. Lots of players followed and gave him gloves and wrist bands. Honestly, by the end of the week-end, Ryan was feeling like the MVP of the team. I've never seen a group of people go out of their way to make a weekend so special for a child dealing with a serious illness."

The best part was, Ryan seemed to make it special for the players, as well. "We all felt it," said Lofa Tatupu, a starting linebacker at the time. "When we put him up on our shoulders after practice, it was great to see the smile on his face." Leinart not only became Ryan's favorite player, he became his new pen pal, the two continuing to write each other even after the quarterback moved on to the Arizona Cardinals in the NFL. Ryan's mom, Amy, couldn't get over the way her stricken son was treated. "It's done a lot for his morale," Amy says. "Mention USC, and Ryan's face lights up. It's amazing the way the guys treated him. Coach Carroll was incredible. I'm terribly impressed."

Later that year, Ryan, now considered USC's good-luck charm, and his dad flew to Miami and helped the Trojans celebrate a 55–19 victory over Oklahoma and their coveted BCS Championship. The Davidsons and Carroll kept communicating after that, and Ryan kept battling, even after the cancer continued to reappear. "He's been told five different times that the cancer is back, and every time is the same," says Kirby. "He crys and hugs everyone for ten or fifteen minutes, and then it's done. He starts cracking jokes and just moves on."

It is some four years later now, and the jokes are hard to come by. The latest diagnosis from the doctors is not good. The cancer has reappeared yet again, and, despite all the hopes and prayers from his family and friends all over the country, this time, unlike the three previous tumors that were removed, this one is inoperable.

So a new trip is arranged, allowing Ryan, now a spindly fifteen years old, to come to California again and see the team he loves so much. They fly West on a Wednesday and arrive at USC on a Thursday afternoon before the Arizona State game. Carroll is deeply immersed in practice when someone whispers to him that Ryan Davidson and his dad are in the house. USC's head coach immediately turns around, spots Ryan, rushes over, and gives him a huge bear hug. "Ryan, look how tall you are," he says. Ryan's face is beaming. Carroll takes Ryan's hand and escorts him out to the middle of the field with him, something not many coaches would do in the midst of a pressure-filled season.

After practice is over, Ryan again finds himself in the middle of the field, surrounded by the Trojan players who are shouting "Let's go, Ry-an . . . Let's go, Ry-an . . ." Ryan is loving it. Afterward, he looks up at a writer and says, "That was so cool." A few moments later, Rey Maualuga, the menacing-looking All-American linebacker, comes over. The 6'2" 250–pound Maualuga is considered one of the more intimidating players in the country, but you'd never know it as he speaks in a soft, soothing voice to Ryan. "You coming to the game, Saturday?" he asks. Ryan nods yes. "You got a front row seat, or are you in the VIP section?" Ryan shakes his head and giggles. "You let me know where you're sitting. When I make a big hit, I'll point to you." Now it's offensive line coach Pat Ruel's turn. "You enjoying all this, Ryan?" he asks. "I'm still kinda processing it all," Ryan answers. "That's OK," says Ruel, "some of my linemen are the same way."

After practice is over, Ryan and his dad are taken to a campus pep rally that traditionally ends with the playing of the team fight song, "Conquest," and a player climbing a ladder and leading the band. This time, it isn't a player, though. It is Ryan, beaming as he waves the Trojan sword and the band plays USC's favorite music. Later, back near his office, Carroll, who realizes the seriousness of Ryan's latest diagnosis, can't get over how good it was to see him again. "It was awesome to have him here," the coach says. "He won our kids over. He's been just a warrior. You have to understand the courageous attitude he's had about this whole thing. He's given strength to his family and friends. They told me that the last time he was given the news about the cancer reappearing, he was the one reassuring the doctor, telling him it was OK. Can you imagine that? On the way home from the hospital that day, he was telling his folks he had to raise money to help other kids that might have to go through this. We're lucky he's fallen in love with the Trojans. We're lucky to have him. He's really been a treasure for us."

Carroll didn't let it end there. He arranged to have Ryan be an honorary captain for the Arizona State game, and he was escorted by quarterback Mark Sanchez, Brian Cushing, and the other USC captains to midfield for the pregame coin-flip. A few minutes earlier, in the locker room, Sanchez points to his face and the word RYAN that is written on his eye black, and Maualuga shows Ryan his name is on his wrist band. After the game, a 28–0 victory for the Trojans, Carroll, who rarely gives out game balls, presented one to Ryan, while the players surrounded him in the Coliseum locker room and again chanted his name. "Then they made Ryan dance, and Coach Carroll joined him," says Kirby. "It was unbelievable."

A few minutes later, in his usual postgame press conference, Carroll talks about it. "We never give out game balls, but we did today," he says. "We gave one to Ryan Davidson. We hope he had a beautiful weekend. I love the fact he might have had a beautiful weekend because of us. Ryan, you back there? Wave. See, there he is." Everyone laughs.

An hour later, in the middle of an almost empty locker room, Ryan and Kirby approach Carroll one final time to thank him. Before they can, the coach, knowing this might be the last time he sees the frail teen-ager, grabs him and hugs him tight. "You stay well," he says, his voice choked with emotion. "You take care of yourself."

The few people still left in the room seem to be fighting back tears of their own, but one look at Ryan Davidson's smile takes care of that. Those lucky enough to see it will remember it for what it has always been: A shining beam that will warm everyone connected with the USC football program for years to come.

Ryan Davidson died on February 19, 2009, with his family and friends close by. It was the day of his sixteenth birthday.

IX

Game Seven: Raising Arizona and Keeping an Eye on the BCS

In their normal Sunday afternoon meeting at Heritage Hall, Pete Carroll doesn't spend much time reviewing the Washington State game with his assistants. There is no need for that. Everyone knows the 69–0 rout of the undermanned Cougars was more like a glorified scrimmage and meant little, if anything, in the overall scheme of the season.

What does matter, though, is Arizona. The 5-2 Wildcats, slowly building their way toward becoming a conference contender under Mike Stoops, had upset Cal 42–27 the night before, and all of a sudden, USC's upcoming trip to Tucson in six days was fraught with all kinds of Pac-10 and national title implications.

"This," Carroll tells the coaches scattered around him at the table of the War Room office, "is a championship game." No one argues. USC–Arizona has evolved, in many ways, into the Pac-10 Game of the Year. The Trojans and Wildcats are two of four teams tied at 3-1 in first place in the conference. For USC, having won or tied for the Pac-10 championship the past six seasons under Carroll, a loss would probably end that streak. More important, it would knock the Trojans out of the BCS title game picture. The coaches swear they don't pay any attention to the

Bowl Championship Series standings that appear for the first time this weekend, but don't let them kid you. They all watch them. They all know what is going on. Despite the early season loss to Oregon State, 5-1 USC opens up at No. 5 in the standings. That is the good news. The bad news is that three of the four teams above them are undefeated and playing in conferences that are stronger than the Pac-10 this year.

So what's it all mean? Well, to have any chance to make it to the BCS title game in Miami in January, the Trojans have to win out. They have to finish the second half of their season 6-0, and right now, the biggest obstacle in their way appears to be the most intimidating road game left on their schedule—Saturday night in Tucson, Arizona.

It is homecoming for the U of A, as they like to call it in Arizona, and even early in the week, the frenzy is beginning to build at the only school in the Pac-10 that has never been to the Rose Bowl. Local writers in the Tucson area have been busy pointing out that if the Wildcats win this game against USC to go 4-1 in the conference, they would become the favorites to make it to Pasadena for the first time. For Stoops, in his fifth year at the university, this is the game that can turn his program around.

A typically intense, defense-minded coach, Mike is regularly known as "the other Stoops" in college football circles. His brother, Bob, is the more celebrated head coach at the University of Oklahoma. Mike coached on his brother's staff and helped him win the national championship in 2000. Along the way, he became one of the hottest head coaching prospects in the business. When Arizona beat out a number of interested schools to hire him, the general feeling in Tucson was that the Wildcats were on their way. Some five years later, the road to championship contention has been cluttered with obstacles, causing Stoops to sometimes come off more prickly than a local cactus. He found the talent flow in Tucson isn't what it was in Norman, Okla., and he has struggled to 3-8, 3-8, 6-6, and 5-7 records in his first four years on the job. "It's been more difficult than I thought it would be," Stoops admitted, and heading into the 2008 season, he was widely described as one of the coaches around the country who was on the hot seat. If he didn't win this year, they were whispering at Pac-10 Media Day, he could be out looking for work by the end of the season.

So Stoops, whose roots are all on the defensive side of the line of scrimmage, brought in a new offensive coordinator in Sonny Dykes from Texas Tech, where they regard the only good football as one that is constantly flying through the air. Things started out well enough. The new, more wide-open 'Cats mugged Idaho, 70–0, in their opener, then beat up on Toledo, 41–16. Just when the town was starting to get excited, though, Stoops's kids lost at New Mexico, 36–28, and the muttering began anew. A convincing 31–10 victory over injury-marred UCLA was followed by a 48–14 romp over Washington. Then another road trip resulted in a 24-23 loss to Stanford, and Wildcats fans thought, "Here we go again." Happily for Stoops, the critics were silenced when his team overcame a 17–7 halftime deficit with a roaring comeback to knock off No. 22 Cal and set the stage for a Saturday night game that could be the biggest in school history.

"This has a lot of significant meaning for us in the Pac-10," Stoops says, in a phone interview early in the week. "We have not been relevant in the Pac-10 in the past eight to ten years, so that part makes it really good for the people, and I'm happy for our players and our coaches that we actually get to play in a big game." Rose Bowl talk is rampant in Tucson, but Stoops, who has yet to take this team to any bowl, isn't buying into it. "We haven't really talked about it," he says. "We don't even bring it up. Our kids understand what comes with being on top, so I don't really spend any time with it. If you're able to win against USC, it gives you a game-breather on top of them. You've beaten them head-to-head and you have the advantage if you end up tied with them. It's significant in a lot of ways."

It is significant at USC, too, only the scope is much larger. For the Trojans, under Carroll, getting to the Rose Bowl is still nice, but since the advent of the BCS, they have had a bigger prize in mind. The loss to Oregon State still rankles their coach, particularly those disastrous first thirty minutes. Any time it is brought up, he grimaces as if something he just ate isn't agreeing with him. He knows the knock against him now is that he can't seem to get through a Pac-10 season unscathed. Maybe that's why, more than ever, he appears energized by the challenge ahead. History suggests one thing is clear about Carroll's USC teams: they all seem to get better as the season progresses. After October 15, his teams have gone 40-4 in the second half of his past seven seasons, not including his first rebuilding year. There are indications the same thing is taking place this season. Since allowing Oregon a field goal late in the second quarter of their game on October 4, Carroll's kids have outscored the opposition by the staggering total of 138–0. His defense, in particular, is now playing like the one everybody was touting as his best ever back in August.

"It's been a good run for the defense," he says, "and we've had some great challenges in there and really big-time field position challenges, which shows the mettle of the team and their attitude and progress coming through and all that. It's fun for the kids and fun for the coaches, and it's a source of pride when you can put a little string like that together, and it's unusual that it happens. Our goal is to have some fun with it, but now it's on to the next challenge."

The unit is led by linebackers Rey Maualuga and Brian Cushing, the two preseason All-American candidates. But on a midseason All-American team picked by the *Sporting News* this week, it is tackle Fila Moala and strong safety Kevin Ellison who make it, not Maualuga and Cushing. All four could conceivably win the honor by the end of the season, and all eventually will be high draft picks, as will speedy 6'3" 230–pound free safety Taylor Mays, the All-American from a year ago who regularly makes pro scouts swoon. This is a group that is definitely playing like the best defense in the country. "It doesn't give you a breather," says Arizona State coach Dennis Erickson, admiring the overall speed of the unit. Stoops, who has been poring over tape of the Trojans, agrees.

"They're big, fast, and physical—that's the first thing you realize," he says of the defense. "They make you earn it on the field. When you're good at all the positions, that's what makes it hard. They're very sound and very fundamental, too. They're not just big, strong, fast athletes, it's their technique, and the way they're coached, I think, that tells you what they are."

As good as the defense has been, it hasn't faced a proven, healthy quarterback yet this season. This week it will. Arizona has Willie Tuitama and the most balanced team the Trojans have seen. "This is the best group Mike has had," says Carroll. "It has star power, great schemes, and a coach who is all jacked up. This is going to check us out and it's going to be very hard to hold them down at all. They have scored a ton of points already on most everybody they have played." Quarterback Tuitama is the Pac-10's most experienced player at the position. "He's a really good all-around athlete who is a classic pocket type," Carroll says. "He has a big arm for the down-the-field stuff and a nice touch on the short passes. He is well ahead of where he was before. He's experienced now and been through a ton of games and been through all kinds of situations."

Mark Sanchez, his USC counterpart, has not. As well as he has played this season, and he's been the Pac-10 Player of the Week three different times in the first half and has 19 touchdown passes in six games, Sanchez has yet to win a truly big game on the road. A year ago, he couldn't get the Trojans past Oregon in Eugene, although he was somewhat hampered by a strangely conservative game plan early. Then, earlier this year, there was that frustrating experience at Oregon State. Now he gets another opportunity, coming off a flawless performance against outclassed Washington State with his knee no longer bothering him and his confidence clearly growing. All that won't mean much once he trots onto the field in Tucson and faces what could be the loudest, most hostile crowd yet.

"It will be similar to the Oregon game last year," Sanchez says. "The [Arizona] fans are tough. You've got to be ready to battle their crowd noise. They're on top of you. You're right next to the student section during warmups, and they get on you pretty good, even getting personal and stuff. But we can't worry about that. We just have to worry about our game plan. If we get amped up and focused, not many teams can play with us."

Subtly, Carroll has made some midseason changes up-front on his offense. Tackle Nick Howell, the son of former USC lineman Pat Howell, and guard Alex Parsons were rushed into the lineup when injuries kept Butch Lewis and Zack Heberer out of the Washington State game. But now Lewis and Heberer are back, and Carroll has told both they will need to compete to win back their jobs. As the week goes by, it appears that is not likely to happen. Carroll and offensive line coach Pat Ruel believe Parsons and especially Howell give the Trojans a toughness they didn't always exude before. "Nick brings a physical presence that is exciting to see," says Carroll. "He's also played with a minimal amount of mistakes that could plague someone without much starting experience. So he just was knocking people around and it showed very well." Offensive coordinator Steve Sarkisian hints at a new USC game plan. "Howell and Parsons make us better at driving off the football," he says. "We're not as big in the middle as some teams, so we have to be successful running outside. We tried to focus on that last week, and we did it well."

The Trojans had three different tailbacks rush for more than 100 yards each against Washington State's shredded defense, and the suspicion is they will try to emphasize running the ball against Arizona, a team that is only ranked sixth in the Pac-10 against the rush but second against the pass. The more they run, of course, the less time Arizona's potentially explosive offense will be on the field.

For Carroll, this is a chance to showcase the aforementioned trend that he started in his second season at USC. His teams have consistently gained confidence and momentum in October and November. "It's something we have always stressed," he says, "to improve as the season goes on when we play the biggest, most meaningful games." Considering the growing pressure for him and his team to make it back to a BCS title game, it's been a while since they've played one any bigger or more meaningful than this.

By the time the Trojans take the field on a warm, pleasant Saturday night in the desert, it is clear that the setting will be every bit as emotional as expected. In the Arizona student section, the kids are howling hours before kickoff, and when USC comes onto the field for pregame warm-ups, the decibel level shoots up dramatically. Sanchez, who had talked about the taunting he expected from the students, is getting more than his share, most of it in loud expletives. He pretends he doesn't hear, but he is smiling and shaking his head as the noise continues to grow. The crescendo builds until kickoff, and when USC's David Buehler knocks the ball out of the end zone, Tuitama and the Arizona offense take over at their own 20 and the entire Arizona Stadium rocks with noise. Much of it is silenced moments later when the Trojans' defense forces a quick three and out. If that's a portent of things to come, these fans won't be happy.

Arizona's ensuing punt bounces into the arms of USC's Stafon Johnson, who makes a couple of quick jukes and cuts and bursts into the clear. Some 54 yards later, he is dragged down on the Wildcats' 25, and Sanchez and Co. are in business. The groan from the crowd quickly turns to cheers when Arizona's defense rises up and stops USC, mostly because Sanchez appears too "amped," as he likes to call it. He has receivers open on two of the first three plays and misses them. The Trojans have to settle for a David Buehler 43-yard field goal attempt. The kick, barely in Buehler's range, is good, and USC takes a 3–0 lead two and a half minutes into the game.

The next fifteen minutes or so are dominated by defense. Sanchez relaxes some and begins hitting a few passes, but he misses one pivotal first down when he forces a pass instead of running for it with plenty of space in front of him. Arizona moves the ball some, too, utilizing lightning-quick tailback Keola Antolin and another one of those familiar USC facemask penalties to position

Jason Bondzio for a 30-yard field goal to tie the score at 3 early in the second period.

Then a startling thing happens. At perhaps the pivotal point of the USC season, Carroll suddenly changes his philosophy. Johnson rips off a nice run or two, and instead of going back to his stubborn routine of tailback roulette, alternating players at the position on every down, the coach leaves the sleek junior in the game. The result is an old-fashioned type of Trojans' ground-hugging drive, dominated by Stafon pounding away, behind crisp blocking from the offensive line. Johnson, clearly into a rhythm, slices through for 8, then 9, then 7, then 4 more yards on 1 carry. Carroll sends Mc-Knight in for one quick 12-yard gulp to give Johnson a breather, but Stafon returns to top off the drive with a 2-yard power surge into the end zone.

Now it is 10–3, and USC's suffocating defense takes over. Antolin, the 5'8" waterbug of a tailback, seems Arizona's only real threat offensively. Then Mays, the Trojans' lethal-hitting safety, nails him with a hit so vicious it seems to crackle through the warm desert air. Antolin wobbles off the field with help from the trainers and is not seen again the rest of the evening. Tuitama tries to muster a drive near the end of the half, but much to Stoops's dismay on the sideline, the Wildcats are out of time-outs and the quarterback is forced to waste a precious play by spiking the football. With the final seconds ticking on the clock, Bondzio attempts a 48-yard field goal. It is wide left.

Any USC momentum that is building is quickly squashed early in the third period when Sanchez, scrambling out of the pocket, is blindsided and sacked by defensive end Brooks Reed and fumbles the football. It is recovered by the Wildcats' Donald Horton Jr. at the Trojans' 15. Four plays later, backup tailback Nic Grigsby squirts through for 5 yards and the first touchdown USC has allowed in more than 12 quarters. It does more than tie the game, it awakens the frenzied crowd.

Now it is Sanchez's turn to respond. He finds Patrick Turner for a 15-yard gain, then hits Damien Williams, his favorite receiver, for 19 more. With a second and 10 on the Arizona 30, he drops back to pass, and Arizona's Nate Ness bursts in on a safety blitz. Just as he is about to get to Sanchez, Johnson, pass protecting from his tailback spot, cuts him off and cuts him down, flipping him helmet over heels with a sensational block. Sanchez takes advantage, finding fullback Stanley Havili wide open down field in the area left unprotected by Ness. Havili cradles the soft 30-yard spiral and steps into the end zone untouched for a 17–10 lead. Ness needs help from the trainers to make it off the field, while on the USC sideline, Johnson, clearly playing the finest all-around game of his college career, is being wildly congratulated.

The rest of the evening is dominated by the Trojans defense that systematically imposes its will on Arizona and Tuitama. Carroll makes some halftime adjustments that slow down the Wildcats running game and shut down Mike Thomas, the dangerous receiver who made some key first-half plays. But mostly, it is the ferocity of the USC pass rush, led by Clay Matthews, Kyle Moore, and Everson Griffen, that overwhelms the Wildcats and overcomes another shaky night of Trojan penalties (10 for 68 yards). With 5:55 to play, Stoops becomes desperate enough to go for it with a fourth and inches on his own 37. When a beaten-down Tuitama is straightened up and stopped short on the play, you could almost feel the desert wind coming out of the Wildcats' sails. By the end, Arizona's senior quarterback looks like a prizefighter who has had enough. His passes have no snap and his body language has no bounce.

Buehler eventually misses a field goal for the first time this season, a relatively easy 30-yard kick that would have made it 20–10, but by then, it didn't seem to matter. USC's defense is not about to let the Trojans lose this game. Both the clock and any Arizona enthusiasm slowly run out amid a final five-minute blizzard of crisp tackles and brutal sacks. It ends 17–10 in favor of USC, and all Carroll can do afterward is gush about his defense.

"I'm just so proud of those guys," he says. "They're just so tough and they won't give in. Defense is what gives you a chance to win every time." Moore, the senior defensive end, wants to talk about the huge stop of Tuitama on fourth and inches. "We knew what was coming," he says. "We just had to get down low. If we keep playing great defense, teams won't beat us."

How good was the defense on this soft October night? Well, Arizona had scored 283 points in its previous seven games. It would have finished this one with three if Sanchez's fumble hadn't provided the field position for the only Wildcats touchdown of the night. Tuitama, the Pac-10's most experienced quarterback, was limited to just 88 yards passing and Arizona managed only 188 yards overall.

USC's offense had something to do with this victory, too, especially Johnson, who finishes with 83 yards rushing in 19 attempts to go with his 54-yard punt return and the highlight-reel block of the USC season so far. "The line made some great holes and it was up to me to make plays," Johnson says. "I just felt good tonight." He'll feel even better when the team watches tape of the game, and they replay that brilliant cut block and all his teammates whoop and holler in admiration.

"We're still moving, still improving, I like it," says Carroll, smiling. "It will be good to get back to the Coliseum." USC does not have to leave the state again the rest of the regular season. The only road games remaining are November 15 at Stanford and December 6 against UCLA in the Rose Bowl. Its chances to make it seven Pac-10 titles in a row look good, but even amid the happy vibes from this hard-earned victory, the opportunity to get back to a BCS title game seems to be diminishing. A late fumble by Ohio State freshman quarterback Terrelle Pryor leads to a 13–6 victory for unbeaten Penn State, a team that now looks like it will finish the season 12–0. If it does, with eighty-two-year-old coach Joe Paterno poised to go for a final shot at a national championship, the Nittany Lions would be difficult to keep out of Miami in January. Then there are Texas and Alabama, both of whom are still unbeaten, and Georgia, Oklahoma, and Florida, all with one loss. All five play in conferences that are more competitive this season than the Pac-10 and therefore more computer friendly when it comes to those controversial BCS standings.

USC still has the incentive to win the rest of its games and finish the season 11-1. But as Halloween approaches, there is no denying the fact that the inexplicable, early-season loss at Oregon State continues to haunt Carroll and the Trojans.

Pete Profile

Coaching Roots

The coaching tree that sprouted Pete Carroll has roots embedded in all different areas of the country, with influences that are as varied as his football-rich resume.

The foundation was set not far from Carroll's hometown of Greenbrae in affluent Marin County, where the nearby ferry takes daily commuters across the bay to San Francisco. The high school was Redwood High and the coach was Bob Troppmann, an ex-Marine who taught football for fifty years and is retired now. Carroll played for him for four years and spent eight years as a counselor at the Diamond B Football camp, the first of its kind in California, according to Troppmann. "That was extremely important for me," Carroll says. "It had a big impact on me." Troppmann remembers a skinny teenager who couldn't get enough of the game. "He was always around," Troppmann says, "sort of a gym rat of a football guy. Back then he'd be a listener more than a talker. But he was always sort of hyper, like you see him on the sidelines now." Interestingly, it was Troppmann who used to pump his team up with quotes from Maxwell Maltz, M.D., the author of *Psycho-Cybernetics*. Troppmann says his game slogans sometimes would be "Win one for Max." You can almost see the track marks from Maltz to authors like W. Timothy Gallwey, *The Inner Game of Tennis* guru whose theories

Carroll has come to embrace. Among other things, Maltz wrote, "People who say life is not worthwhile are really saying that they themselves have no personal goals which are worthwhile." It is no coincidence that Carroll wound up writing his Masters' thesis on psychologist Abraham Maslow, who specialized in the field of positive psychology.

Carroll's actual coaching career began at his alma mater, the University of the Pacific, where he spent three years working as a graduate assistant concentrating on the wide receivers and secondary and making all of $3,000 in annual salary. He lived in a free apartment and ate cafeteria food, but he was on a staff with people such as Jim Colletto, Walt Harris, Ted Leland, Greg Robinson, and the late Bob Cope, all of whom eventually would be successful coaches and administrators. "It was Bob Cope who helped get me to Arkansas," Carroll says. Pete didn't want to go, but Chester Caddas, the head coach at Pacific, convinced him, telling him if he did, he'd be coaching in the Rose Bowl in two years. Carroll finally gave in, spending the following season as a grad assistant for Lou Holtz, barely earning a living but enjoying the opportunity to work on a team that won the 1978 Orange Bowl. He followed that up by working a season for Earle Bruce at Ohio State, where, exactly two years from when Caddas made his prediction, the Pacific coach received a phone call. "It was New Year's Day," says Caddas, "and Pete called. They were playing in the Rose Bowl."

Next stop on the Carroll coaching express was North Carolina State, where he worked three years as defensive coordinator and secondary coach and reconnected with the man who would shape everything about his coaching technique and philosophy. "Monte Kiffin has influenced what I've done in coaching more than anyone else on the planet," Carroll says. The venerable Kiffin, who just left his job as the extremely successful defensive coordinator of the Tampa Bay Bucs to join his son, Lane, on the staff at the University of Tennessee, remembers meeting Carroll for the first time in 1977, when Kiffin was the Arkansas defensive coordinator. "Pete was a grad assistant, and he was about twenty-five at the time, but he looked more like eighteen," Kiffin says. "He sat in the back of the room and didn't say a whole lot. But you could tell he had an unbelievable mind for football. I used to like to ask questions of the grad assistants to find out which ones were willing to work. The more questions I asked, the more Pete kept answering. I told Holtz at the time: 'He won't be here very long.'" He wasn't, but a few years later, Kiffin became head coach at North Carolina State, and one of his first hires was Carroll, who became his defensive coordinator. Eventually, the two would be together on five different staffs, including the Buffalo Bills and Minnesota Vikings in the NFL.

"Monte Kiffin took me under his wing and, as one of the greatest defensive coordinators in America, taught me everything I know today," says Carroll. "We're still very close. He had a huge effect on me as a coach and otherwise. I feel unbelievably lucky to have had him as a mentor and a friend." Kiffin sounds just as impressed with his now wildly successful protégé. "If you interview Pete Carroll, you're going to hire him," Kiffin says. "First, he's very, very smart. He is a great motivator who has great respect from his players. I know what they said about him in the NFL, that he couldn't coach pro players, but he got a bad rap. It's the biggest fallacy in the world. The pro players love him." Kiffin and Carroll are both defensive coaches first. They can talk X's and O's for hours, and they still do on the phone to this day. "I've always been a defensive guy, so we're always talking about formations, new things offenses are doing, how to stop the new spread coverages, everything like that. You know what makes Pete so unique? He made sure to learn everything about the front seven. A lot of guys who are secondary coaches, they only learn those four spots, but if you don't take the time to learn the defensive line and linebackers, you'll never stop the run. And if that happens, opponents will rarely pass."

The more Kiffiin talks, the more he sounds like a Carroll fan. "He keeps offenses so off balance," he says, after watching USC's defense on tape. "He's always adjusting. He'll never fall behind the times. He and I are alike in that way. You can't rely on what you did in 1972 or 1982. You'll fall behind if you do that." Kiffin's relationship with Carroll has stretched well beyond the coaching offices. His son, Lane, was Carroll's bright, young offensive coordinator before leaving to become head coach of the Oakland Raiders. "Our families spend a lot of time together and our kids all know each other," says the elder Kiffin. "We have a special friendship, but even if we didn't, I'd respect him. Our scouts all come back from Southern Cal, and they say they're so impressed by what the Trojans are doing at practice. He teaches kids to compete, and they play so hard. That's why high school kids all want to go there. They know they're going to get better. Pete knows what it takes to get to the NFL."

After working for the Buffalo Bills as defensive coordinator, Carroll moved to the Minnesota Vikings, taking the same job under Hall of Fame coach Bud Grant, who still remembers his initial interview with USC's current coach. "You know, coaches come in all different shapes, sizes, and dispositions," says Grant. "There is no mold for coaches. What struck me with Pete was that he was a very gregarious guy. In a half hour, we must have covered about ten subjects." It didn't take Grant long to see Carroll's serious side. "I like to test my young assistants to see what they're about," Grant says. "I like to give them a timeline. One day, during the offseason, I told Pete that by tomorrow I want him to give me a paper on the Khyber Pass. I told him I wanted him to find out about it, write it down, and give it to me. Lots of guys I tried that with were confused. Not Pete. He went to the library, did the work, and came back the next day and gave it to me. That's the way he was. He could approach a project and do it without any strain. Some always strain. They don't make the best coaches. Pete knew what he saw and he'd go about the task and get it done. It never felt like he was under pressure. He did his job in a happy manner, and that's good. I like happy coaches."

Grant thinks head coaches need to have a certain intangible. "It's an instinct you have to have," he says. "A lot of excellent coaches can't be head coaches . . . the thing that helps Pete is his ability to see the whole picture. Some head coaches don't have that ability to be able to stand in the middle of the practice field and know everything that is going on. You have to be able to do that and make the tough decisions. Pete can do that." Then there is the people part of it. "Managing people is the same whatever you do," Grant says. "You have to get the best out of them, keep them motivated, make corrections, and do it all in a manner that is beneficial to the team or the company. Pete knows how to manage the best people."

Maybe the ultimate compliment paid Carroll by Grant was his attempt to convince ownership of the Vikings that Pete should be the team's head coach at one point. "The ownership was kind of in flux at the time, and they were trying to make a decision on whom should be the next head coach, Denny Green or Pete. Roger Headrick [Vikings executive] called me. I told him Pete is the obvious candidate. I told him I know Pete Carroll and I gave him my unequivocal endorsement for Pete. I told him he'd do an outstanding job. So much for my recommendation. I think the league was pushing for minority coaches, and Headrick was new to this business with no football background whatsoever. I think he wanted to be in good with [Paul] Tagliabue [the NFL commissioner]. So they hired Green."

Grant is happy Carroll has found success at USC. "Pete and I still talk," he says. "He'll just call and say what's going on. It is always good to hear from him. You know, X's and O's are a big part of football and you can absorb all that like a sponge, but it's what you do with it that counts. Pete has all that stuff at his fingertips, and he knows how to make decisions. The best committee is a committee of one. That's what he is."

Carroll still talks about the two years he spent as defensive coordinator with the San Francisco 49ers, under George Seifert. "It was special to be working near home, where my parents and friends lived," he says. "I had known George and studied under him for years, and it was a fantastic challenge to work in that system. In my last year there, Bill Walsh returned to the organization, and it was fabulous to have the source of all knowledge nearby. I never hesitated to pick his brain and to ask how and why things worked. That experience helped me to formulate a plan for how to be a head coach and how to put all the pieces together."

All the coaches who employed Carroll bring up his curiosity, his hunger to learn. They all talk about how he constantly asked the why and how of things. Troppman, his high school coach, remembers that

Carroll was always the guy in the huddle drawing plays in the dirt or off somewhere working on new drills.

"It was obvious from the beginning," says Troppman. "Pete was born to coach."

X

Game Eight: "Slu" Is on the Job, but Defense Steals the Spotlight

I just laugh when outside people call and try to solicit attention with Pete," says Dennis Slutak. "They say all they're asking for is thirty minutes of his time. Hey, I'm considered his right-hand man, and I'm lucky if I get five minutes."

Slutak, better known as "Slu" to everyone in the USC Athletic Department, is the chunky, good-natured, thirty-six-year-old ex-special teams coach who is director of football operations for the Trojans. That's a nice way of saying he is in charge of just about everything off the field for this football team. Meals, hotels, travel accommodations, security, making sure there are enough qualified officials for practice sessions, he does all that and more. "If you ask Coach what my job description is, he says it's anything and everything," says Slutak, chuckling. "There are a lot of details and a lot of moving parts, but I love it."

It also means being a first-class passenger on the Pete Carroll Express. "You just get on board and hold on," Slutak says. "He is hands-on with everything that has to do with the program. He has an energy level unlike anyone I've ever been around. His mind transcends football, and the wheels are always turning. He could be on vacation on the beach in Hawaii and call me with some random idea about something we won't have to deal with until five or six months down the road. He tells you that it's all part of trying to do something better than it's been done before."

Slutak glances at his cluttered desk in the office on the same Heritage Hall second floor as all the coaches and shakes his head, still amazed how a supposedly calm, composed middle school teacher in Palm Beach, Florida, got here from there. Credit Norm Chow, of all people. "I finished my graduate degree working on the staff with Chow at North Carolina State," Slutak says. "After I got into teaching, a mutual friend of ours called and said Norm, who was now the offensive coordinator at USC, mentioned something that might be right up my alley. "They were looking for someone to work with special teams and specialists, so I came out for an interview, and Coach [Carroll] offered me a graduate assistant job. I wasn't looking for it, but I said to myself, 'Do I want to keep escorting around teenagers with hormones bouncing off the walls, or do I want to get back into coaching at a premier institution?' It was a no-brainer for me. I coached in 2003 and 2004, when we won two national championships. It was a great way to start, but obviously, I was looking for some kind of full-time position that would pay a better salary. About that time, Coach [Ed] Orgeron [USC's defensive line coach] got the Mississippi head coaching job, and he offered me a position as special teams coordinator. I talked to Coach [Carroll] about it, and he encouraged me. He said 'You've got to do it,' adding that he didn't have any full-time spots open. So I actually took the job and went to Oxford, Mississippi, for about five weeks. Then the job I have now opened back here, and Coach called me about it. I had to decide, did I want to stay in Oxford and keep coaching, or come to L.A., a place I loved to live, and go into administration? My graduate degree is in administration management, with the idea of doing this some day. So I figured, why not do it here?"

Now he's a bachelor in L.A., living the good life, at least when he can find the time, which isn't often. "I get here between seven and eight in the morning and leave about eight at night Monday through Wednesday," Slutak says. "On Thursday, Coach wants everyone out of here after practice. But basically, this is a seven-day-a-week job, and in the offseason, well, that's the craziest time for me. I've got a ton of things going on."

All of it is worth it, Slutak says, for the opportunity to work with Carroll. "It's amazing the impact his vision has had on all of us on the staff," he says. "He instills a competitiveness in you. He tells you that a lot of people will tell you no. He pushes you for ways to make them say yes. He forces you to maintain a certain focus and intensity. I think a lot of us around here were at our lowest of lows after the Oregon State game, but I was there to listen to his talk to the team afterwards, and I automatically felt better about what was ahead. He brought us back to life. It's uncanny."

Carroll sounds just as impressed with his director of football operations. "Slu is very efficient and diligent," he says. "He's basically our quality-control guy in so many important areas. He's been a great factor in any success we've had." So how does Slutak manage to communicate with this man whose time is so limited? "No problem," he says, laughing. "I text him like everybody else."

It is easy for Slutak to count his blessings this particular week, especially when he and everyone at USC hear that Tyrone Willingham, the head coach of this Saturday's opponent, the University of Washington, has been terminated as of the end of the season. A stern, but disciplined man with the kind of strong moral character you expect to find in an Army officer, Willingham is generally well-liked and respected by everybody in the industry. The announcement from Washington officials, not unexpected in light of the Huskies' poor overall record and woeful 0-7 start this season, comes on the Monday of its upcoming game with the Pac-10's strongest opponent. "It's always a very difficult thing for any coach to look at ending his tenure at a university," Willingham says in a telephone interview, adding that a coach knows what to expect when his team can't win. "When you are 0-7, close doesn't get you anything," he says, when it's mentioned a few games were less than blowouts. "We've had some games that we've done things well, but we've never done it in unison. We've never had offense, defense, and special teams really all performing at the same high level at one time, and that will be one of the things we will be seeking to see how we can get all of those areas to get together and perform well. I think the football team will find a way to regroup and challenge itself to be better than this here."

For all intents and purposes, Willingham's season went into a permanent nosedive when Jake Locker, the most talented quarterback in the conference and one of the finest all around players in the country, was lost for the year with a broken thumb on September 27. USC's Carroll is quick to concur. "I thought he was the best freshman to enter the Pac-10 [a year earlier] since I've been here," the Trojans coach says. "I thought he was the most impressive single football player to come in the conference. He's a great player. He's talented. He's a leader. He's tough. He'll take the hit when he has to make the play. I just admire the heck out of that guy. It's rare that a guy can control the game as much as he did. He basically did it by adding the throwing game to his ability to run. He's really fast. He's really tough. There just aren't very many quarterbacks like that. He's playing like Tim Tebow, with that kind of effect and that kind of style. It's just been unfortunate he's been banged up so often."

Not surprisingly, Carroll has empathy for Willingham and knows that his Husky team could play with more emotion against USC in an attempt to demonstrate how it feels about its coach. "I think a team could go one or two ways, yeah," Carroll says. "I think with the leadership that they have and the strength of Tyrone, the way he's always handled his teams and all—we've seen him in different settings, Stanford, Notre Dame—they're going to be tough. They're going to bring their best. He's an incredible guy. I know he's affected all their young guys' lives through the recruiting process and building of their program. I know they have a really strong feeling about representing and doing a great job for him."

Meanwhile, an intriguing subplot surfaces at USC, where the name of offensive coordinator Steve Sarkisian, who turned down the

Oakland Raiders head coaching job two years ago saying he wanted to become a college head coach, already is being mentioned on the list of candidates to succeed Willingham. Asked about it by reporters who are wondering if Saturday's game could be a big-stage audition for the position, Sarkisian doesn't deny his interest. "I'd look at it and assess it," he says. "It's obviously been one of the premier jobs not only in the Pac-10 but in the country, so you'd have to look at it." At thirty-four, Sarkisian is widely viewed as one of the country's hottest head-coaching prospects, something his current salary of $704,500 at USC, tends to confirm. It isn't every assistant coach who ranks as the school's fifth highest-paid employee.

Carroll, who is always enthusiastic about his assistants moving up, is quick to endorse Sarkisian's credentials. "They'd be lucky to get him," he says of his offensive coordinator. "Whenever you have a chance to hire a guy that brings a major aspect of the team like the offense, that's huge, because you know what you're getting."

The irony is, Sarkisian's candidacy coincides with a new wave of criticism on Internet chat boards and blogs directed at his play calling. Especially late in the game at Arizona, there were some calls, including a first-down pass with five minutes to play and USC looking to run out the clock, that did seem questionable. Asked about his decision making in that game, the coach everyone calls "Sark" admits he personally reviews all his calls after games. "I look at every call upside down and inside out to see if I would have done something different here or there," he says, "and inevitably, there's anywhere from five to seven plays I would change. That's not necessarily the same five or seven plays other people would change. You can't go in trying to satisfy people. You've got to satisfy the team and get the win."

The offensive coordinator at USC is under almost as much scrutiny as the head coach, and the pressure is magnified by the huge number of fans who remain enamored with Chow, the scholarly gentleman who held the job during the Carson Palmer, Matt Leinart glory years. He now occupies the same position at crosstown UCLA. When Sarkisian isn't defending his play calling, he is trying to explain the rotation at tailback that has been further confused midway through this 2008 season by Stafon Johnson's breakout game at Arizona. Should the junior who was the clear player of the game in Tucson now be anointed as the new No. 1 at the position? Many now think so, but C.J. Gable, one of the many other tailbacks in waiting, disagrees, and in the *L.A. Times* this week, he vents for the first time. "I'm angry and I don't understand," he says, referring to his meager five carries in Arizona after rushing for 109 yards and three touchdowns at Washington State. "But I'm not going to cry about it."

This is a situation Carroll cannot avoid, not when he recruits so many tailbacks who are regarded as four- and five-star players (in high school recruiting parlance, a five-star player is the highest ranking you can give). In 2007, there was an even bigger waiting list with as many as ten gifted tailbacks on the roster. It is human nature for all these kids, most of whom were the top running backs in their hometowns, if not in their home states, to be upset when they see their opportunities dwindling at USC. Not even the soothing words of a talented coaching politician like Carroll can eliminate the frustration many of these kids and their families are feeling.

All of the conjecture concerning Willingham, Sarkisian, and the ongoing tailback controversy is overshadowed in the middle of Thursday's practice when safety Kevin Ellison suddenly goes down in the midst of a drill clutching his right knee. The senior, who just recently was named to the *Sporting News* midseason All-American team, watches the rest of practice sitting on the trainer's table, then rides a cart to the locker room afterward. Carroll announces X-rays and an MRI exam have been scheduled. The results come back the next day. Ellison has suffered torn cartilage in the knee and will undergo arthroscopic surgery immediately. Estimates are he will be out from two to four weeks in a schedule with five regular-season games remaining.

Twenty-four hours before a game the Trojans are favored to win by more than 40 points, the shock waves are still being felt in the USC locker room. Ellison is not only a team leader, he has been the most consistent player on a defense considered among the best in the country. He is the one who is always there to make a clean tackle of a back who has busted into the open field or to come rushing in to knock down a pass to a seemingly open receiver. It is Ellison, not the more hyped middle linebacker Rey Maualuga, who is the glue that has held this extraordinarily cohesive unit together. Will Harris, the junior who will replace him, is a good football player, but he is not Ellison.

The news of the injury is exacerbated by the fact that defense has been the anchor of this football team. While the offense and Sanchez, the emotional quarterback, struggled somewhat in Tucson, it was the take-no-prisoners defense that dominated one of the two most important Pac-10 games the Trojans have played this season. Ellison's absence shouldn't be felt to a great extent against Washington, but there are still some dangerous games remaining on the schedule, beginning the next weekend when Cal comes to the Coliseum. That's when this defense, which has been so strong and overpowering, figures to get its next great challenge, one it unfortunately will be forced to face without the strong safety who has been its steadiest player.

First, though, there is the matter of Washington, a winless team that arrives at the Coliseum on a homecoming Saturday when Los Angeles feels more like Seattle, with dark clouds hovering and a steady rain pelting the field in the hours before kickoff. Once the game starts, the weather is the least of the Huskies' problems. Willingham's punchless team opens with a long series of three and outs, unable to even come within shouting distance of a first down, while USC's Sanchez, energized by the prospect of playing at home against a suspect defense, begins by going five for five on the Trojans first drive, culminating it on a quick 4-yard dart for a touchdown to Patrick Turner with less than five minutes expired. A few minutes later, the Trojans quarterback pump-fakes the Husky secondary into biting on a hitch pass, then finds Turner running free near the 5-yard line and hits him with a soft, floating spiral for a 32-yard touchdown play to make it 14–0 after just 10½ minutes of the first period.

It is merely a portent of things to come, with USC beating up on Washington as easily as it did on Washington State a few weeks earlier. All facets of the Trojans offense are working, with Gable, the surprising tailback starter after he spoke out publicly concerning his frustration a few days earlier, rushing for a couple of first-half touchdowns and Sanchez going 15 of 17 for 167 yards and his two TDs in the opening half. All of this is framed by another spectacular effort from the first-team defense that holds the Huskies to an astonishing 35 total yards in the first thirty minutes, allowing just two first downs, one of them by penalty. It is 42–0 at intermission, and Carroll, if he truly wanted to impress the BCS pollsters, could roll up 80 or 90 points by the end of the game. But he doesn't. He floods the field with reserves early in the third period, playing just about everyone on the roster, and mercifully holds the final score down to 56–0.

"We wanted to make a big deal for our seniors with homecoming and all," Carroll says, "and it all worked out great. We had a real good energy and focus, the kind we must have, no matter who we're playing." That, in case people aren't paying attention, is a direct reference to that disastrous evening when they weren't focused at Oregon State. The only negative on this particular afternoon for USC is a return of those nagging penalties. The Trojans are flagged ten times for 90 yards, and while it hardly mattered against Washington, it remains a disturbing habit. "It was a good, sharp day in every way but the penalty situation," Carroll says. "We still have to work to get that cleaned up."

The old defensive coordinator didn't want to talk about the penalties, though. He wanted to wax enthusiastic about this defense, the one that just recorded its third shutout in four games. The one that has allowed just one touchdown in the past eighteen quarters, and that only because of a turnover on its own 15-yard line. "This is the best run we've ever had defensively," he says, meaning no other USC team in his tenure has been better. When you consider his past defenses have consistently ranked among the best in America, that is saying something. "This is a fantastic group that is really, really playing now. Our linebacking corps is really special. The four, and I'm including Clay Mattews in that, is the best group we've had by far."

Then Carroll gets this glazed look in his eyes and begins talking about a 1949 defense at his alma mater, the University of the Pacific, of all things. "When I played there [in the early '70s], we looked at film of that team and it never allowed anybody to score against them," he says. "I always wondered what it would be like to coach a team like that, a team that gives up nothing every week. You know, to have a team where guys just can't score against you. This is an exciting time for us." The performance of the defense is even more impressive when you consider it pitched this third shut-out without Ellison, its captain and leader at strong safety. Harris, an athletic junior, stepped in and played extremely well, just as cornerback Josh Pinkard did earlier in the season, when starter Shareece Wright went down with an injury.

"That's even more encouraging," Carroll says. "A great player like Kevin is injured, but a Will Harris comes in and plays great. He was active, aggressive, and almost had himself a couple of picks. You lose your captain and one of your best players, and someone comes in plays well in his place. That's how you become a great football team." Maualuga, who dispensed one of his strongest performances, smiled and said, "I still think this defense has yet to show its best."

One sideline observer was duly impressed. Sedrick Ellis, the two-time All American at nose tackle who was the best football player on the team a year ago, liked what he saw. "The defense is doing really well, as expected," said the current New Orleans Saints starter. "At USC, you always know the guys waiting to take over are going to be good. It's what you expect to happen here." The second half of the Washington game was of little significance except, as Ellis hinted, it provided a glowing peek into the Trojans' future. Chris Gallipo, the redshirt freshman who will take over for Maualuga at middle linebacker next year, intercepted a pass and returned it 50 yards in the fourth period. Safety Drew McAllister, a true freshman who could also start in 2009, picked off another pass to help preserve the shutout. On offense, promising freshman Marc Tyler, the son of former UCLA and Rams star Wendell Tyler, took advantage of his first real opportunity in a USC uniform to rush for 85 yards in the final two periods, demonstrating again the endless depth this team has at tailback.

Later, in the USC locker room, Carroll took time to talk to two of the weekend's prized visiting recruits, linebacker Jarvis Jones from Columbus, Georgia, and Frankie Telfort, an all-around star at Gulliver Prep in Miami, Florida. Both are among the most sought-after high school players in the country, and Carroll would love to add them to his list of early verbal commitments, a group already regarded as one of his best yet.

Unfortunately, the whole upbeat feel of homecoming weekend officially ends on Sunday, when the latest BCS poll comes out and the Trojans drop from No. 5 to No. 7. Texas Tech's thrilling comeback victory over previously unbeaten Texas moves the Red Raiders all the way up to No. 2, and Florida's pummeling of Georgia allows the Gators to slip in at No. 5.

"We're playing really well now," says Carroll, feeling that old momentum that has allowed him to go 24-0 in November games, but also sensing the frustration of USC fans. "We're playing hard and we're playing focused. We've missed only two quarters of playing like that all season [against Oregon State]. Unfortunately, they're still hanging there."

Pete Profile

The Inner Game of . . . Football?

There is more to coaching football for Pete Carroll than X's and O's. There is a whole lot more.

Carroll is deep into the psychology of the sport, fully involved in what is going on his athletes' minds and how he can help them to relax and focus, shaping their thinking to fully concentrate and produce to the best of their ability. If it sounds simple, it is not. Carroll has been studying this aspect of athletics since he was a graduate student at University of Pacific, where he wrote his Masters thesis on psychologist Abraham Maslow's field of positive psychology. Maslow believed people were motivated by unsatisfied needs. When those needs were met, only then could they achieve self-actualization to maximize potential.

Later, as a graduate coaching assistant at Pacific, Carroll became enthralled with W. Timothy Gallwey's *The Inner Game of Tennis*.

"I recognized the obvious benefits of Gallwey's teachings early on," Carroll says, and he has since proved it by writing the forward to Gallwey's latest paperback edition of his book, which, by the way, has sold more than eight hundred thousand copies since it was first published thirty years ago. The two have become fast friends and now communicate regularly.

So maybe it was inevitable that, on a soft summer night six weeks before the start of 2008 fall camp, Carroll would decide to organize a semiprivate discussion group between himself and Gallwey, inviting fifty or so of his closest friends and associates, a smattering of his assistant coaches, and me. In the Varsity Lounge of USC's Heritage Hall, a temporary stage is set up with two comfortable-looking lounge chairs and microphones. Four rows of chairs fifteen across are lined up facing the stage with a serious crew of technicians in the back of the room, taping the proceedings for a DVD that will be available at a later time.

After a brief cocktail party with servers offering cool drinks and hot hors d'oeuvres, the stylishly dressed crowd, made up of both men and women, makes its way into the lounge, while Carroll and Gallwey take their appointed seats on stage.

"I want to welcome everyone," says Pete, flashing that now familiar smile. "In essence, we're just here to have some fun talking." He proceeds to tell how his interest in Gallwey's work began. "I took the book very much to heart," he says. "In philosophy and theory, we've connected for a long time. This is extraordinary. I'm the real winner here tonight."

Gallwey, a former National Hardcourt tennis champion as a teenager, is a distinguished-looking gentleman with slicked-back hair whiter than Carroll's tousled, mixed gray. He has written a series of best-selling books on the "inner game" and has spent much of his time the past twenty years introducing his approach to corporations looking for better ways to manage change. He begins his part of the conversation by describing how he discovered the inner game.

"I was an educator studying higher education, and I found that it wasn't changing much over the years," he says. "So I left and started teaching tennis. One day, I was about to do this, I was about to go out there and say, 'You should do this and you shouldn't do that,' and it suddenly seemed like a very boring system. I was teaching a student with a bad backswing, and I had no energy to start telling him what to do. So I just waited, and pretty soon, his backhand started dropping lower by itself. I thought to myself, 'Oh my God,' and the inner game started in that next moment. I realized I was more committed to teaching than to the student actually learning. I was upset he had learned by himself. That changed my perspective, and I began thinking what would happen if I became more interested in learning than teaching.

"That led to the question of what is going on inside the head of a person as he is about to hit the ball. It started my theory about Self 1 and Self 2. It's been an interesting journey. I realized I didn't have to do much teaching at all. By getting students to focus their attention on something quiet, their mind started functioning better. I call it a person's performance equals his potential to perform minus interference." Gallwey said eliminating interference is all about something he calls ACT. "That's Awareness, seeing truth in how things really are, with Commitment, your vision and passion, and Trust, the ability to have faith in yourself."

Carroll says his trick was to try to adapt Gallwey's methods for individuals into a team concept. "What happens is we want to see how our whole team [all the players] actualizes their knowledge. Our whole thing is based on one simple thought: We want to win forever. Winning forever is not necessarily winning all your games, although the fans and certainly the alumni would like that to happen, but it's about having a blast, having fun, enjoying the heck out of it by finding out how good you can be. Competition is my central thing. Competition gives us the mentality we can live in. We want to make it fun, but put it in a competitive mode."

Carroll points out that he doesn't agree with the old Vince Lombardi theory that winning is everything. "For me, winning is being the best you can be," he says. "The better the other team plays, the harder they make you play, and that makes you better. We use the phrase here that practice is everything. We try to make practice as much fun as possible and get players to work against the best players we can find. We feel if we do that we can instill and orchestrate confidence."

Gallwey smiles as he listens to his friend wax enthusiastically about his approach. "Interference is that shadow that stands between who you really are and who you can be," Gallwey says. "It's an ignorance. It is not a fear of failing. It is a fear of what it's going to mean if you fail."

Just as some in the audience begin to blink as the level of conversation seems to grow deeper, Carroll talks about a key moment in one of USC's games with Cal, one of its more intense Pac-10 rivals. "We're late in the fourth quarter, and there's a pivotal fourth-and-one play for our defense, with the game on the line. So I call a couple of our key defensive players over and I say, 'Can you believe how loud it is? What a great moment.' They were expecting me to tell them what defense to run and they look at me kind of crazy, but what I was really doing was trying to get them all on the same page. Get them to relax and focus."

Gallwey nods. "What you did is that they had their own mindset on fourth and one, but by saying, 'Wow, what a moment this is,' that shifted no fear in their thought. It made them realize that win or lose, this is a moment [to remember]."

"I like to visualize what a player can be," Carroll says. "I like to share my vision with them. Once that vision is set, I try to get the player to not only envision it, but to be even better than I envisioned. Once when I started out at Pacific, we had a lousy team. I mean, we sucked. But as a defensive backfield coach, I told them I had a vision. I told them we're going to lead the nation in interceptions. They thought I was crazy, but sure enough, we wound up having a heckeva year."

"That's the trust idea," Gallwey says. "You get a person surprised at the level of their performance. You get a player to say, 'Wow, who was that?' The answer to the question is, that was you."

"It's like in the military," Carroll says. "In these elite Special Forces units, they convince them they are absolutely prepared for whatever happens. It comes out of great discipline. That's where extraordinary performance shocks you. It allows you to fly."

"To do the flying," Gallwey adds, grinning, "you first have to trust."

"On Fridays, I tell our guys, 'You don't have to make the greatest plays ever,'" Carroll says. "Just play the way you're capable of playing. Just go out and play. When we do that, I think we're unbeatable."

After a brief break, Carroll opens it up with questions, but first he wants to ask Gallwey a few questions of his own. "I'm curious about the discipline of a coach," Carroll says. "What elements does that take."

"I don't think of myself as a disciplinarian," Gallwey says. "I think it has to be spontaneous. The discipline is putting yourself in the other person's shoes you are coaching. Then try to react. I think you do it intuitively. Leave no room for doubt in your voice. Real discipline is listening to your heart rather than your head."

Carroll nods in agreement. "We have this given sense at USC of what we can be," he says. "We try to draw focus to who the players can become. It's a real cool distinction. Very cool. It's the same with my staff. My coaches have to be fully convinced they're in a great setting. They have to be able to express their individuality. They have to know they have a future. All these things, they're sending messages to our players. I can feel great about myself, but it's no good if they don't feel that way, too."

Now it is Gallwey's turn to give a knowing nod. "Is there an inner game of anything?" Carroll asks. "Anything that is human," Gallwey says. "Everyone has potential, but things interfere. As long as you're human, though, there is an inner game of anything."

The talk turns to goals. "I never wear a ring," Carroll says. "I don't cheerlead for what already happened. I try to keep our goals sensible. For our players, the only real goal is to own the Rose Bowl. Winning the National Championship is out of our control somewhat." That statement, coming in early summer, is more prophetic than Carroll ever suspected.

"Performance goals are somewhat limited," Gallwey says. "Enjoyment goals are not."

Carroll laughs. "I'm so screwed up, one of my favorite lines is from Jerry Garcia. It goes: 'I don't want to be the best one doing something. I want to be the only one doing it.'"

As the session winds down, the coach and the author take a few questions from an obviously enthralled audience, then Carroll leans over and shakes Gallwey's hand.

"This has been so much fun for me," he says. "It's been a great thrill."

"I really appreciate you giving me the chance," Gallwey says. "I feel the same way."

Spontaneous applause breaks out, then the two are quickly surrounded at the front of the stage, shaking hands and signing autographs before the doors to Heritage Hall open and all of them slowly stroll out into the warm June night.

XI

Game Nine: A Presidential Vote, a BCS Rant, and a New Challenge from Cal

I'm voting for Obama," he says, and those of us standing around him try not to be too obvious about our jaws dropping in unison. It is not so much that Pete Carroll, the liberal-minded coach who grew up in the San Francisco Bay Area during the wild Haight-Ashbury era, would vote for Democratic candidate Barack Obama for president. That is not a surprise.

The surprise is that he would publicly announce it, considering he is the head coach at USC, the rich, private university that has long had a huge conservative Republican majority as its base. Football coaches, in general, rarely divulge their political leanings, but for Carroll to do it, then to expound on it, well, it comes as more than a slight shock. "It's time," he says about Obama. "I'm excited for it, for everybody. Most of all, I'm excited to be represented by him around the world." At his Tuesday press conference, on November 4, the day the first African American will be voted in as president, he is asked about it again. "I voted for Obama today," he says, "was excited about it, fired up for it." He announces it as his press conference ends and he stands up. "That's a good one to end on," he says. As he is walking out the door, he turns to me, smiling, and says, "That should make me popular in Orange County, huh?" Orange County is known as one of the more conservative areas in the state, if not the country.

Thinking about it later, you realize it is not so much that Carroll is flaunting his politics as it is a measure of his job security. Only a coach who understands how overwhelmingly popular he is with boosters and alumni would come out and make statements like this. Then again, it seems to be Carroll's week for venting. Earlier, both during and after that same Tuesday press conference, it is as if he can hold it in no longer. He finally lets loose in an uncharacteristic rant about the current BCS poll system.

"I think it stinks," he says. "I don't think it's the way it should be. The really interesting thing is, who is making these decisions? You guys can't even talk to the people that are calling the shots. You can talk to people that have opinions about it, who say they know somebody that might have a play in it, but we don't even know who this is. It's kind of like the Wizard of Oz. Somebody's behind that screen there, but we don't know who it is." The more this 2008 season goes by, the clearer it becomes that the weakness of the Pac-10 is working against USC's chances to get to the BCS title game with one loss. Representatives from both the Big Twelve and Southeastern Conference, with stronger overall teams, are likely to be picked ahead of the Trojans should they also finish with just one defeat. "I don't understand how the thing works," Carroll says. "I don't really know. Maybe you guys will have an answer for it one of these days. Maybe you know and I don't. What is the criteria of the process? Is it to pick the team that has the best season, that has the season that you like the most and feel best about voting for? Or is it the best team at the end of the year, the team that would win a playoff system if you did have it? . . . I think there's a difference there. I think it's difficult to understand really what is behind everybody's choices. That's why I can't give it any concern because I don't know how it works. I don't know how the computer thing works. I don't get that part of it. I don't get how the computer knows how good another team is. I don't understand that. I don't know how they can evaluate who you're playing and stuff and all that." At that point he pauses, as if setting up his audience. Then he breaks into a big grin. "That's why I'm coaching football," he says. The place erupts in laughter.

It is no laughing matter, though, and Carroll knows it. His patience with the system is wearing thin, because for the third year in a row, a mind-blowing upset by a huge underdog has derailed his chances of even getting a shot at a third national championship. In 2006, it was a painful loss to 3-touchdown underdog UCLA. In 2007, it was the watershed of all upsets, a 24–23 defeat at the hands of 41-point underdog Stanford, at the Coliseum, no less. Of course, this season, there was also that mind-boggling 27–21 disappointment against Oregon State, a mere 25-point 'dog. It is not like Carroll isn't aware of it, or hasn't thought about it a million times, trying to figure out why it happens. "Yeah, I've worked really hard at it," he says. "Every game you work to make sure you've covered all of the aspects that can affect your performance. A big part of it is the mental side of it. A big part of it is what's happened before. Have you left it behind? Does it affect you? All that. In particular, coming off a high-profile win like the one we came off of [against Ohio State], that was an issue that I could see coming for months ahead. I had set my sights trying to make sure I didn't leave any stone unturned to get it prepared and it still happened . . . I mean, I don't know that it's rocket science, but man, it will get you once in a while. But that's what we deal with. I love this challenge. I'd much rather be fighting that challenge of the game that you fall out on rather than trying to be 6-5 or something like that. . . . Things get you. It's not always what you can control. Sometimes it's those other guys playing really well and doing really good things. A lot goes into it. You know, I guess I'm glad we're not a machine because we would have no feelings. We do get affected by stuff sometimes and we don't control it as well as we'd like. That's the great challenge we face. We'll keep working on it, see if we can figure it out."

This must be the week for psychoanalysis at USC. Earlier, Carroll mentions the talks he and his assistants have been having with Mark Sanchez, their gifted but still sometimes fragile quarterback.

In the Arizona game two weeks ago, Sanchez missed a wide-open Patrick Turner on a pass that would have been an early first-quarter touchdown, and he seemed to go into a funk about it for much of the rest of the game, although he did come back to throw the winning touchdown pass. Carroll, offensive coordinator Steve Sarkisian, and even graduate assistant Yogi Roth, the young coach who wants to grow up to be Carroll, have been preaching to Sanchez. "I think Mark is really, really good and on the verge of being a great football player," Carroll says, after Sanchez's thorough carving up of woeful Washington. "It's important to know when something doesn't go good that it's not necessarily a bad day.

"I had the same conversation with Carson Palmer and with Matt Leinart his senior year. They're so prideful, and they want to be great. I told him [Sanchez] you've got to recognize how good you are and bounce back when you have a bad play." Sanchez credits the talks with his improved performance against Washington. "I've been talking to the coaches about focusing my emotions, as to what the team needs," the quarterback says. "Like that time in the game [at Arizona] when I threw deep to RoJo [Ronald Johnson] when I could have tripped and fell down for the first down. I think I'm an emotional kind of guy. It's so much fun out there, I can't help it. I have to show it when something doesn't go well. Coach Carroll has talked to me about it. He said you've got to get to the point where you know something good is about to happen right around the corner, not just in the game, but in life. It put things into perspective for me." Roth, the sort of New Age coach on the staff, also approached Sanchez, likely on Carroll's behalf. Sanchez says Yogi came to him and asked, what kind of player do you really want to be? "First thing that came to mind was, I want to win," says Sanchez. "I am a winner . . . that's what I want to do." Roth told him, that's the way you should think. "That's what you are, that's who you are," Roth said. "Be that, trust that, feel that way."

All this touchy-feely business eventually gives way to a typically raucous pre-Cal team meeting on Thursday afternoon in the tiny amphitheater on Heritage Hall's first floor. The noise rising to a crescendo in the room stuffed with large, muscular athletes stripped down to cutoff T-shirts, football pants, and raging testosterone quickly quiets when Carroll enters wearing a gray hoodie with USC emblazoned on the front. "Do you guys know what 'rips it' means?" he asks. "Well, let me tell you. Rips it is when you see Kevin Ellison only three days after knee surgery and he tells you, 'Coach, I'll be ready to play next week.' That's what rips it means. Or Garrett Green sprinting down to make contact on the kickoff team at the 7-yard line. Yeah, that's what rips it means. How about Barack Obama's campaign manager, David Plouffe? That guys rips it." Several of the players hoot at that point, loving the fact their coach is a fan of America's first African-American president. "Or Jeff Byers, up for not one, but two national academic awards. That rips it." The players begin chanting at that point: *"Jeff! . . . Jeff! . . . Jeff!"* Byers smiles and waves them off. "OK, OK," says Carroll, "now you guys know we have only two turns left at the Coliseum [this year]. Yeah, only one more before the last one. You got to make the most of it. This feels right for us. It just feels right. This game is really about the running game. We need to run well on our side, and we need to shut down their running game. They have two terrific running backs, but their quarterbacks are up and down. Their coach doesn't want to throw. We have to make them throw. We have to be ready and focused. All right, let's go out and have a good practice. Everyone on the field at four."

USC opens as a 17-point favorite, but the line grows to 22 as the week plods on, an indication that oddsmakers, unlike much of L.A. and the rest of the country, are taking notice of a defense that is developing into one of the finest in Trojans history. For some reason, maybe because no one has come up with a colorful nickname for this group, there is hardly been any notoriety about what is happening with this defensive unit. After eight games, it leads the nation in scoring defense (7.1 points) and total defense (211.63 yards). It has allowed one touchdown in the past 18 quarters, and that only after a turnover on its own 15-yard line against Arizona. One measly touchdown has been scored against it at home all season, and in the second half of games, there have been just two touchdown drives by opponents, the aforementioned one for 15 yards and another for 2 yards. "It is, at this point of the season, the best defense we've had here," says Carroll, and that's saying something. His defenses, littered with future high NFL draft choices, have consistently ranked among the top in the nation.

The linebacking corps led by All-Americans Rey Maualuga and Brian Cushing has grown stronger with the solid performance of Kaluka Maiava on the weak side and surpising Clay Matthews, who, as a hybrid linebacker/defensive end, has made as many big plays as anybody. The Fili Moala–led defensive line, with three starting seniors and a mix of young reserves, has gotten better every week. That said, the real key has been the ability of the cornerbacks to play receivers one-on-one, allowing Carroll's defenders to be more aggressive with blitzes and freeing up the safeties, Ellison (before his knee surgery) and Taylor Mays, to make more plays. Even injuries haven't stopped this defense from improving. When Shareece Wright went down at a corner, Josh Pinkard stepped in and provided an even tougher, more physical presence, and when strong safety Ellison, the captain and the unit's best player, was injured before the Washington game, Will Harris moved in and played remarkably well. "I felt so bad when Kevin went down, my heart hurt," Harris says. "Thank God it's not serious. But I also looked at it as my opportunity, and I knew I had to grab it. The great thing about our defense is that we depend on each other. I think that's what makes us so good. Everybody helps everybody else out."

Cal, rated No. 21 nationally, will provide a much sterner test than the Washingtons and Washington States. Although the same Arizona team that was limited to 10 points against USC rumbled through the Bears on the way to a 42–27 victory. "We've been up and down," Coach Jeff Tedford says, in a phone conference with reporters. "We haven't put a big game together yet. We're young in some areas, but we're developing every week." Still, Tedford, one of the better X's-and-O's coaches in the country, usually plays Carroll's teams competitively. He comes to the Coliseum with a defense ranked No. 23 in the country, and an offense that features the best breakaway threat in the Pac-10 in tailback Jahvid Best (6.8 yards per carry) and another speedy runner in his backup, Shane Vereen. Cal's quarterback play has been inconsistent for much of the season, and just when sophomore Kevin Riley seemed to have taken over the position, he suffered a concussion in the victory over Oregon. So senior Nate Longshore, who has a strong arm but is relative immobile in the pocket, has reemerged and will start against the Trojans.

Kickoff arrives on an early fall evening framed by a dazzling California sunset, the gathering darkness streaked with bright ribbons of red. The game quickly settles into a battle of defenses and a flurry of penalty flags. Carroll talked about the importance of the running game, and the Trojans, led by a seemingly inspired Maualuga at middle linebacker, immediately put the clamps on Best, the Bears' darting little tailback. Meanwhile, their own tailbacks, typically shuttling in and out, pound away early and manufacture a 56-yard drive that climaxes with David Buehler's 27-yard field goal.

Next time it gets the ball, USC seems on the verge of opening a commanding lead. The offensive line is punching holes up front and C.J. Gable, Joe McKnight, and Stafon Johnson are pounding away for big chunks of yardage. Then, inexplicably, on a third and 2 in four-down territory at the Cal 35, the Trojans choose to pass. Sanchez is sacked for a 3-yard loss and Carroll decides to punt. For all the physicality this team demonstrates on defense, it stubbornly refuses to play the same way on offense, even when it is clearly muscling an opponent. The way it is dominating the line of scrimmage, one or two run calls on third and 2 almost assuredly would provide the coveted first down. Instead, Sarkisian, the finesse-minded offensive coordinator, inexplicably calls a pass. End of drive. To say this kind of stuff drives USC fans and Internet bloggers crazy would be an understatement.

A few minutes later, Cal's most effective, and as it turns out, only real drive of the evening is helped along by another surge of

USC penalties, particularly a 15-yard roughing the passer call on Cushing and a blatant pass interference by Maiava. It allows the Bears to go 63 yards to position the lyrically named Giorgio Tavecchio for the tying 35-yard field goal.

In the second quarter, Sanchez, who is clearly being told to stay conservative against a Cal defense that leads the nation in interceptions, finally gets into rhythm, hitting tight end Anthony McCoy for 20 yards, Damian Williams for 30, and then firing a C.C. Sabathia–like fastball into the end zone, where Patrick Turner makes a spectacular diving catch for the 19-yard touchdown. The half ends 10–3, and the game stays that way for most of the final two periods. Cal's Tedford switches quarterbacks at the intermission, and Kevin Riley comes in and makes some nice throws, but trying to put a scoring drive together against this USC defense is like running into a brick wall. At one point in the third quarter, the Bears' Nyan Boateng breaks clear into the Trojans' secondary on consecutive plays and seems ready to catch a couple of Riley passes when free safety Mays, all 6'3" and 230 pounds of him, crashes into him so hard it separates him from the ball and sends a collective shudder through the Coliseum. It's like a replay of a Ronnie Lott's Greatest Hits highlight reel, and it sets the tone for the rest of the balmy evening. USC's stingy defense is not about to give up any more points.

Offensively, though, the Trojans cough and sputter, with those nagging penalties, some rushed Sanchez passes, and a McKnight fumble all conspiring to keep the game close. It isn't until late in the final period that they manage to piece together a 73-yard drive behind some Sanchez passes and Gable runs. On a third and 2 at the Cal 6, Sarkisian calls—what else?—a pass, and this time Sanchez finds Ronald Johnson for the first time all night with a quick 6-yard dart for the touchdown that makes the final score 17–3.

It is a tough, grinding, somewhat satisfying victory for the Trojans, but one overshadowed by the fact they are plagued once again by all those penalties, a total of ten for a staggering 105 yards. In the locker room afterward, it is almost as if Carroll and the players are trying to defend themselves, noting the fine line between aggressiveness and carelessness. "I think the more physical you are, the more chance you have at getting them [penalties]," Mays says. "Any time you're that aggressive, you're going to have some," Cushing says. "But we've got to cut down on them, or they'll hurt us down the road." Carroll isn't happy with the penalties, but he is enthralled by the way the defense holds Cal to 165 total yards and Best, the Pac-10's second-leading rusher, to 30 yards in 13 carries. "I don't see any reason things should change," Carroll says. "The defense is playing crazy, lights out. I don't think we've ever had a streak like this."

The streak is getting to be remarkable. The defense now has allowed one touchdown in the past 22 quarters. It has given up only 60 points in nine games, the best of any USC defense since 1962, the year of legendary John McKay's first national championship team. In their opponents' last 62 drives, the Trojans have allowed one TD, that coming after a turnover on their own 15-yard line against Arizona. "We were actually disappointed that we gave up a field goal tonight," Cushing says, in the winning locker room. "We want to shut everybody out now."

Yet the BCS polls remain unimpressed. A 17–3 victory doesn't win over any voters on the same weekend Texas Tech is blowing out Oklahoma State, 56–20, Texas is mugging Baylor, 45–21, and Oklahoma is bludgeoning Texas A&M, 66–28. The only good news for USC is that Penn State was knocked from the ranks of the unbeaten, losing to Iowa, 24–23. So the Trojans move up one spot, to No. 6, in the BCS standings, which doesn't really mean much and still seems to put them beyond reach of an eventual BCS title game.

When asked about his team's lack of style points, or the idea that instead of playing to win he was playing not to lose against Cal, Carroll bristles. "Part of it was because Mark [Sanchez] was schooled all week long not to give up the ball against them," he says. "That was a big concern for us, the fact they had all those interceptions, and it was a big challenge for Mark. He had to really school it down. You guys don't have to be satisfied by the way we won, but I am. I don't care about impressing anybody. I don't want to win a popularity contest. I just want to win games."

He has three more to win, against Stanford, Notre Dame, and UCLA, to give him a new, eye-popping NCAA record of seven consecutive seasons of eleven or more victories.

Pete Profile

The Free Spirit

It is the day before Halloween, and USC is wrapping up an otherwise uneventful Thursday afternoon of practice heading into the Washington game. The players gather around Pete Carroll as they usually do at the end of drills, but their attention is diverted by offensive line coach Pat Ruel, who suddenly starts screaming at the other end of the field.

He is shouting angry words at one of the cameramen who tapes practice at the top of a fifty-foot crane that sits above an equipment truck across the street from Howard Jones Field. Everyone is watching as Ruel shouts and the cameraman shouts back. Then, as a collective gasp goes up from the field, the cameraman falls, tumbling toward the concrete below with his arms flailing. "Oh my God!" one of the players yells. Others put their hands over their eyes. On the sidelines, Adam Maya, a young writer from the *Orange County Register*, appears to have the blood drain from his face. The fence surrounding the field is covered, so no one can see the result of the fall. Everyone can only imagine.

A panicked-looking Brennan Carroll, the coach's son and the team's tight ends coach, bolts across the field and out the door to see if he can help. He is followed by an onrushing Steve Sarkisian, the offensive coordinator. A few emotional moments go by and a young woman bursts through the door onto the field. "He caught him! He caught him!" she shouts. "Oh my God, he caught him!"

While everyone stands there stunned, in walks Will Ferrell, the popular actor and noted USC alum, dressed in some kind of Captain Marvel costume, with the presumed cameraman, who turned out to be a stuntman, in his arms, trying not to smile. Turns out, unbeknown to the players and everyone else at practice, a large cushion had been set up outside, allowing the stuntman to land safely.

Just call it a typical Pete Carroll prank. "We thought we'd try to have some fun for Halloween," the coach says, grinning. The players are laughing and joking about it, but later, some admit they thought it was for real. "It felt awful," says fullback Stanley Havili. "Seriously," says freshman defensive tackle Armond Armstead, "I thought we just watched a dude die."

The regular Carroll-watchers laugh and say this was nothing. You should have been here a few years ago when he pulled the LenDale White stunt. White, now a tailback for the Tennessee Titans, was the "Thunder" in the "Lightning and Thunder" tailback combination that also featured Heisman Trophy winner Reggie Bush. On this particular afternoon, White gets into a presumed angry argument with a coach during practice and stalks off the field. Ten minutes later, a great commotion is heard on top of the three-story building directly behind Howard Jones Field. It appears to be White, still in uniform, wrestling with somebody as angry words are exchanged. The two disappear for a few moments, then the next thing everybody sees is White, still wearing his uniform, falling off the building. Many of the players honestly believed White had committed suicide. Turns out, much to everyone's relief, it was just a dummy with White's uniform on. He was in on the gag the whole time. Carroll actually took some heat for that one, with many feeling the stunt was in bad taste.

Nevertheless, the coach didn't care. To him, it was just another example of trying to have some fun. Having fun is a big thing in Carroll's life. "It's that Peter Pan thing, man," says Dave Perron, one of his closest friends. "He's Peter Pan in some ways. He's got this wonderful, childlike way about him." The proclivity for pranks apparently started at an early age. His friends still talk about his favorite stunt in high school. He'd cruise the Marin neighborhood in a red Valiant, then slide over to the passenger side using his left hand to steer and his left foot on the accelerator. He would honk and wave at people, all of whom did massive double takes watching the driverless car cruise by them.

Carroll sharpened his prankster skills in his time as a defensive backfield coach in Minnesota. "That's why we got along so well," says Bud Grant, the legendary former head coach of the Vikings. "I loved pranks as much as he did. With Pete around, it seemed like we had one every day. His best stuff was with Floyd Peters. He was a former Marine who was very straitlaced and disciplined. Pete was totally different, a free spirit. I think Pete understood Floyd better than Floyd understood Pete. Anyway, this one time, Pete arranged this deal where he pushed a dummy off a building, and everyone thought it was Floyd Peters. It was pretty extravagant." Well, at least we now know where Carroll came up with this falling-off-the-building/crane idea. "You might ask how does that help you as a coach," says Grant. "It helps you become a team. It is a bonding thing. I don't know how to explain it, but if you laugh at yourself, you're OK."

If nothing else, you have to give Carroll points for creativity. Another time at USC, he coerced his celebrity buddy-in-playfulness, Ferrell, to walk into a team meeting dressed as Ricky Bobby, his character in the movie *Talladega Nights*. Ferrell proceeded to deliver a hilarious, twangy attempt at an inspirational speech, but that's not the only thing that had the players roaring. Next to Ferrell, standing there with an impish grin on his face, was Carroll, wearing a NASCAR jumpsuit. The players really loved that.

Then there was the day this past spring when Carroll was in the middle of a serious talk with the players before practice. An officer from the Los Angeles Police Department interrupts the discussion by walking into the room. He whispers something in Carroll's ear, and the coach looks over with a furrowed brow at Everson Griffen, his young defensive end. "Everson, you need to go with these guys," he says.

Griffen, looking solemn, stands up and is escorted out as Carroll and his assistants exchange serious glances at one another. The other players in the room look concerned and worried. Griffen eventually comes back and announces he was booked on assault of a freshman. Then Carroll douses the lights and plays a video of Griffen manhandling freshman tackle Matt Meyer in practice. The place explodes with laughter.

"He wants to make it fun," says USC Sports Information Director Tim Tessalone. "It's loose, but he feels when people enjoy what they're doing they are apt to stay in line more often. You talk to any of his ex-players. They all tell you how much fun they had in the program."

That is part of the reason Carroll is coaching in college, instead of the NFL. "There is a level of seriousness that gets a little crazy in the NFL," he says. "It's still a game. They lose track of that in the NFL sometimes."

Fun is something Carroll manages to find every day at USC. You watch him for any length of time during the season, and you realize the thing you see him do more than anything else is throw the football. He throws it before practice. He throws it during practice. He throws it after practice. He throws it around during meetings. You suspect, before he goes to sleep at night, he sits up in bed tossing a football in the air. After one November weekday practice this season, Carroll pauses to sign autographs for two preteenage boys from the inner city. After he signs one's T-shirt and the other's football, he says, "OK, let's see what you got." The kids get wide-eyed when he instructs the first somewhat thinner boy to go out for a pass. He does, and Carroll throws a soft spiral that the kid catches in stride. The other slightly plump boy goes out and Carroll's pass floats just beyond his reach. "Let's try it again," Carroll says, and on the next pass the young man makes a pretty one-handed snag. "That's what I'm talking about," Carroll says, as he turns and casually walks toward the team beat writers who have been waiting impatiently, the usual twenty to thirty minutes after practice, for their daily interview.

"Is there anything you like better than throwing a football?" one writer asks. "Nope," says Carroll, with that trademark grin.

Well, maybe an occasional elaborate prank, you're thinking. He'd probably like that better. One day, I ask Carroll if they ever make a movie of his life, what actor would play him. He never even hesitates.

"Will Ferrell," he says.

XII

Game Ten: The Defection of a Tailback and a Nightmare Revisited

Todd McNair has a quiet, soulful kind of presence that makes him come off as part running backs coach and part favorite uncle. He is especially close with his tailbacks, that always supersized group at USC that seems to need his constant stream of soothing words and sensitive cajoling. You'll see him hugging one here, then playfully tapping another on the helmet there. More than a few times during a typical season, you'll find him off in a corner with a disgruntled backup who wants to know what is going on.

He calls it his "family," and on this cool November Tuesday afternoon you can see the pain on his face following practice. A member of the family has left. Broderick Green, the 240-pound redshirt freshman from Arkansas who seemed to have the style and potential of a young Jerome Bettis, has announced he intends to transfer at the end of the semester. Green is saying the health of his maternal grandmother, who suffered a stroke last year, is the primary reason, but everyone around the program knows his lack of playing time influenced him just as much, if not more. This is becoming a major issue in Pete Carroll's otherwise overpowering program now, because Green is the second tailback in two years to depart. Emmanuel

Moody, who arrived with just as much hype out of Texas, transferred to Florida, where he has played somewhat sparingly for the highly ranked Gators this season, after sitting out last year.

"It's tough at times, you know," McNair says. "They all come here thinking they're the best, and they get frustrated. I've been there myself. I try to share my experiences with them." McNair was a high school star in Pennsauken, New Jersey, then a running back who was good enough at Temple to earn All-American honorable mention in 1987. He spent eight seasons in the NFL as a journeyman running back and special-teams player in Kansas City and Houston. "You feel the loss with a kid like Broderick, but at the same time, that's what our program is about. It is about competition. The NFL is like that. You've got to learn to excel in that kind of environment. When you come here, you know how many tailbacks there are."

They all know, but amazingly, under Carroll they all still come. There were no less than ten on the roster in 2007. There were six starting this season. Now there are five, and that's not counting latecomer Curtis McNeal, a stubby little true freshman who is likely to be redshirted. Carroll's philosophy is that you can never have enough gifted tailbacks, and he refuses to name a starter at the position. Even when Reggie Bush was juking his way toward the Heisman Trophy, he shared time at tailback with LenDale White. At least then, Carroll stuck to two primary runners. The past three seasons, he has shuttled four or five in and out. Green had only one major opportunity this year, sent in during garbage time in the second half of the 69–0 rout of Washington State. He made the most of it, though, rushing for 121 yards and scoring 2 touchdowns. The next week, at Arizona, he was back on the bench, never given the chance to touch the ball. That's when the whispers first started. He was unhappy. He was thinking of transferring.

Carroll understands, but he is adamant about his approach. "It's a challenge," he says. "I don't want them [the tailbacks] to be pushing it at every turn, but I wouldn't want them to be really satisfied and comfortable with not playing, either." The tailbacks, whether individually or as a group, remain a constant topic of conversation among the USC bloggers and Internet junkies. Before he was injured earlier, Allen Bradford, a consistent standout at practice, was rumored to be unhappy with his lack of playing time, as well. Then there is Joe McKnight, who is one of Green's closest friends on the team. McKnight is always in the middle of the USC tailback controversy because he is one of Carroll's highest-profile recruits, a nationally known high school superstar who stunned everyone in his home state of Louisiana when he bypassed LSU for the Trojans two years ago. Some feel, because of the political implications, because his success might convince other celebrated five-star recruits from out of the area to consider USC, McKnight has become one of Carroll's favorites. It's not like the sophomore with the often breathtaking moves lacks talent. It's just that sometimes it seems as if he gets breaks some of the other tailbacks, most of them from the general L.A. area, don't. McKnight has struggled with a series of nagging injuries all fall, the latest a strained toe that has kept him on the sidelines for a couple of weeks. He was held out of the Washington game supposedly because of the toe, but later, Carroll confirmed a story in the *L.A. Daily News* that reported even if healthy, McKnight would have been held out because of academic issues.

So it's no wonder, when practice is over, that Carroll bristles some when I bring up the tailbacks as we walk from Howard Jones Field toward Heritage Hall, amid the strange sound of all the nearby music students warming up their various instruments. It's hard to ask serious questions when some guy is belting out notes on his tuba. "Does it worry you that another of your tailbacks is leaving?" I ask, trying to be heard over the noise. "No," he says, and you can tell he is irritated. "What about the charge that you have too many tailbacks on the roster at one time?" He shakes his head and grimaces. "Look, we have three right now, and four guys in the program that are healthy," he says. "Shoot, you need every single guy at that position. It's a hard business and you have to keep people healthy. Tailback is a very high-risk position." He will get no argument there. At USC, the position couldn't have a much higher risk factor.

Part of Carroll's edginess this week has to do with the tailback situation. The other part has to do with Stanford, Saturday's opponent in Palo Alto. Thinking about coach Jim Harbaugh and the Cardinal (the color not the bird) is like revisiting a nightmare for Carroll and the Trojans. It was only a year ago that the biggest upset of Carroll's tenure occurred, when the 41-point underdog visitors from the Farm came from behind with 17 points in the final period to knock off No. 2–ranked USC, 24–23 and snap the Trojans' thirty-five-game winning streak at the Coliseum. It is now commonly referred to as one of the greatest upsets in college football history, and it nags at Carroll more than people will ever know. "I was pissed about it then, I am pissed about it now, and I will always be pissed about it," he says, although he'd never admit as much at a function as public as his weekly press conference luncheon. It all started when Coach Harbaugh, the feisty former Michigan and Chicago Bears quarterback, opened fire before practice even started in his rookie season at Stanford. He announced that sources had told him 2007 probably would be Carroll's last at USC before jumping to the NFL. Later, at his first Pac-10 Media Day, Harbaugh proclaimed USC could be the greatest team in college football history.

Publicly, Carroll laughed off both proclamations, but privately, he wasn't happy with either of them. The quiet assumption was that he would try to rub it in Harbaugh's face if he got a chance. The opportunity never came, however, especially after John David Booty, the Trojans' star quarterback, fractured the tip of the middle finger on his throwing hand in the second period of their early October game. Carroll decided to leave Booty in, and it didn't seem to matter when USC took a 9–0 lead, then threatened again in the final moments before halftime. But with a fourth and goal at the 1-yard line, Carroll somewhat arrogantly disdained the field goal that would have given his team a 12–0 advantage. Instead, he went for the touchdown. Tailback Chauncey Washington was stopped short of the end zone, and the Cardinal raced off to the locker room with a measure of hope and a shred of momentum.

Although Mark Sanchez was warming up on the sideline, Carroll decided to stick with Booty, broken finger and all, in the second half. It is a decision that continues to haunt him to this day. "I should have taken John out," he says. "It was my fault. I should never have let him play the second half." Not only did Carroll let Booty play, he had him throwing deep passes over the middle. It is no wonder that he suffered four interceptions, the most in a game by a USC quarterback in twenty years. Stanford, down 16–7 after three periods, rallied behind those turnovers and Tavita Pritchard, a quarterback starting his first college game. With the final seconds ticking down and the Trojans still clinging to a 23–17 lead, Pritchard hit on a fourth-and-20 pass to Richard Sherman. Then, on fourth and goal, the suddenly cool quarterback found Mark Bradford with a 10-yard touchdown pass that became one of the most famous in Stanford history.

It was a game marked by a series of uncharacteristically poor coaching decisions, especially for someone of Carroll's stature. Leaving Booty in with a fractured finger on his passing hand was obviously the big one, but disdaining that gimme field goal at the end of the half proved to be another. Then there was the strange, non-blitzing strategy on defense against a young quarterback starting his very first game. Why not come after Pritchard early and try to rattle him? Why give him time to slowly gain some bravado? Finally, there was the late touchdown pass after a long time-out, when USC failed to put its best cover cornerback, Terrell Thomas, on Bradford, the Cardinal's clear go-to receiver. "We kept waiting for someone to signal us to switch," Thomas later said, "but the signal never came."

As it was, the game not only knocked the Trojans from the ranks of the undefeated, it eventually cost them any chance of squeezing back into the BCS title game at the end of the season. Other than that, it was just a wonderful fall evening for Carroll. A year later, with the rematch approaching, comments from both coaches are cryptic, at best. "They came through and made the plays they had to make, and it was a great finish for them. It wasn't for us," Carroll says, and you can almost see him biting his lip.

"Both teams will have fire in their eyes and will be ready to play this football game," Harbaugh says, making it sound more like an old, clichéd recording. "Our team plays very hard. They compete. Our team understands how good USC is."

The difference between that game and this one is the new, overpowering USC defense, a fact oddsmakers seem to note by establishing the Trojans as 23-point favorites on the road. Carroll's defensive unit is now allowing the least points per game (7.7) of any USC team since 1952. This is also November, not October. Carroll is 25–0 in the second-to-last month of the year, and maybe even more significant, his teams once again have established a remarkable dominance in the second half of games. In the nine games played so far in 2008, USC has managed to outscore the opposition 143–13 in the final two periods. "It's all about finishing," says Sanchez. "Coach Carroll preaches that to us all the time. It's about finishing games and finishing out the season as strong as possible."

It is also about conditioning. It has to be. How else to explain the fact that USC's teams always seem to be gaining energy at the ends of games, while opponents seem to be gasping for breath? John Wooden, the legendary former UCLA basketball coach Carroll openly admires, always said one of the most important aspects of coaching is to make sure your team is better conditioned than your opponent. For Carroll, his main ally in that regard is Chris Carlisle, an intense, rumpled-looking forty-six-year-old who serves as the team's strength-and-conditioning coach. Carlisle has an interesting storyline of his own. In December 2000, while he still worked for the University of Tennessee and just before Carroll called him for an interview, he was diagnosed with Hodgkin's disease. "I decided to fly out for the interview and tell him [Carroll] after I got here," Carlisle says. "So I did. After he was finished interviewing me, I said, 'I need to tell you something.' I told him about the cancer, and he said, 'Will it make you a different coach?' I told him no. He said, 'Can you be here on Monday?' Later, he told me he thought I was worth the chance. For a long time in my first year here, only Pete and I knew about it. He helped me through it.

He believed in me when times were tough, so my loyalty to him is undying."

One of the more remarkable aspects of USC's success is its ability to win so regularly with facilities that you wouldn't wish on your lower-level Division IAA school. There is no plush athletic dorm, and the practice fields are rudimentary, at best. As for its weight room, well, it is stocked with most of the requisite equipment, but it is housed in a somewhat dingy area in the basement of Heritage Hall. At Notre Dame, the weight room area is 25,000 square feet of gleaming surroundings. At Nebraska, the area seems almost as big as the city of Omaha. At Florida and Texas, it is 20,000 square feet. Arizona's facility is 21,000 square feet, Oregon State's is 20,000. Even UCLA's is 15,000.

USC's weight room is 9,000 square feet, and although university officials keep promising an upgrade and some architectural plans for a state-of-the-art facility already have been drawn up, a frustrated Carlisle just kind of shrugs and makes do as best he can. His only mistake is that the Trojans' superb conditioning makes higher-ups wonder why he can't continue to get by with what he has. Fortunately, he has Carroll, the gregarious salesman, working for him, and he's confident the head coach will find a way to improve the situation. Nobody in the program is more impressed with the head coach than Carlisle.

"The thing about Pete is he knows everything that is going on, but he allows you to do what you do best," he says. "He's not a micromanager, he is a microleader. With his words, he paints murals, but he doesn't give you a blueprint. He adds color to it. He brings in a kid like Taylor Mays, and he tells me, here's what I want him to be. We construct a program to bring that out in him. For instance, his speed was God-given, but his ability to change direction and maintain speed, that's something we've been working with him on. We have drills that emphasize that. You never have a sit-down meeting with Pete. You know how he is; everything is on the fly. But he tells me this is what we need to do, and he allows me to use my tools to do it."

Carlisle is very aware of the team's success in the second half of games. "I'll take about 2 percent of the credit for that," he says. "But if Coach Carroll believes in what I do, the athletes believe in Coach Carroll. That makes my job easier. He's told me this is our basic goal: We want to prepare these kids for the highest level, so they can practice at the highest level and play at the highest level. The best kids are the ones who drive this [conditioning] program. It all started with the Carson Palmers and the Troy Polamalus and the Matt Leinarts. When the best guys work hard, the second-level guys, like Matt Cassel, work hard, too. When the freshmen come in, they're all five-star rated and everything, but most of them haven't trained. A guy like T.J. Bryant comes in, and he sees what Mays and Josh Pinkard and those guys are doing, he sees how hard they're working, and he knows he has to catch up to play at their level. It's an evolution, not an accident."

Speaking of accidents, the idea, on this particular November Saturday, is not to repeat the one of a year ago. On an unseasonably warm fall afternoon in Palo Alto, Stanford alums and boosters can still be seen walking around Stanford Stadium wearing T-shirts that read: BIGGEST UPSET EVER. No one has to remind Trojans fans, who annually make their beloved Bay Area trip by the thousands, to which game that refers. Hours before the TV-dictated four o'clock kickoff, Town and Country Plaza, the folksy strip mall across from the stadium, is full of fans wearing USC colors. At Kirk's Steak-burgers, one of the more popular laid-back luncheon spots, a prominent USC alum is shaking his head over Carroll. He wasn't upset at his coaching. He was angry about his political leaning. "He made a big mistake announcing he was voting for Obama," says the alum. "He made a lot of big donors angry and that could cost him." Another alum sitting nearby smiled and said, "If Pete keeps going 12-1, it won't matter who he's voting for. The donors won't care."

Once the game starts, all anyone wearing USC colors cares about is the way the team is playing. It is not encouraging. In fact, it begins to feel a lot like that first half in Corvallis. The defense that has played so superbly in the past two months looks lethargic, allowing Toby Gerhart, Stanford's bullish tailback, to ransack it almost at will. The Trojans' offense, meanwhile, shrivels into your basic nonentity, going three-and-out on its first three possessions. The first quarter ends with Stanford ahead 10–3 and the Cardinal outgaining USC 149 yards to 6.

The second period is a bit better, with the Trojans finally utilizing what clearly appears their best weapon, their tailback-fueled running game, to drive 80 yards for a touchdown. C.J. Gable returns a kickoff 93 yards for another, but USC fans feel fortunate their team is tied at 17 after a shaky first thirty minutes. In the second half, Steve Sarkisian, who is being widely second-guessed by fans at this point, finally relents and begins calling plays that pound at the Cardinal with Gable and Stafon Johnson, his two excellent running backs, interspersing some Joe McKnight in there, as well. The Trojans move ahead 24–17 heading into the final period, and then all that Carlisle-inspired conditioning starts to pay off. USC begins to wear down Harbaugh's overmatched defense, finishing with an impressive 243 yards rushing in the second half to win, going away, 45–23.

Afterward, some of the USC players seem as perplexed as the fans. "We knew the run was there all along," says Gable. "We kept trying to tell them [the coaches] that. Thank goodness we finally went to it more in the second half." Carroll, always sensitive to criticism of Sarkisian, was quick to come to his defense. "We kind of mixed around so much early in the game we couldn't find the running game," he says, "but once Sark went after it, I thought he just figured it out and then did a fantastic job of changing the night." Even for Carroll, that one seemed like a stretch. They couldn't find the running game? Was it hidden under the luggage on the team bus, or what? So what happened when they finally "found" it? "A lot of the guys' eyes lit up," says center Kristopher O'Dowd. "That's what we wanted."

A team searching for its offensive identity all season long finally seems to have discovered it. Most fans believe USC should run first and pass later. A 60-40 split, run over pass, fully utilizing the skills of tailbacks Johnson, Gable, and McKnight, could allow this offense, stacked with talented athletes, to operate at optimum level. Unless, of course, Carroll feels otherwise. "We're not changing anything," he says to reporters the next day, in what seems to be a reaction to all the criticism. "I don't know what we're going to call in the next game. Nobody knows that."

What everyone does know is that even though the Trojans are now 9-1 and cruising once again through November, nothing has changed in the BCS polls. There are no major upsets of teams ahead of USC in the standings, and the deeper it gets into the season, the less chance the Trojans have of climbing past them into the BCS title game. So the mood around campus on Monday is somewhat bittersweet. USC finally showed its dominance over Stanford, and the Trojans reaffirmed their role as a superbly conditioned second-half team, having now outscored the opposition 171–19 across the final two periods this year. It was also Carroll's eighty-fifth victory in his first hundred games at USC. Still, none of that seems to matter, because Sarkisian and the play calling are under fire again from the bloggers and Internet columnists, as well as the alums and even the student newspaper, the *Daily Trojan*, while the ugly BCS situation continues to fester.

Oh well, somewhere in the bowels of Heritage Hall, at least Chris Carlisle must be feeling good about things.

Pete Profile

The Alumni Fave

It is noon on the Monday after the 69–0 bludgeoning of Washington State, and we're whizzing across the USC campus in a four-seat equipment cart, cutting by startled, football-savvy guys who wave and beautiful, fashion-resplendent coeds who can't figure out why we seem to be careening directly at them. A relaxed Pete Carroll is riding shotgun up front, while Ben Malcolmson, his online director and all around Man Friday, is driving. I'm in the backseat with Eric Espinoza, the director of video operations. We are heading for the weekly Monday Morning Quarterback Club at the plush, relatively new $140-million Galen Center.

As we get to Figueroa, the busy main street that runs between campus and the Galen Center, we are forced to stop at the light. A silver four-door pulls up alongside, either a Lexus or a BMW. It's impossible to tell from the angle. The driver, a middle-aged gentleman, rolls down his window and asks for an autograph for his wife, who is sitting alongside him. Carroll smiles, jumps off the equipment cart, and, much to the surprise of his two startled fans, opens the back door and plops down in the backseat while he scribbles the autograph. The driver and his wife are amazed. Espinoza isn't. "Happens all the time," he says, grinning.

When Carroll gets to the door of the Galen Center, it is locked, so he's forced to wait while somebody finds an employee to open it. "Most football coaches don't like these types of functions," I say to Carroll. "How do you feel about them?" He thinks about it for a moment and shrugs. "I don't mind, but your time is so limited on game weeks, it makes it tough." Not that he'd ever let any of the people who pay forty dollars a pop for lunch and a half-hour commentary by the coach know that. Once he gets in and is introduced, he turns on the charm, like a politician at a preelection rally. The crowd, a mostly elderly group with a smattering of younger business types mixed in, gives him a rousing ovation as he walks out to what would normally be the basketball floor, wearing a black sweater with the USC logo and khaki pants. "How many of you went to Washington State for this game?" he asks after accepting the microphone. A surprising number of hands pop up. "That's great. It was one of the most unusual games we've ever been involved in. Washington State is just not ready. They're just not equipped to compete right now, and we took full advantage of it. But this week will be a different story. It's a big game for Arizona, and they tell me they're going freaking crazy over there. I just got off the phone with their media, and they are so full of themselves right now. Golly," he says, and, much to the delight of the boosters, his smile tells you he is not exactly intimidated.

"Well, let's take a look at some of the good stuff from this past game," he says, and the lights dim and Espinoza puts his computerized highlights up on a screen. Carroll immediately goes into his gushing mode. "Ohhhhh, good hit there by Cary Harris. . . . Nice job there by Armond Armstead. See how he stays on his feet. Nice job. . . . That's pretty good defensive play right there. We get that running back pretty good. . . . This is Garrett Green on special teams. Garrett is one of the great kids on our team. He'll do anything you'll ask . . ." It goes on like this for a few minutes, but Carroll has to cut his part short. They've asked him to appear across the street at a memorial for Craig Fertig, the beloved, former Trojan quarterback and broadcaster, who died a few days earlier. "I have to leave a little early," Carroll says, smiling, "but we have a special guest for you. It's Steve Sarkisian, our offensive coordinator. I want you to be really nice to him. Throw him a lot of softball questions. Then tear his ass off." With that, Carroll laughs, waves, and strolls off the floor. The applause for the head coach lasts so long Sarkisian has to shuffle his feet and wait until it diminishes before he can start.

It is the way it goes at every alumni function for Carroll. Other head coaches seem to dread the interaction with the sometimes fanatic alums and boosters. He seems to thrive on it. "Best at it I've ever been around," says Paul Salata, the high-profile booster and donor who was a former USC wide receiver before gaining a measure of fame as the originator of the NFL's Mr. Irrelevant concept. "At all these functions, he is the last guy to sit down. He knows you, he knows your wife's name. It's amazing. He met my wife once on a trip to Nebraska. Next time he saw her, he says 'Hi, Carolyn, how is everything going?' It's uncanny. And when he talks, well, he's like a salesman. That's what he is, a professional salesman."

Jim Hardy, the former Trojan quarterback who starred for Jeff Cravath, marvels at how Carroll has transformed the atmosphere at USC. "He includes everybody," says Hardy. "When Larry Smith was here, he didn't want any of the old guys at practice. Pete wants everybody here. He invites us all out. He makes us feel like we're part of the program."

To really appreciate the way Carroll works a room, though, you have to see him in action at the various Trojan Clubs he visits on a regular tour he makes every summer. "Our alumni see him as someone who is very confident but humble," says Roger Rossier, president of the Orange County Trojan Club. "He comes over, shakes your hand, talks to you. He's not distant like a lot of the other coaches we've had here. He is down-to-earth. He makes people feel comfortable, whether they're affluent or not, whether they're big donors or just fans. When he visits us every year, he gets there early and walks around the room and shakes everybody's hand. It doesn't come off like he's looking for votes. He seems sincere. Do I ever hear any grumbling about him? Sure. People complain after a loss like the one to Stanford last year or Oregon State this year, but I think we're jaded. People aren't even satisfied if we win 28–3 or 28–7. They want us to pour it on. He has won so much he's spoiled us."

"Personable" is the word alums and boosters use most often when describing Carroll. "That's what he is," says Clifford Rowe, president of the L.A. West Trojan Club, "he is so personable. He has that great ability to remember names. I usually go up to him and say, 'Hi Coach,' and identify myself. He always laughs and says 'I know who you are, Clifford.' I guess I have a little different perspective than most. I was a ball boy and manager back in the John McKay and John Robinson eras. Carroll is so interactive in practices. McKay distanced himself from players and coaches. There is a clear distinction between the two. Pete is the same way at our functions. He's so comfortable. He seems to enjoy dealing with alumni and boosters. I think that distinguishes him from a lot of other coaches."

Bob Hopkins, the longtime leader of the Trojan Club of the Desert, is most impressed by Carroll's enthusiasm. "The guy is just so gregarious," Hopkins says. "He exudes enthusiasm. I don't think the same was true of his recent predecessors. The overwhelming opinion of our members is that he is just an exceptional human being. When he visits us, he brings along his assistants and makes sure he answers all our questions. There is just so much dynamism associated with him. I think that makes a big impression on the other gender, if you know what I mean. You can see why he's such a great recruiter.

"We don't always have great turnouts, but when he's coming, we never have any trouble selling out," Hopkins says. "Put it this way: If it were up to the folks out here, Pete could run for president . . . or at least governor."

XIII

Game Eleven: A Great, Historic Rivalry or an Annual Mismatch?

Pete Carroll has no one to blame but himself. He has taken the greatest intersectional game in college football and turned it into an annual dud.

USC vs. Notre Dame used to be the pinnacle. It was Yankees vs. Red Sox, Celtics vs. Lakers, Ali vs. Frazier. It was two of the most successful teams in the sport—one with twelve national championships, the other with eleven, both with seven Heisman Trophy winners—meeting every season, either in the picturesque, fall environment of historic Notre Dame Stadium in South Bend, Indiana, or in the cool, late-November glow of the legendary old saucer known as the Los Angeles Coliseum. This was a game filled with extraordinary players and iconic coaches, from the Four Horsemen, Johnny Lattner, Alan Page, and Joe Montana to O.J. Simpson, Anthony Davis, Matt Leinart, and the Wild Bunch. It was Knute Rockne vs. Howard Jones, John McKay vs. Ara Paraseghian and, yes, in the modern, updated version, it was supposed to be Pete Carroll vs. Charlie Weis.

That last projection hasn't worked out too well, though. Carroll has taken over this rivalry the way he has taken over so many other facets of college football. He has turned this once competitive series into a mismatch. After losing at Notre Dame in his first rebuilding season, the USC coach has won his past six games against the Irish, only one of which was close, and rolled up scores of 44–13, 45–14, 41–10, 44–24 and 38–0 along the way. In three tries against the Trojans, Weis, the rotund, crew-cut former offensive coordinator of the three-time Super Bowl champion New England Patriots, has had only one close shot at them. He came within seconds of a Golden Dome–rocking upset of an unbeaten USC team that had won twenty-seven games in a row, only to lose when Leinart completed a dramatic, fourth-down 61-yard pass and then lunged his way into the end zone, with the help of a controversial Reggie Bush push, on a quarterback sneak. The final score was 34–31, and the Fighting Irish's effort that day was so impressive, Notre Dame officials quickly rewarded first-year coach Weis with a ten-year contract worth more than $30 million.

Three years later, after two lopsided losses to the Trojans and an ignominious 3-9 season in 2007, Weis arrives at late November of his fourth year with a shaky 6-5 record, coming off yet another surreal loss, this time to a 2-8 Syracuse team. As a measure of how far the competitive level between Notre Dame and USC has widened, oddsmakers have installed Carroll's team as an astounding 32-point favorite against the once proud Fighting Irish. No one can remember a larger point spread in the long, rich history of this series. Then again, this game isn't about the so-called rivalry anymore. It is more about the growing national speculation regarding Weis's job status and USC's continued, if somewhat futile, attempt to move up in the BCS standings. Most of the reports filtering out of the Midwest suggest that if Notre Dame is unable to keep the final score of this game somewhat respectable, Weis conceivably could be fired as early as Tuesday of the following week.

In L.A., meanwhile, the Thanksgiving week environment is not nearly as incendiary. After a semirelaxing bye week, Carroll opens preparations for Notre Dame by trying to pump up a game even he knows has lost much of its old luster. "This game is as high on a scale you can get as a Trojan," he says. "These are two storied, legendary programs in college football. I don't think there are many rivalries with this much distance between the two schools involved. I think it is unique in that regard. There are a lot of close-proximity rivalries in college football, like ours with UCLA, for example, but this one, this has more of a classic aspect to it." Weis, for his part, is still trying to get over the image-shattering loss to a Syracuse team regarded among the worst in the nation. He said he felt sick to his stomach immediately after the game, and now he needed to get his team out of its self-pitying mode and ready for a battle with No. 5–ranked USC. "We don't have any choice," Weis says. "We have to go to work and get ready for this game, or it could be a very long night at the office."

In USC's coaching offices, meanwhile, a startling admission is heard. After ten games and any number of critics suggesting the alternating tailback system is ridiculous, Carroll and offensive coordinator Steve Sarkisian finally appear to have given in. "We've decided to allow the tailbacks to play entire series rather than alternating every play or two," Sarkisian says, and you could almost hear the huge sighs of relief echoing across the vast, USC-attuned megalopolis. "We're trying to let them find their rhythm," Sarkisian says, "and we feel that might be easier if they stay in for four, five, six, maybe seven snaps in a row." In the background, it is easy to spot the smiles of tailbacks C.J. Gable, Stafon Johnson, and Joe McKnight peering out from under their facemasks. On the rare occasions the Trojans have let one tailback stay on the field for that long, it has resulted in a much smoother running game. McKnight was the primary runner in the victory over Ohio State, Johnson was the pivotal ball carrier for almost the entire game-winning series at Arizona, and Gable stayed in during much of the turnaround series at Stanford.

"It's easier for us to get into our groove," says Gable, the quasi-starter who has been quietly politicking for such a change. "It's working good so I hope we stay with it." Whenever reporters asked about staying with one runner, Carroll always argued against it, but not anymore. "We've been trying to give them a little bit more of a feel than just onesies-twosies type stuff," he says. "We all know every running back wants to stay on the field. I don't see it being anything to write in stone forever. It's just what's happening right now and I kind of like it. It could change Saturday."

Lots of things could change Saturday. In the ten days or so since the Stanford game, USC's sluggish offense has been the No. 1 topic in town. Or at least tied at No. 1 with the controversy over whether the Dodgers should re-sign free agent Manny Ramirez. Did the Trojans really rediscover their old, trusted, run-first philosophy in Palo Alto after a terrible first half? And what about Mark Sanchez? The quarterback who had appeared so aggressive, energized and, yes, exciting early in the season has been kept carefully under wraps since suffering a fumble and interception at Arizona. It's as if Carroll has decided that his brilliant defense is so effective, he is better off playing it safe on offense. Sanchez was barely allowed to throw downfield against a Cal defense that led the nation in interceptions coming in. A week later, the once fiery leader at quarterback attempted only 17 passes in Stanford Stadium, often looking hesitant and frustrated in the process.

I ask Carroll about it on Tuesday, and you can see in his eyes that it's not a subject he is anxious to discuss. I wonder if by preaching so much ball safety and conservatism, they haven't taken away a huge part of Sanchez's big-play ability. "Yeah, that comes up in a lot of different areas," Carroll says. "It's the same with any individual player. You have to go through stages and growth, especially at quarterback. You have to do that before you find the best of yourself. Mark is in the middle of all that. He is very receptive and introspective. Right now, he gives us a chance to win every game. We ask our quarterback to be kind of a point guard on offense. A big aspect of that is not to give the ball away. We really curled things up for him against Cal. We were responsible [for the conservative play]. I think he's doing what is asked of him. I wouldn't be surprised if in these last few weeks we give him a chance to throw the ball and make plays."

Later, following the afternoon practice on a cool, rain-threatening day, I ask Sarkisian if he sensed Sanchez being hesitant or reluctant against Stanford. "Yeah, he could have been," Sarkisian says. "We placed so much emphasis on not turning the ball over, he could have been. I don't feel it this week, but you know, he hasn't thrown a pick since Arizona. We're pretty happy about that."

One former prominent USC player reveals to a reporter that Sanchez has called him, complaining that the coaches "are in my head" and that he is confused about exactly how they want him to play at this point. If that is the case, the always politically correct quarterback doesn't admit as much to writers after Tuesday's practice. He does, however, admit that his focus on not turning the ball over continued at Stanford. "Absolutely, it carried over in that game," he says. "When things are tough like that, it would be my chance to force a throw, to gamble regardless of down or distance. But I don't do that anymore. I find myself playing smart and conservative." I ask him if that conservative approach has robbed him of his confidence to make big plays. "No, not at all," he says. "I'm not worried about it one bit."

Others are worried, though, especially those who still harbor hopes that USC can sneak its way into the BCS Championship Game. They think the Trojans need to showcase a high-powered offense with plenty of flashy Sanchez passes to get there. Realistically, however, Sanchez could throw for 1,000 yards in the final two games and it might not help. With so many other one-loss teams, especially Oklahoma, Texas, and Texas Tech in the Big Twelve and Florida in the Southeast Conference, along with still unbeaten Alabama, the road is littered with too many bumps for USC to overcome. You never say never in the tumultuous world of college football, but at this point, the Trojans need Auburn to upset Alabama, Oklahoma State to beat highly favored Oklahoma, Florida State to knock off much more talented Florida and Missouri to beat whomever it meets in the Big 12 title game. Even with all that, USC is no lock to get one of the two final BCS bids. Carroll continues to get asked about it, and his answer is always similar. "I keep postponing thoughts about that," he says. "I don't need to think about it to keep me amused."

Thanksgiving week is always a nostalgic time for the Trojans coach. Invariably, he brings up the Turkey Bowl, the pickup game he and a collection of his friends played every year on the holiday at Greenbrae School, near his home. If they were lucky, they had enough for an 11-on-11 game of two-hand touch that often lasted until dinner time. "Oh man, I loved playing in those games," Carroll says. "I still think I have to rank as the all-time quarterback of the Turkey Bowl. I haven't been able to play in it for a number of years now." Then he looks up and breaks into that fun-loving smile that has become famous by now. "They do know, however," he says, "that one day I'll be back."

Thanksgiving Day for the USC players is controlled by the team's first family. Nick and Maddy Sanchez, parents of quarterback Mark, invite all the out-of-state players who can't get home for the holiday to join them for a huge day of turkey and camaraderie. "We're having sixty-two people over this year," says Maddy, Mark's stepmom. "We'll have four turkeys and forty pounds of ham. I think there are about fifteen players from out of the area who are coming."

Now if only this once-great football rivalry can avoid being a turkey. The last Saturday in November is a typical fall day in Southern California, sun-splashy warm and into the high 70s during the afternoon, turning into a relatively cool night, although temperatures still hover at a pleasant 67 degrees at kickoff. The rising tension between these two longtime rivals can be felt outside the Coliseum locker rooms before warm-ups, when barking and taunting can be heard from both sides. By the time the two teams make their way down toward the tunnel exit out to the field, the pushing and shoving heats up and a near brawl erupts. A few minutes later, an unfortunate thing happens for Notre Dame. The game starts.

Whatever fight is left in the Irish is quickly squashed by the best college defense in America. It becomes a signature game for the Trojans, who had three shutouts and were leading the nation in almost every major defensive statistical category coming in. On this night, they literally stop everything Notre Dame tries in its tracks. The Irish can't run, they can't pass and, by the time the second half arrives, you're amazed they're even allowed to step into their huddle without a growling USC defender waiting to wrestle one of them to the ground. Clausen, Notre Dame's promising sophomore quarterback, looks like he is back at nearby Oaks Christian High still trying to make the varsity. He never has time to catch his breath, let alone to spot an open receiver. Golden Tate, his favorite target, is surrounded by cardinal jerseys most of the night, and whatever passes for the Irish running game doesn't emerge until late in the fourth quarter when USC has its reserves in the game.

This is how bad it gets before then: Notre Dame goes the entire first half without a first down and doesn't squeeze its first one out until the final play of the *third* quarter. USC outgains the Irish 265 yards to 9, that's right, 9, in the first half and 360 yards to 38 after three periods. On Senior Night at the Coliseum, linebackers Rey Mauluga and Brian Cushing reinforce a legacy that will have them remembered as perhaps the best combination of linebackers in the school's glorious history. They are everywhere on the field, pillaging through the Irish offense almost at will. Their fellow linebacker, Kaluka Maiava, and Clay Matthews, the senior Carroll calls the poster boy for Trojan overachievement, can be seen making tackles from sideline to sideline. It proves to be not so much a game as a gruesome display of ferocity on defense. Clausen is sacked four times and almost sacked on a half dozen other occasions. He finishes with 41 yards passing, just 9 yards less than the Irish manage rushing for the night. It could have all resulted in USC's fourth shutout of the season, except the beleaguered Weis, already down 31–0, orders his team to kick a field goal on fourth and 3 from the Trojans' 23 early in the fourth quarter.

Offensively, the evening begins less than auspiciously for USC's Sanchez, whose first pass attempt, a quick slant, is intercepted by an alert Robert Blanton. In previous weeks, Sarkisian, the Trojans' offensive coordinator, would immediately put his quarterback under wraps. Not this time. This is not edgy Cal or a dangerous Pac-10 team that must be faced on the road. This is mediocre Notre Dame, and the USC coaches are confident holes can be found in this secondary. They are right. Sanchez gets hot, completing 15 of 17 at one point and finishing a more than respectable 22 of 31 for 267 yards, with 2 touchdowns and 2 interceptions.

Although it is never completely fluid, with the usual flurry of penalties (eight for 80 yards), the USC running game does have its moments. The surprising plan announced earlier in the week, the one that had Carroll and Sarkisian switching to a system allowing the tailbacks to stay in for an entire series, lasts about as long as a Notre Dame rush attempt. On the Trojans' first 79-yard scoring drive, McKnight, Gable, and Johnson all have carries. The most memorable run of the evening is a weaving, back against-the-grain, second-quarter beauty by McKnight, who covers 55 yards for his first rushing touchdown of the season and the longest so far for USC this year. Still, the most effective USC tailback in this game is Marc Tyler, the young fourth-stringer who went to high school at Oaks Christian with Clausen. Tyler carries the ball seven times in the fourth quarter and churns out 58 yards, juking and sliding his way past tired Irish tacklers to put yet another name up on Carroll's endless depth chart at the position.

The final score winds up 38–3 in a game that really isn't that close. There are two lingering reactions as the players from both teams mingle in the middle of the field before heading back to their respective locker rooms. First, this USC defense really might be the finest in the tradition-rich history of the school, and, second, Charlie Weis's job has to be in serious jeopardy. New Notre Dame athletics director Jack Swarbrick is approached on the field and asked about Weis's status. "You evaluate based on the available data, and we have new data coming in all the time," he says. In other words, the media is advised to stay tuned in South Bend.

Meanwhile, the news filters out of the Northwest that Oregon has pummeled Oregon State, 65–38, meaning that USC has clinched at least a tie for its seventh consecutive Pac-10 title and is one victory away from claiming yet another Rose Bowl berth. The accompanying upsets the Trojans needed from around the rest of the country didn't happen. Alabama prevailed over Auburn, Oklahoma outscored Oklahoma State, Florida cruised past Florida State, and, earlier on Thanksgiving Day, Texas gunned down Texas A&M.

All of it leaves the USC players feeling as if they've just finished their ample holiday dinners but are now being deprived of their just desserts. The most frustrating part is that this extraordinary defense Carroll has put together won't get a chance to face the ultimate test. Because of the current BCS setup, it won't be allowed to go head-to-head with a Texas, an Oklahoma, or a Florida. It will have to be satisfied with facing a strong but less offensively imposing New Year's Day rival in Penn State. Most of the players, clearly warned ahead of time by Carroll, go out of their way to say the politically correct things in the locker room.

Kyle Moore is different. The senior defensive end is not the best player on this great defense. He is, however, easily the best talker. He is a smiling, unpretentious twenty-two-year-old who is never afraid to speak his mind. When the team inexplicably went away from its basic 4-3 defensive set, switching to a 3-4 in that disastrous first half at Oregon State, he was the only one who spoke out about it afterward. Same thing happened at Stanford, when the team again switched to a 3-4 early, falling behind in the first half. "Why did we do that? I don't know," Moore says, shaking his head in dismay, knowing those first thirty minutes at Corvallis cost the Trojans everything. Unlike the other players in the room who are trying to convince reporters they're looking forward to the Rose Bowl, Moore smiles when the question is asked. "Would I rather play against Florida or Texas? Yeah, of course I would," he says. "I want to go against one of those teams that scores 40 or 50 points every game and see how we'd do. The thing is, those teams also give up 30 or 40 points every game. I'd love to see USC-Florida or USC-Texas. I'd like to see how those teams would do against our defense, but you know, that one half at Oregon State got us. One half is going to keep us out of the Natty [national championship game] this year, and that hurts."

If nothing else, part of the frustration is eased by the performance of Sanchez, who clearly needed a confidence boost after the coaches had played a bit with his mind following the Cal and Stanford games. "Was I more relaxed tonight? Sure," the quarterback says. "I think I learned to let my mistakes go. Earlier in the season, those two mistakes [on interceptions] might have got me, but after hearing the coaches tell me to just play, let it rip and have fun, I was able to snap back and it felt like I was just playing free out there."

For Maualuga and Cushing, the two fierce linebackers and Butkus Award finalists who have become close friends, as well as the other prominent seniors, it was an evening of joy mixed with nostalgia. "All the good things that have happened in my life have happened right here," Maualuga says. "All the bonds we created here have been special." Cushing seemed to thrive on the fact the barely Fighting Irish struggled so mightily to scratch out yards. "Were you aware it took three quarters for them to get a first down?" he is asked. "I was," he says, grinning. "I'm not sure the rest of the defense was. When we heard the roar from the fans [when Notre Dame finally got one], I think we all knew."

Carroll, who lives for great defensive performances, no longer holds back when describing this particular unit. "Halfway through the season, I think we began to realize what we had," he says. "We saw that not many teams could do much against us. I didn't know how far we could take it, but we're playing the best defense we've ever played right now. Nobody ever played any better than this."

Which is why there was such a tormented tinge to the postgame proceedings on this strange November night. Sadly, the best defense in the history of the school and one of the finest ever seen in college football never will get a chance to find out just how good it really can be.

Pete Profile

The Son Also Rises

He never calls him by name. He always calls him "Coach," as in "Coach always has the final say in recruiting," or "As long as I'm having fun and Coach is here, I'll continue to do this."

The fact that the coach in question happens to be his father doesn't seem to matter to Brennan Carroll, the thirty-year-old assistant coach in charge of tight ends who also manages to serve as USC's recruiting coordinator. "I always call him Coach when people are around," says Brennan. For the moment, Pete Carroll and his son, who is built like the tight end he once was for the University of Pittsburgh, are living a bit of a dream, working and plotting together to help build what has been the most successful college football program in America.

"It's a cherished opportunity," says Pete. "It's one that I really love. It's fun competing with him. He is my most loyal confidante and he is important to me in that regard." Brennan feels the same way. "It's always great to be around your family," he says, "but it's even more so when you're competing at such a high level. It's cool."

It has worked out pretty well considering Brennan never had thoughts of following his famous father's cleat marks and going into coaching. That wasn't even on his radar when he was serving as a reserve tight end, as well as a key special-teams player, at Pitt. It wasn't considered after he received his bachelor's degree in social services there in 2001, either. "I didn't want to get started in coaching and get pigeonholed," he says. "I was working for the NFL youth football program, still trying to decide what to do with myself." Than Dad called saying he needed a graduate assistant. Since he had no other immediate plans, Brennan took the job and spent two years in that role before being elevated to a full-time assistant in 2004. Two years ago, when Lane Kiffin left to become the Oakland Raiders head coach, Brennan was given the added responsibility of coordinating the Trojans's recruiting. He must be doing all right in that regard, considering USC continues to rank near the top in the annual recruiting ratings nationally.

Along the way, Brennan's mind-set seems to have changed some. When he first took the job, he was determined not to make it his long-range profession. "It's a hard life to put your family through," he said at the time. "I didn't see a lot of my dad growing up. He was always off doing his thing. This is his goal, and I'm here just helping out for now. It's not an ego thing for me. I have no drive, no passion to be a head coach. I don't want to run my own team. I don't really see myself doing this at forty."

Now, some five years later, he talks somewhat differently. "I really don't know about my future," he says. "I'm thinking I'll be here as long as Coach is here." Memo to Brennan: That could be a while. Of course, now that he is no longer the fun-loving bachelor with a pad in Manhattan Beach, now that he is married and busy building a family of his own, Brennan's priorities may have been altered. He is being paid handsomely and he is an important member of perhaps the most respected program in the country. "What Coach does out here is fun," Brennan says. "They call it business, but it's fun."

Brennan seems to be having as much fun as anyone. It is his voice you can always hear in the back of the meeting room, hooting and hollering when a big hit shows up on the screen, or when "Coach" is trying to fire up the troops. He is the one you can see trotting around the practice field with his cap on backward, like all the kids on campus. Let's not forget, that Peter Pan syndrome runs in the family. "I'm not complaining," Brennan says. "Oh yeah, I'm enjoying it. I'm having a blast out here."

He seems to be working out OK in the coaching department, as well. Tight end Dominque Byrd was a star on the undefeated team that won a national championship in 2004 and was selected as a third-round draft pick following the 2005 season. Fred Davis, who succeeded him under Brennan's tutelage, became a first-team All American and a second-round NFL draft selection.

"It's been a fun experience playing for BC," says Anthony McCoy, the Trojans' current starting tight end. "My coaches in high school were a lot more serious. The players and BC are always clowning on each other. You know, watching film on him when he played, stuff like that, but techniquewise, he has helped me a lot, especially when it comes to my footwork. I'd have to say he got me where I am today."

For Brennan, some of the best moments of the season are those he gets to spend around his father. "He's always the last one out of the locker room after games," he says. "I'm the second-to-last one out. We usually get to spend some time talking then."

Football and sports, in general, always have been lively topics in the Carroll family. Brennan's mom and Pete's wife, Glena, played volleyball at the University of the Pacific. His sister, Jaime, was on the USC women's volleyball team and, of course, Dad has always been deeply involved in his favorite sport. "It's great now for Coach, but it's taken him some fifty-odd years to get there. It's a hard life, man."

What makes it easier now is the steady stream of five-star recruits USC seems to land every year. Brennan, as the coordinator, has a pivotal role, one he seems to cherish. "I'm kind of like the GM," he says. "It's my job to help find the personnel. You know, trying to get the right guys to fill the right spots." Along the way, Brennan has been able to watch his dad do one of the things he does best. "What makes Coach so successful is that it is easy for him to speak to people. He's very good with the parents, especially. He says the easiest thing is to tell the truth. He doesn't make stuff up. He doesn't make false promises." A big part of it, of course, is the evaluation. From the hundreds of top prospects on their lists, they have to trim down to the players they think will be best for their program. "If I like a guy and Coach doesn't, well, we don't offer him. Coach always has the final say," says Brennan.

Both his professional and personal life seem to have stabilized in the past year. "I've been married for over a year now," he says. His wife, Amber, played volleyball at North Carolina, in Europe, and on the AVP beach tour under her maiden name, Amber Willey. On February 23 of this year, they welcomed a son, Dillon Brennan, to the family, making Pete a grandpa for the first time. "Life is different now," Brennan says. "Different, but better. The whole process for me now is very enjoyable. Being a part of this staff is a lot of hard work, but all the work you put in for the week is well worth it when you win the game on Saturday." Brennan says it's great for him and great for his father. "Right now," he says, "I'm just happy to be taking the ride with him."

"Coach" seems happy about it, too.

XIV

Game Twelve: Chow Returns, but Carroll's Defense Rules

T he coffee table starts shaking first. Then the large bay windows and the sliding glass door begin rattling. Soon the entire family room of Norm Chow's plush Manhattan Beach home is rocking and rolling. It is your prototypical 5.8 California temblor, and Chow, who never had experienced one before, is more than a little startled.

"What the hell is going on?" he says. "It's an earthquake and a pretty good one," I tell him, being an experienced Southern California native. "But don't worry, it will be over soon." A long minute or so later, the room finally grows quiet and still, and Chow, nervously gulping down some extra coffee, is able to relax, make a couple of calls to ensure his family members are all right, and then resume our interview. It is a warm, late-July day, and I am there to try to get to the facts behind his post-2004 departure from USC and Pete Carroll. Many theories had been advanced as to why the man most people consider the finest offensive coordinator in college football history and the game's most successful, defensive-minded head coach would part ways. Chow accepted the same offensive coordinator position with the NFL Tennessee Titans, and while he received a hefty pay hike, those close to him said he never wanted to leave USC. He loved what he was doing, and his home was only twenty minutes away. Why would he want to take a job where he'd be separated from his family and have to live in a hotel for the greater part of the year? Both Carroll and Chow insisted publicly that they parted on amicable terms, but everyone knew there was more to it than that. It is my job to find out. This book wouldn't be complete without an explanation of what was really behind the most notable breakup of the Carroll era. I'd grown to know Chow well when he was at USC, and I felt he trusted me. Now is the time to press him on it.

"OK," I say, "now tell me the real story." Chow, who had just been hired as the new offensive coordinator at USC's crosstown rival UCLA, takes another long sip of his coffee and sighs. "It was right after the [2004 national championship] season," he says, "and Pete called and said he wanted to go to lunch. So we met at this place in the South Bay. I thought we were going to talk about recruiting and his plans for next season. Then he tells me he is planning to make some changes on the staff. I was stunned." The changes involved taking the play calling duties away from the coach most people considered the finest play caller of the modern era. Carroll apparently was describing it as a "promotion" for Chow, but in essence, young Lane Kiffin was being moved up to join Steve Sarkisian, a Chow protégé who had left to be an Oakland Raiders assistant and was now returning, as co-offensive coordinators. Chow, despite whatever new title they were giving him, basically would have been relegated to coaching the quarterbacks.

To hardly anyone's surprise, it was not long after he and Carroll met that Chow announced he was accepting a new position with the pro football Titans. "Look, I'm grateful to Pete," Chow says. "He gave me a chance to coach in the Pac-10. It was time for me to leave. Obviously, there were other guys on staff he felt were ready to do what I was doing." He tries to make it sound OK, but the pain on his face is obvious. How do you promote two unproven play callers to replace the best one USC, or maybe anyone, ever had? It is not an easy thing for Chow to talk about.

It is now four months later, and USC and UCLA are preparing to meet in their annual crosstown showdown. The 10-1 Trojans are on the cusp of another Pac-10 title and Rose Bowl invitation. The 4-7 Bruins are suffering through a difficult first year under new coach Rick Neuheisel. Injuries knocked out their first two quarterbacks before they ever played a game, and the offensive line has been in shambles, leaving Chow with little, if any, weapons to work with offensively. Oddsmakers have installed USC as an overwhelming 33-point favorite for the game in Pasadena, and while the usual competitive vibe to this game is missing, much of the old controversy is not. The Chow–Carroll story has been revived, especially with the news late in the week that Sarkisian has accepted an offer to become the new head coach at Washington. Many Trojans alums and boosters still harbor bitterness over Chow's departure. They feel their favorite team might have won at least one and maybe two more national titles if Chow hadn't been nudged out the door.

With my notes from that July meeting at Chow's home still relatively fresh, I approach Carroll in Heritage Hall before a Tuesday afternoon practice. I tell him how Chow had explained the situation to me and ask him if his version is correct. "Yes, that's accurate," he says, "it's very accurate. Because of job opportunities some of our young guys had elsewhere, we had to do something to keep them. We had to switch some duties around." This is more than just a casual comment from Carroll. It is a stunning admission. It is the head coach's first corroboration of what really happened. If I still had been working for a newspaper, I'd have called my sports editor immediately, and the headline on the story the next day would have read WHY CARROLL PUSHED CHOW OUT. Carroll seems to sense it, maybe by the look on my face. "You can write that in the book," he says, "but I don't want to see it written anywhere else this week." In some ways, as I reflect later, that's an even more revealing comment. So now I try to go over the whole scenario in my head. Apparently, in order to keep Kiffin and re-hire Sarkisian, Carroll felt he had to offer them more money and a better position. Clearly, he had to know what the repercussions would be. He must have realized Chow would be looking to move under those circumstances. No matter how he tried to spin it, it would have come off as a demotion to the offensive coordinator who had developed three Heisman Trophy–winning quarterbacks and called plays for some of the most successful offenses in NCAA history. A man of great pride, Chow couldn't be expected to stick around and allow people he perceived as far less capable run the offense and call the plays.

If Chow has any lingering bitterness toward Carroll now, he hides it well. The same can't be said for his feelings toward Sarkisian. The two no longer talk, even though Sarkisian still speaks fondly of their relationship when they were both at USC. Kiffin, who moved on to a stormy year and a half as the Oakland Raiders head coach before being fired, has, interestingly, just this week been named the new head coach at the University of Tennessee, where he signed a lucrative multiyear contract reported to be worth more than $2 million per season. Sarkisian, making more than $700,000 as the Trojans' highest-paid assistant, now will more than double his salary to take over the rebuilding job at Washington.

First, however, Carroll and Sarkisian will be coaching head-to-head against Chow for the first time, providing an intriguing subplot to a game that otherwise appears to be a massive mismatch. "It's going to be a great challenge," Chow says early in the week, knowing he'll be going up against the best defense in the country. "It is going to be almost as great a challenge as knowing what to do when that earthquake hit."

It is another of those bittersweet final weeks of the season at USC, where the Trojans, despite their glittering record, appear to be out of the running for a shot at the BCS title game. The winner of Saturday's Alabama-Florida SEC title match will get one spot, and Oklahoma, having recently moved up to No. 2 in the BCS standings, will get the other if it defeats Missouri as expected in the Big Twelve championship game. Even if Missouri wins, Texas, with a higher ranking in the BCS poll, likely would go ahead of USC. Carroll isn't happy about all that, especially with his defense playing the way it has been in the closing weeks. He calls the performance against Notre Dame, where the Irish couldn't squeeze out a first down until the final play of the third quarter, "pretty close to perfect." He knows the unit that has given up only a miserly 7.8 points per game and just a jaw-dropping 22 second-half points all year would make the Trojans competitive against any team in the country. The problem is, for the third consecutive season, it doesn't appear he'll be able to prove it.

Typically, though, Carroll doesn't dwell on the negative. He talks about the chance to win an unprecedented seventh consecutive Pac-10 championship and chirps about the chance to play another rivalry game. "It just adds to the excitement," he says. "This is a great rivalry. This is one that is so close to home, even in-home rivalries, with people who went to both schools and all that. I think it makes it really fun. It's a thrill to be part of it." To punctuate how he feels about this series, Carroll announces that his visiting team will wear its cardinal home jerseys for the game at the Rose Bowl, even if it means he has to give up two time-outs to do it. The last time the two teams wore their home jerseys was 1982, the final year they shared the Coliseum. When UCLA moved its home games to Pasadena, the tradition stopped. Now Carroll wants to start it again. Technically, it violates an NCAA rule, but eventually the news comes down from NCAA headquarters that the Trojans only will be penalized one time-out. UCLA's Neuheisel, who agrees with Carroll's move, says he will call a similar time-out early, so neither team will be at a disadvantage. "I think wearing the home jerseys is a great decision," Neuheisel says.

Once that is cleared up, USC receives another minijolt. Vidal Hazelton, a little-played junior wide receiver who had been battling injuries, announces he has filed papers to transfer. It is the second such defection in three weeks. Tailback Broderick Green had earlier announced his similar intention. Hazelton's loss won't have a major effect on the Trojans. He'd been beaten out by Damian Williams and Ronald Johnson at flanker and had made only fleeting appearances in games this season. Nevertheless, he had started a year ago, was responsible for one of the highlight-reel plays of 2007 against Notre Dame, and had arrived in Southern California as one of the more hyped recruits in his class. What his departure does, especially coming on the heels of Green's, is give recruiters from other schools reason to make athletes wary of coming to USC. "You go there, you'll never play and eventually you'll have to transfer," they'll tell kids. "Come with us and you'll play immediately."

Carroll can't do much about it. This won't make him stop recruiting great athletes. It is just the price you sometimes pay for having top-5 national recruiting classes year after year. "This is a very difficult program," he says after the Hazelton news breaks. "It's not for everybody. It's because of the competition issues here, and he also has some health issues with his family. I'll try to help him all I can." John Morton, the low-profile wide-receivers coach who is a candidate to succeed Sarkisian as offensive coordinator, is the one closest to Hazelton. "Am I surprised about the transfer? A little bit," Morton says. "We were working on some things. I thought he was improving. When you lose your No. 1 job, you struggle. He was fighting back, but the other guys ahead of him were making plays. When you make plays, you're going to play. You see the stats of those two other guys. They're having a heckuva year."

Meanwhile, the stars of the USC defense, seniors Rey Maualuga, Brian Cushing, Fili Moala, Kaluka Maiava, and junior Taylor Mays, are preparing to play what probably will be their last regular season game at USC. Mays could come back for his senior season, but he is already projected as a first-round draft pick and likely will leave early. The four of them, along with injured Kevin Ellison, have been the heart of what many believe is one of the greatest defenses in recent college football history. What they remember about playing UCLA in the Rose Bowl is the 13–9 upset the Bruins pulled off in 2006, the one that prevented yet another Trojans team from getting to the BCS title game.

"You've always got to remind yourself of what happened two years ago," Maiava says. "I remember everyone on the sideline looking around, wondering what was going on. College football is a crazy game. You have to try to prevent those kinds of things from happening again." Moala shakes his head at the memory. "Sometimes your body can be out there and your mind can be somewhere else," he says. "That's what happened to us that day. We just don't want it to happen again."

Carroll is doing everything he can to make sure it doesn't. Even after that performance against Notre Dame, even after the coaching staff watched the tape of that four-first-down, 91-yard masterpiece by the defense, Carroll didn't make it a big deal. "He hardly even talked about it," says secondary coach Rocky Seto. "He came in and said, 'Nice job. Now let's get ready for UCLA.' It was pretty amazing."

Then again, maybe not. Carroll says repeatedly that losses like the 13–9 game two years ago continue to gnaw at him. Now he once again has to face a good UCLA defense coached by DeWayne Walker, the first assistant he hired when he arrived at USC. "DeWayne is a really good football coach," Carroll says. "He's got a lot of stuff up his sleeve. His style can give you a lot of problems. They played great defense against us in that game." It was the first UCLA–USC game Carroll coached without Chow in the booth upstairs calling plays. Kiffin and Sarkisian, in their first season, were roundly criticized for not making adjustments, especially in the second half of that game. Now it will be Sarkisian on his own, going one-on-one against Walker on defense, while Chow will be calling the UCLA offensive plays against Carroll. If these two teams don't present particularly enticing player matchups, the same certainly cannot be said of the coaches.

Game day dawns with the kind of weather the Pasadena Chamber of Commerce loves to brag about. By kickoff, it is 75 degrees with the nearby San Gabriel Mountains presenting their usual breathtaking backdrop and the famous old saucer in the Arroyo Seco glistening in the afternoon sun. Throw in the frisky marching bands and the splashy home colored uniforms, and the Rose Bowl seems to be basking in its Saturday finest.

After all the week-long hype about the coaching soap opera, it seems only fitting that Chow would strike first. USC's C.J. Gable fumbles on his second carry of the game, and UCLA recovers on the Trojans' 20 yard line, as the Bruin home crowd, with the memory of that 13–9 mega-upset two years ago still fresh in their mind, goes wild. Two rushing plays get nothing against the stubborn USC defense, then Chow springs one of his typical timely surprises. UCLA quarterback Kevin Craft tosses the ball to wide receiver Dominque Johnson behind the line of scrimmage. As the Trojans defenders react to the ball, Johnson steps back and lofts a soft pass back across the field. Tailback Kahlil Bell races out of the backfield and out-jumps two USC players to catch the ball for a touchdown that sends Bruins fans into spasms of delight. It is 7–0 UCLA, and USC fans immediately get that "Oh, not again" feeling.

They needn't have worried. Even after David Buehler misses the first of what would be three errant field goal attempts, the Trojans quickly regain control of a game once again dominated by Carroll's defense. As he has all season long, the coach trusts Mauluga, Cushing, Mays, and the returning Ellison to take over. They overwhelm Craft, surround Bell, and basically force UCLA into a long, dreary series of three-and-outs. The Bruins have had trouble consistently moving the ball all season against average defenses. This is not an average defense. This is the nationally rated No. 1 defense everyone wants to see play a Florida, an Oklahoma, or a Texas. Sadly, it doesn't appear it will happen, and on this picture-perfect Pasadena afternoon, the Trojans defenders take out their frustration by limiting UCLA to seven first downs and 157 yards, much of that collected late in the fourth quarter when Carroll fills the field with reserves.

USC's offense, meanwhile, delivers a performance that is, in many ways, a microcosm of this season. It has flashes of brilliance, with Mark Sanchez dispensing some of his patented fastballs and Joe McKnight juking his way for some significant yardage. But there is no rhythm to it, no consistent flow, nothing that stamps it with a true identity. It is as if Sarkisian, in his final regular season game as Trojans offensive coordinator, is still searching to find the offense he wants. USC produces 21 points in the first half, but only 7 in the second, and a game that really should have been a blowout ends with a relatively tame 28–7 final score. For Sanchez, though, the afternoon turns into a personal proving ground. A chippy, Walker-designed UCLA defense comes after him hard, delivering three late hits that result in penalties and more than a few more that don't. He gets up staggering at one point and bleeding at another, but he hangs in there, refusing to come out even after his throwing shoulder goes numb for a few minutes. He waves off the trainer and keeps playing, demonstrating the kind of toughness teammates and coaches admire, especially in a quarterback. Afterward, in the visiting locker room in the catacombs of the Rose Bowl, Sanchez can be seen with just a towel draped around him, his body marked with welts and bruises, and three deep gashes along the left side of his face. "It looks like I got bit by a vampire," he says, smiling.

Jeff Byers, the senior guard and cocaptain, looks across the room toward Sanchez's cubicle and shakes his head. "Mark was a stud out there today," he says. "He was running around, diving headfirst. Mark is crazy, man, but this kid showed us how bad he wants to win." He also showed the coaches something else. He showed them they probably overreacted earlier in the year when they tried to tone him down and make him play conservative football. Sanchez isn't that kind of quarterback. He is an emotional, fiery player who loves to take chances. Sometimes, that attitude will produce an occasional mistake, but more often, as it did against UCLA, it will produce some big plays. He is the anti–John David Booty, who was effective and more error-free as Sanchez's predecessor but also someone who rarely threw the ball successfully 40 or 50 yards downfield. Booty would drop straight back and hardly ever move in the pocket. Sanchez always seems to be moving, using his better athletic ability to sidestep tacklers and give his receivers extra time to get open.

It is interesting a few days later that Sanchez is voted first team All-Pac-10 by the conference coaches. He is one of only two Trojans who make it on offense. No less than six USC players are honored on defense, including Maualuga, who is named Pac-10 Defensive Player of the Year, making it three straight seasons a USC player has captured that honor. Sedrick Ellis, the nose tackle now playing for the New Orleans Saints, won it the previous two seasons. A few days later, Maualuga is named USC's first winner of the Chuck Bednarik Award as the nation's outstanding defensive player.

Standing by himself in the middle of the locker room after everyone has left on Saturday, Carroll turns to me and a couple other writers and talks about what this game and this season really means to him. "By far, the favorite aspect for me is that this makes it seven Pac-10 championships in a row. I love that part," he says. "That's what we're trying to do above all else, win championships. We're trying to be consistent. We're trying to show that we can stay right up there near the top year after year. We're trying to 'win forever,' as I like to call it." Someone mentions this is the seventh consecutive year his team has won eleven or more games, a record unprecedented in NCAA history. Carroll looks up and grins. "I like it," he says. "I like it."

Unfortunately, for most USC fans, the game, like the season, leaves a bittersweet afterglow. For the third straight year, they won't be going to the BCS Championship Game, and while they're annoyed about the loss to Oregon State, they're angry that this defense, maybe the finest defense in school history, won't get a chance to prove how good it is, or how much better it might still be. The players know it, too. They put on a brave face afterward, but you can hear it in their voices. "It's just not going to work out," Sanchez says. "It's unfortunate, but that's how it is."

Maualuga, who will leave a USC linebacker legacy befitting the Junior Seaus and Richard Woods and Mike McKeevers before him, doesn't try to hide his disappointment. "We feel we could match up with anybody," he says. "We would love to show people how good we are. We would love to play teams like Florida and Oklahoma, but until they put in a playoff system, we'll have to stick with what we have now."

In one area, at least, what they have is about to change. Sarkisian prepares to leave immediately after the game for a Monday press conference in Seattle, to introduce him as the new Washington coach. The speculation is already rattling through the chat rooms about his possible successor. Carroll admits Morton, the low-profile wide receivers coach, is the likely favorite. "That's the way I'm leaning right now," the head coach says. It is an indication that the somewhat controversial pass-first, run-later philosophy will continue at USC, something more than a few critics won't like. Then again, when you've won eleven games for seven seasons in a row, you don't have to worry much about critics.

Now Carroll will concern himself with his next challenge, an 11-1 Penn State team that appears considerably stronger than the Illinois and Michigan teams that were so easily dispatched in previous Rose Bowls. Maybe more intriguing, in the aftermath of the Chow-Carroll hype, will be the matchup between Joe Paterno and Carroll. College football's all-time winningest coach against the coach with the best winning percentage (87-15 overall and 81-9 in the past seven seasons) of the modern era.

Joe Pa going head-to-head with the fun-loving USC coach who wants to win forever. No, as BCS bowl consolation games go, this might not be a bad one at all.

XV

Bowl Game: A Staff Shake-up and a Classic Coaching Duel

The first few days of USC's Rose Bowl preparation are dominated by what is happening off the practice field. It is not just the fact that offensive coordinator Steve Sarkisian is working part-time for the Trojans and the rest of the time for his new employers, the University of Washington. It is that the Huskies' aggressive new head coach is trying to lure some of Pete Carroll's top assistants to go with him.

Rocky Seto, the secondary coach and a strong Carroll loyalist, is offered the job as defensive coordinator at Washington, a position that would be a clear career upgrade. Yogi Roth, the ambitious young grad assistant in charge of quarterbacks, is also offered a full staff position by Sarkisian, as is Dennis Slutak, Carroll's director of football operations, who would serve in the same capacity but with the added title of associate athletics director that would likely include a hefty raise. For his part, Carroll already is molding his new staff, promoting wide receivers coach John Morton to offensive coordinator and hoping to add Carl Smith as the new quarterbacks coach. That part isn't going as smoothly as Carroll had hoped, however. Smith, a longtime college and pro assistant, is someone Carroll trusts, someone who has served as an unofficial adviser to the Trojans coach in the past, someone who, unlike many of his present assistants, would not be afraid to speak up if he didn't agree on certain strategic moves. Fact is, Smith is apparently speaking up already. He reportedly wants to come to USC only if he is named the new play caller, which makes it awkward for Carroll to explain to Morton why, as the new offensive coordinator, he wouldn't be calling plays. "We hope to have it all settled soon," Carroll says, "but we still have some things to work out."

The rest of the decision making doesn't take as long, except a new, last-minute curve is thrown into an already complicated picture. Slutak announces he is accepting Sarkisian's generous offer to leave for Washington. Roth, who also was offered a spot on Lane Kiffin's staff at Tennessee, declines Sarkisian's offer, but hints he will be leaving USC to do something else away from football. Seto, meanwhile, after considerable soul-searching, decides to stay with Carroll, who shows his appreciation by promoting the former grad assistant to assistant head coach in charge of defense. The hitch is that the open defensive coordinator's job at Washington is then offered to Nick Holt, who holds the same job at USC. Why would Holt even consider the same position at a rebuilding school? Because Carroll, the noted defensive guru, makes the big defensive decisions for the Trojans. At Washington, Holt presumably would make those decisions for a new head coach whose strength is offense, not defense.

Carroll tries to slough off any concerns and can't wait to talk about Seto, the one coach who is staying. "Rocky is a great story for us," he says. "He's grown up in this program. It's been kind of a thrill to watch him mature. He's earned this spot. It is fun to watch guys on our staff reach a status where other teams come after them. Now Rocky will be someone I will rely on to keep us on track defensively, to make sure we keep doing what we believe in. I'm happy for him. The guy has earned it."

Standing in a sun-splashed end zone after the first Rose Bowl practice session, Seto looks like the happiest man on campus. "It was a tough decision, a very tough decision," says the thirty-two-year-old Seto. "My wife and I did a lot of talking and praying about it." Eventually, Seto says he reached out to a surprising source for advice. He called John Wooden, the legendary UCLA basketball coach he had met and visited in the past. "Coach Wooden really helped," Seto says. "He asked me, 'Rocky, are you happy where you are?' I said yes. He said, 'So what's the problem?' Then he reminded me the most important thing is to put your family first. My wife and kids all love where we live and what our life is like now. I decided Coach Wooden was right. We're so happy here, why change it? I am living a dream." The added title and the obvious pay raise that comes with it clearly helped the decision-making process, as well. "You have to understand where I've come from here," Seto says. "I was a lowly grad assistant. I was the guy who picked up Coach Carroll at the airport when he flew in for his interview. That was my first task, driving him here for his interview. Now to be someone who will serve as his sounding board on defense, someone who has worked with him long enough so that he trusts me to keep pushing his philosophy, well, I feel very fortunate."

A day later, everyone seems focused on the task at hand, getting ready for an 11-1 Penn State team that appears considerably stronger than the Illinois and Michigan clubs USC dispatched with relative ease in the past three Rose Bowls. Both the Trojans and the Nittany Lions would prefer to be playing in the BCS title game, but that doesn't lessen the challenge that is headlined by the duel between the coaching giant from Happy Valley, Pennsylvania, and the man from downtown L.A. who seems on the cusp of succeeding him as the college game's preeminent force. This is all about Paterno vs. Carroll, the venerable, eighty-two-year-old Joe Pa against the energized rival who is twenty-five years his junior.

The contrast between the two is evident at Rose Bowl media day at L.A.'s downtown Marriott Hotel. Both teams are scheduled to appear wearing their jersey tops, so they can be easily identified. No one has trouble identifying Paterno, who arrives first and looks surprisingly spry for someone who is coming off hip replacement surgery only a few weeks earlier. He settles into a chair at the head table at one end of the large, second-floor ballroom that is humming with conversation between media members. "Hey guys, you want to shoot the bull, get out!" rails Paterno, sounding more like a curmudgeon than he really is. Once the questions begin, the real Joe Pa surfaces. His answers are clear and concise, his mind remarkably sharp. With few, if any, lines on his face, he looks more like he is sixty-two than eighty-two. Someone asks about the three-year extension he just signed, a somewhat surprising move for somebody his age. "We prolonged the thing until it became a recruiting issue," he says. "Kids wanted to know. We needed a contract. . . . It has helped in the sense that some kids know when I tell them that I'll be around three, four, or five more years, that is probably a reality." Five more years? A head coach at a major college power at age eighty-seven? Well, if anyone can do it, he can. Paterno talks about the fifty-seven-year-old Carroll as if he were a young whippersnapper. "There are two or three young coaches out there who have changed the whole game of football," Jo Pa says. "Pete's right there at the top of it."

Only when the discussion turns to where Paterno will coach from during the game does he begin to sound his age. "My only problem is my leg gets tired," he says. "I don't have any pain. It just gets tired. Whether I can make it three and a half hours on the sideline, I don't know. People are worried I'm going to get hurt on the sideline." Later, it is announced he will do his coaching from the Rose Bowl press box on New Year's Day. Wherever he does it, his players won't mind. "It's an honor and privilege to play for someone who is a legend," says safety Anthony Scirrotto, who seems to echo his teammates' sentiments. "He's taught us all a lot. He's just a great guy, really down-to-earth. He might be eighty-two years old, but he is a twenty-five-year-old man at heart." As Paterno is about to leave his spot behind the microphone to head for practice, someone wonders if he wants to give the media a New Year's message. "Happy New Year?" he says, grinning. "I don't give a damn about your New Year, but I hope mine is happy."

When it is USC's turn to face the media, Carroll slides into the same chair Paterno occupied just a few minutes earlier and shakes his head when asked about his legendary counterpart who began as an assistant at Penn State a year before USC's coach was born. "He is extraordinary," Carroll says. "I don't know how he does it. My body is feeling pretty rickety as it is. I don't know how he does it at his age. I can't even fathom it. He's like a modern version of Benjamin Button, or something." Carroll says he admires Paterno because he has discovered the secret to what USC's coach is most anxious to pursue. "It is finding ways to continue winning," he says. "Maintaining a level of excellence, being successful over a long period of time. That's what he's done, and that's what we're trying to accomplish here." Going against a coach with an all-time best 383 victories and a 23-10-1 bowl record is not an enviable task. Carroll seems to recognize that it is Paterno, and not any of the Penn State players, who is the most intimidating factor in this game.

As the practice schedule heads into its final days at USC, Carroll first makes news by elevating Aaron Corp to No. 2 on the quarterback depth chart, ahead of Mitch Mustain, the final move in a season-long shake-up behind Mark Sanchez at the position. Then the Trojans learn that Stanley Havili, the fullback who might be the most underrated player on the team, will be ineligible to play in Pasadena because of academic issues. The discouraging news is exacerbated by the lack of depth at the position. Carroll says sophomore Rhett Ellison, junior Adam Goodman, and freshman D.J. Shoemate will alternate at fullback, but all of them represent a major dropoff from Havili, who has been especially dangerous making big plays as a pass catcher out of the backfield. Losing such a proven weapon only furthers speculation that this could be a low-scoring, defense-dominated game. "It should be a chess match," says Carroll, who doesn't need much encouragement to let the best defensive unit he's had in eight years at USC decide the outcome of a game the oddsmakers favor the Trojans to win by 9 or 10 points.

In a game that will have little effect on the final national polls, it is USC's defense that could, in fact, have the most to prove. Despite being ranked No. 1 in the nation in almost all the usual statistical categories, despite having three legitimate All Americans and as many as six players who could be selected in the first two rounds of the next NFL draft, this is a unit that has failed to gain widespread national attention. Maybe it is because it doesn't have a flashy nickname. Maybe it is because it hasn't compiled many of the more sexy numbers usually associated with a great defense. It has a modest 28 sacks and has created only 26 turnovers in twelve games. Only twice during the season have touchdowns been produced directly from the defense. The best thing this astonishingly fast, cohesive group does is shut opposing offenses down, not partially, but completely. It has given up just 11 touchdowns and 22 second-half points in twelve games. Its pass efficiency rating of 81.46 yards per game is 12.71 better than Florida, the second-place team in that category. Its 8.28 yards allowed per completion would be a new NCAA record. Maybe best of all is the fact that the 7.8 points it has allowed per game is not only the lowest in twenty years, but in this wild, high-scoring era, it is an astounding 19.4 points lower than the national average, the largest differential since the NCAA started keeping records in 1937.

"The best part is, we think the best is yet to come," says smiling Rey Maualuga, the hulking middle linebacker who won the Chuck Bednarik Award as the best defensive player in the country. A year ago, Maualuga, who is among the fastest linebackers in the country, played at around 270 pounds in the Rose Bowl and was named the game's defensive MVP. Safety Taylor Mays and outside linebacker Brian Cushing also made All-American teams this season. Tackle Fili Moala and safety Kevin Ellison, the most productive of all the defenders before the knee injury he suffered that will keep him out of this game, are likely high NFL draft choices, along with Clay Matthews, the hybrid pass rusher/linebacker who might be the unit's most consistent playmaker. "I'd have to rank this USC defense right up there at the top," says Paterno. "They hustle, they're in good position, and they take advantage of every mistake you make. They're big and they can run. It is one of the better defenses I've ever seen, and they're consistent."

In most of the pregame hype, Penn State's defense has been overshadowed by USC's, but it has some impressive credentials of its own. It is fourth nationally in points allowed (12.4), sixth in pass efficiency (97.3), eighth against the rush (95.9) and fifth in total defense. "I think our defense played some real good teams this year and has done very well," says Scirrotto, one of the starting safeties. "They're the No. 1–rated defense, and I respect that, but we think we're pretty good, too." It is a game that could come down to which offense can produce the biggest plays. USC's overall speed will be a major factor, but the Nittany Lions have a dangerous gamebreaker of their own in wide receiver Derrick Williams, who is utilized in all sorts of formations. The quarterback matchup will be interesting, as well. The Trojans' Mark Sanchez is capable of putting up big numbers if Sarkisian and Carroll aren't too conservative with the game plan. Penn State's Darryl Clark, meanwhile, is a big, effective runner with a strong arm, but he has to prove he can consistently throw the ball accurately, or the Big Ten champs will become one-dimensional, something you don't want to do against this USC defense.

"I don't think people realize that Penn State is just as worthy as all those other teams that were trying to make it to the national title game," says Carroll. "They were one point away, just one lousy point, from finishing undefeated and making it to the title game. On offense, they can do everything offenses do today, working out of a basic two-back set and utilizing a lot of shotgun stuff. Their quarterback moves around, too. And they use Derrick Williams all over the place. Defensively, they're really sound and really good, a lot like Ohio State. It is probably as good a defense as we've played. I just think this is a really cool matchup. We're so dead even in most areas. So now let's go out and play and see what happens."

What happens first is that New Year's Day dawns the way it always does in Southern California. No matter how much rain or mudslides or general gloomy weather arrive with winter, January 1 always comes up like they designed it on a Hollywood movie set. The skies are clear, the sunshine glows, and the temperatures hover near 70 degrees in Pasadena, warming the crowd that huddles through the chilly night to get good seats for the Tournament of Roses Parade. A few blocks away, in the glimmering Arroyo Seco, where the Rose Bowl resides, the picturesque San Gabriel Mountains offer the perfect backdrop, and all the folks who made the 2,500 mile trip from Pennsylvania couldn't be happier.

The ninety-fifth renewal of this historic game begins the way most people expected. Both defenses force three-and-outs on the first possession, and the 93,293 spectators settle in for a suspenseful defensive battle. USC gets its offense rolling by running the ball on the next possession, using C.J. Gable and Joe McKnight to pound away for a couple of first downs. A potentially damaging sack of Mark Sanchez, an ensuing fumble and Penn State recovery near midfield is nullified by an offsides penalty. Buoyed by a second chance, Sanchez continues to drive the Trojans offense until, on a first and 10 at the Nittany Lions' 27, he finds Damian Williams with a rocket that the junior wide receiver catches in stride for a touchdown and a 7–0 lead. Penn State comes right back with a solid drive of its own, led by Clark, an athletic quarterback with a knack for getting the ball away just as USC's defenders are about to pounce on him. Despite a penalty that wipes out one big pass to Deon Butler, Clark finds the shifty little wide receiver again for 28 yards to get the Big Ten champs down to the Trojans' 9. Then, with USC's linemen aggressively busting through, the 235-pound Clark runs a quarterback delay and barges into the end zone to tie the score at 7.

The first quarter ends with this looking like the kind of competitive, close Rose Bowl Game that hasn't been seen in a while. Looks can be deceiving, though. Soon enough, the Trojans' skilled wide receivers start finding gaping holes in Paterno's Cover Three zone defense. For one of the few times all season, Carroll and Sarkisian let Sanchez loose, allowing him to throw at will. With Williams, Ronald Johnson, and Patrick Turner cruising through the open pockets in Penn State's secondary, Sanchez spends most of the second quarter delivering passes that start to look like blurs to the outmatched kids in the vanilla uniforms. Team speed, the one glaring factor Big Ten teams have been lacking, comes back to haunt the conference's latest representative. The harder they try to run down the USC wideouts, the easier it seems to get for Williams and Co. One drive is climaxed by Sanchez's own quarterback draw, the first time he pulled that off all season, for a 6-yard touchdown. David Buehler adds a 30-yard field goal, then Sanchez finds Johnson for a 19-yard touchdown. When Will Harris recovers a Nittany Lion fumble, one of their many sloppy mistakes, at the USC 42, Sanchez again takes advantage, capping off another quick Trojans drive with a 20-yard screen pass to Gable for a touchdown. At one point a few days earlier, Paterno had joked to the media that he'd only seen two movies in the past forty years. One was *E.T.* and the other was *Titanic.* At this point in the game, he must feel as if he is slowly sinking on the same ship as his players. USC finishes with 24 points in the quarter, while its own vaunted defense runs off the field at halftime having limited Penn State to just seven first downs and 7 points. The Trojans outgain Paterno's club 341 yards to 177 in the half and their 31–7 lead appears insurmountable.

To its credit, Penn State doesn't quit. It makes enough adjustments to shut out USC in the third period. Unfortunately, it doesn't score any points itself, either. Nevertheless, at the start of the fourth quarter, the Nitanny Lions put a crisp drive together, with Clark, a much more effective passer than some previous Big Ten Rose Bowl quarterbacks, finding Derrick Williams for a 2-yard touchdown throw. Any chance for Clark and Co. to gain momentum is quickly crushed, however, when Sanchez takes advantage of a blown coverage in that shaky Penn State secondary. Johnson, who has evolved into USC's best deep receiver, sprints into the open by 25 yards and Sanchez's soft, looping spiral downfield catches him in stride for the 45-yard touchdown that makes it 38–14. Sanchez now has four touchdown passes and a touchdown run. He has clearly taken over the game. On the Trojans sideline, the players are already celebrating, bouncing around and slapping each other on the shoulder pads. Whatever intensity they had played with for more than three impressive quarters dissipates in the final ten minutes. Carroll keeps the USC offense conservative, trying not to commit a turnover that could get Penn State back in the game. Still, Paterno's team doesn't give up. It keeps plugging, although Joe Pa frustrates some by settling for a field goal to trim the lead to 38–17, before Clark hits tight end Jordan Noorwood for a 9-yard touchdown pass to make it 38–24. It ends that way when one last valiant Nitanny Lions drive is thwarted by a Cary Harris interception of Clark's final pass in the end zone.

The annual post–Rose Bowl celebration begins on the field, with fans mobbing the players and coaches, and Carroll flashing a smile as wide as the press box when he accepts the Rose Bowl Trophy. Sanchez is asked to lead the USC band and proudly does so, brandishing the familiar Trojan sword as the students begin chanting "One more year! . . . one more year!" The quarterback smiles, understanding that everyone at USC wants him to return for his senior season, instead of opting early for the NFL Draft. He says he isn't ready to make that decision yet, but few, if any, Trojans quarterbacks have exuded as much joy playing at the school.

Afterward, in the middle of the USC locker room, long after he has finished his perfunctory session with the media as a whole, Carroll stands with a few writers, and you can sense the frustration he's felt at the end of the past three seasons rise up again. "In all due respect to those other two great programs [Florida and Oklahoma, who meet in the BCS title game], I don't think anybody can beat us," he says. "Those other two teams are fantastic. I just wish we could keep playing, that's all." Someone wonders why Sanchez, who finished 28 of 35 for 413 yards and 4 touchdowns, wasn't allowed to play this way all season. "We did take a little different approach in the middle of the year," Carroll admits, for the first time. "We realized our defense was so good, we knew it wouldn't beat us. So we played kind of conservative, like in the Cal game. I'm happy for Mark. He had as big a night as any quarterback we've had. You can see him up there with Carson [Palmer] and Matt [Leinart]. He is capable of being the best player in America."

Williams, whose development as the go-to receiver that was lacking a year ago had much to do with this team's success, is asked if he thinks the coaches will ever be conservative with Sanchez again. "Geez," he says, "I hope not." Turner, the senior wideout who enjoyed his finest season, indicates the Trojans saw the Penn State zone and practically drooled at the possibilities. "We saw there were a lot of holes in that type of defense," he says. "We saw that on film, and we have a lot of talented receivers who can take advantage of something like that."

The last player in the locker room is Sanchez, who acts as if he doesn't want to leave. You can't blame him. He is still glowing after the best performance of his still young football career. "We just got in a groove," he says. "Sark [Sarkisian] told me to just go out and play free, just like you did when you were seven years old." Sanchez felt so good he played without the brace he'd worn on his injured knee throughout the season. He admits neither the USC medical staff nor his family was happy with that decision, but it is hard to argue with the results. "My family isn't too pleased with this, either," he says, touching a fledgling beard he'd grown for the game. "I guess I'll have to shave now." Asked what he felt when the fans were chanting for him to stay one more year, he shakes he head and grins. "That was special," he says. "I'll remember that forever. This has all been too much fun and too exciting."

To hardly anyone's surprise, Sanchez is named the Rose Bowl Offensive Player of the Game. Linebacker Kaluka Maiava is selected the Defensive Player of the Game, making it three consecutive years a USC linebacker has captured that award. Maualuga and Cushing won it previously, and now all three senior linebackers finish their careers having taken home one of the more treasured trophies in the sport.

Carroll, wearing a white pullover sweater with no Trojans logo for a change, makes his way out of the locker room, still marveling at the performance of his 12-1 team, still enjoying a fourth consecutive New Year's Day victory in this hallowed, old facility. "The public doesn't get it," he says. "All these people were saying we wouldn't be up for this game. You saw us out there. We weren't going to have a letdown. These guys had a ball playing. You know, it really wasn't a very close football game." No, it really wasn't.

Unfortunately, even the overpowering demonstration does little to ease the frustration of a team and a fiercely competitive coach who honestly believe they could beat anyone in the country. Nevertheless, again this season, just like the two before it, one slipup along the way has prevented them from having the chance.

You can almost see the conflicting emotions on Carroll's face as he opens the locker room door and slowly walks out into the chilled Pasadena night. He pauses when he spots Nick Sanchez, Mark's father, standing a few steps away. He strolls over and the two men smile, congratulate, and hug each other in a fitting, final snapshot to yet another wildly successful, if not completely fulfilled, USC football season.

XVI

The Future: A Quarterback Leaves, but the One Constant Remains

The good-bye is awkward. After all the giddy satisfaction and warm vibes resulting from Mark Sanchez's spectacular MVP performance in the Rose Bowl, no one expected this. No one expected an emotionally torn Sanchez to announce he is leaving the program early for the NFL, and no one expected Pete Carroll, who is usually gracious and upbeat in these situations, to react this way, to allow his disappointment and even his anger to seep through at a somewhat shocking morning media conference at Heritage Hall.

Few have seemed to enjoy playing at USC as much as Sanchez, who was sort of a young Brett Favre when it came to exhibiting joy on the field. He'd sling a blur of a fastball 40 yards downfield for a touchdown, then jump into an offensive lineman's arms and pump his right arm triumphantly. He was not only the leader, he was the emotional catalyst of this team. He loved playing in big games like the Rose Bowl. He loved competing. He appeared to love everything about college football.

Still, maybe it was wrong for everyone to assume that you'd have to drag him away from all that, kicking and screaming. After all, he'd been at USC for four years, he was close to graduating, and all those eager agents out there were telling him he could be the first or second quarterback, and maybe even among the top three players, selected in the NFL Draft, guaranteeing him the kind of money that would make him secure for life. If he waited a year and sustained an injury, he could blow all that. Or, like Matt Leinart a few years earlier, his stock could mysteriously drop and it could cost him millions.

So Sanchez, after what he said were many sleepless nights spent agonizing over the decision, announces he is leaving. For Carroll, it feels like one of those games, not unlike the one at Oregon State this past season, that somehow eluded his grasp even after he'd done seemingly everything he could to avoid it. He'd stayed up with San-chez at the quarterback's apartment until one o'clock in the morn-ing, trying to talk him out of it, but he lost, and no, he isn't taking it well. "We didn't see this decision the same," Carroll says, and you can almost feel the petulance in his body language. "Mark is going against the grain in this decision. We know that, and he knows that. We have compelling information working against the choice going this way." As Carroll speaks, you can see how uncomfortable Sanchez is. When Carroll is done, he doesn't hug his somber-looking quarterback. He quickly shakes his hand and abruptly leaves the room. This isn't the way it happened before. This isn't the way Car-roll reacted when Reggie Bush left a year early. So what makes this different? What makes him come off so upset this time?

Later, after the media crowd disperses, Carroll seems to have cooled off. "I'm not angry at all," he says. "I'm not. I love Mark. I think he's a great kid. I'm disappointed that the information we have wasn't compelling enough to make it clear. I think from our view of it . . . the plight of the early quarterbacks, even the first-round draft picks, is less than fifty-fifty of them being successful. So when it's like that, it's hard to really champion the cause. I just competed to try to get the message across and I had to go hard." So that's what it this is really about. Carroll is doing what he always does. He is always competing, this time trying desperately to talk his star quarterback out of leaving, trying to convince him to stay one more season, maybe win the Heisman Trophy, and, hopefully, lead USC back to the BCS Championship Game. He wanted what was best for Sanchez, whom he definitely feels needs more experience to succeed in the NFL, but yes, he wanted what was best for his team, too.

The irony here is that after most Trojan seasons the past few years, it was the coach everybody was afraid of losing, not the star player. It had only been a few weeks earlier, on the Tuesday of the final week of the regular season, that I had managed to get Carroll off by himself for a few minutes, something that was becoming as difficult as trying to block Rey Maualuga on a linebacker blitz. Finally, after practice, before he could duck off to take a phone call or meet with a player or stop to kibitz with a parent, I get lucky. I manage to isolate him in a corner of the foyer leading to his office on the second floor of Heritage Hall.

"What about the inevitable NFL offers that will be coming your way?" I ask, noting that there seem to be more potential vacancies than ever in Roger Goddell's league. Carroll looks at me for a moment, then smiles, as if he's decided not to give the usual politically correct answer this time. "I'm a logical candidate," he says, and I immediately realize he hasn't said that to anyone in the past. Before the comment fully registers, though, he adds, "Pretty soon I won't be." Now it's my turn to smile, because I get what he's saying. The more he wins and the more plaudits he receives at USC, the more people see how much fun he's having coaching the Trojans while being paid like a Saudi prince and building a plush, new home in one of L.A.'s most desirable locations, the less discussion there will be about him bolting to the NFL. Eventually, all the rumors will fade.

A few weeks later, it's as if his statement becomes prophetic. Jobs open all over the NFL, and except for the whisper of a mention of him being a possible candidate in Denver, his name never comes up. It seems the man with the winningest record in college football finally has convinced people that he intends to stay where he has found the most success. USC fans everywhere are ecstatic at this turn of events, hoping that their annual winter of concern over losing their favorite coach might actually be a thing of the past.

Then all hell breaks loose at Heritage Hall. Not only does Sanchez decide to leave, but in the days leading up to his announcement, before anyone has a chance to really savor another 12-1 season, BCS bowl victory and top-4 finish in the polls—the Trojans finish third in the final Associated Press poll and second in the coaches' poll—Carroll finds himself busy retooling his coaching staff. It proves to be his biggest makeover yet after defensive coordinator Nick Holt belatedly decides to join offensive coordinator and new Washington head coach Steve Sarkisian in Seattle. The move is baffling to some. Why would you leave the most successful program in America to take a similar position for a team that could have been the worst in the country in 2008? The answer is that it probably pays better and gives Holt more freedom to run his own defense. At USC, there is no way he could get that with Carroll in charge.

The widespread speculation over whom Carroll will hire to replace Holt begins immediately. Some think Ken Norton Jr., the former UCLA star who has been wooed by the Bruins in the past, would be a logical choice to promote from within. Others feel Rocky Seto, who's already been promoted once by Carroll, could move up again. Then there is Ed Orgeron, the favorite of so many alums and boosters, who was a force both as a defensive line coach and recruiting coordinator for Carroll during the glory Matt Leinart–Reggie Bush years. Anyway, Orgeron only recently was hired in a similar role at Tennessee by another former Trojans assistant, Lane Kiffin. Carroll settles on Seto, who would probably win if you took a poll to find his most loyal assistant, although he also promotes Norton to assistant head coach in charge of defense. Seto is thirty-two, hard-working, and not the type to be concerned that the head coach will still have final say on everything that has to do with defense.

On offense, receivers coach John Morton is promoted, as expected, to be the new coordinator, but the more interesting move is naming sixty-year-old former staff member Carl Smith quarterbacks coach, assistant head coach on offense, and new play caller. From all accounts, it appears that Smith, who's been an NFL offensive coordinator, tells Carroll he won't take the job unless he is allowed to call plays, and although that makes things a bit awkward for Morton, Carroll agrees. That's great, until a few weeks later when Smith decides he'd rather go back to the NFL and take a job coaching quarterbacks with the Cleveland Browns. Carroll reacts quickly, though, and hires promising, thirty-two-year-old Jeremy Bates, who'd been the quarterbacks coach with the Denver Broncos, where he helped school Jay Cutler, one of the NFL's better young quarterbacks. Bates is given the position of quarterbacks coach and assistant head coach of offense as well as the challenging responsibility of calling plays. Reportedly, he also will be paid more than Sarkisian, who had been making $700,000-plus. Some reports have Bates's salary closer to $1 million.

Carroll rounds out the staff by bringing back a former assistant and NFL veteran, Jethro Franklin, to coach the defensive line. David Watson, the previous defensive line coach, leaves to pursue other opportunities. That opens up a spot, and Carroll, who has stubbornly avoided having a special teams coach since 2001, finally hires another one. He is thirty-seven-year-old Brian Schneider, who last worked with the Oakland Raiders. Carroll then names twenty-seven-year-old Matt Capurro, another former Raiders employee, as the new director of football operations to replace Dennis Slutak, who also left for the University of Washington. Meanwhile, Yogi Roth, the eclectic graduate assistant, has resigned and embarked on a forty-day journey to South America "to spread the grassroots message of Coach Carroll's philosophy." After it's all over, Carroll quietly heaves a tired, postseason sigh. "It's unsettling," he says, "I loved the guys [who left]. I don't like losing them. It makes the new season more difficult."

Sanchez's departure stretches the degree of difficulty even further, although some of the disappointment is offset by Taylor Mays's surprising decision to stay at USC for his senior season and a shot at becoming one of the school's few three-time All Americans. In a year when the defense will face a huge makeover, Mays, the great safety with the prototype NFL body who might have been a top-10 draft pick, will provide someone who can be the foundation. Tailback C.J. Gable, another player who was contemplating leaving early, also announces he is staying, along with Josh Pinkard, the excellent defensive back who has been granted an extra year of eligibility by the NCAA after losing a full season with an injury.

By the time National Signing Day arrives in February, it is clear USC's football program is as potent as ever. Highlighted by Matt Barkley, the No. 1–rated prep quarterback in the nation from Mater Dei High, the same Orange County school that produced Leinart, Carroll's latest star-glazed class includes nine of the top-100 players in America and is ranked second, third, fourth, or seventh in the final national polls, depending on which recruiting service you choose to believe. No less than seven of the eighteen-player class are from out of state. Besides Barkley, the group features Devon Kennard, the No. 1–ranked defensive end in the nation from Arizona, and Patrick Hall, from Oxnard, California, who was considered one of the four or five best in the "athlete" category, meaning he is so skilled he could play offense or defense. Yet it is a measure of the new recruiting standard Carroll has set that most of the Trojan discussion on signing day is centered on the one potentially great player who got away. Manti Te'o, the nation's No. 1–rated linebacker from Hawaii, seemed headed to USC all along. Te'o was aware of the openings NFL-bound players like Rey Maualuga and Brian Cushing are leaving in Carroll's starting lineup, and he is known to have bonded with Barkley at the Under Armour All American Game in December. Yet, in a startling morning decision made on ESPN, Te'o picks Notre Dame over the Trojans. "He's a great player," an obviously disappointed Carroll says. "We battled that one all the way through. But that's the way it goes. You can't get them all."

The Te'o turnaround, perhaps costing USC its chance to finish No. 1 or 2 in the national polls, seems to have bothered the Internet bloggers and twitters more than it does Carroll. "Do you still enjoy the recruiting process?" I ask him, after his long, weary day is over. "Yeah, yeah, it's a blast," he says. "I didn't sleep a wink all night. I called Ed [Orgeron, his former recruiting director who now works the same job at Tennessee], trying to wake him up at 3:30 in the morning. 'What are you doing, sleeping?' I asked. Then he called me at 8:30 trying to catch me taking a nap. He didn't. No, I like the heck out of it. I hate it when you don't get guys you want, but we know that's how it works."

USC's class has some players who could make an immediate impact. Frankie Telfort, from Florida, is described by Carroll as "the fastest linebacker we've ever had." When you realize he's had Keith Rivers, Cushing, and Maualuga, among others, that's an impressive statement. "This kid ran a 4.39 forty the other day," Carroll says, his tired eyes lighting up. Georgia's Jarvis Jones, from deep in football-mad SEC country, wasn't expected to choose the Trojans. Yet at a mature 6'3" 225 pounds, he is a versatile linebacker who should be an early candidate to break into the two deep. Another to keep an eye on is James Boyd, the first USC recruit who comes in as a combination quarterback/defensive end. He started at both positions for L.A. Jordan High, where he was last seen leading the city in scoring and rebounding during basketball season. He is likely to be a pass-rushing end for the Trojans, who will have openings in that area in the fall. "Overall, there are some really dynamic football players in this group," Carroll says. "We're excited about them."

The caliber and depth of yet another highly regarded recruiting class only demonstrates once again that while star players and outstanding assistants come and go, the one most important constant remains at USC. Carroll's presence is what really matters, and as long as he is there, as long as he continues to oversee every aspect of this pristine program, the Trojans will be their usual robust selves.

With Sanchez, Maualuga, and Cushing gone, as well as several other key defensive starters, and with a schedule that might be the most imposing he has faced since he's been at USC, 2009 could be the year his remarkable streak of seven consecutive Pac-10 titles,

BCS bowls, eleven-plus victories, and top-4 national finishes comes to an end. Still, the thing to remember about Carroll is that he rarely, if ever, runs out of talent. A year ago, he had to replace ten players who were drafted by the NFL, seven of them in the first two rounds. All he did was go 12-1 without them. The gaping vacancy Sanchez leaves at quarterback will provide an opportunity for eager, gifted kids who would be starting almost anywhere else. Aaron Corp, who finished the season No. 2 on the depth chart, was the state player of the year in California his senior year in high school, beating out the much more hyped Jimmy Claussen, who went to Notre Dame. Mitch Mustain, like the flashy incoming freshman, Barkley, was a national prep player of the year. One of them is likely to move in and do surprisingly well as the new Trojans quarterback. With a young, reconfigured coaching staff, Carroll will be more active, more challenged and probably more invigorated than ever.

He's like the man he so often talks about emulating, John Wooden, who was always happiest coaching when he didn't have a Lew Alcindor or a Bill Walton and the expectations that went along with them. It is a chance to prove yet again what a difference coaching and teaching can make. Carroll, like Wooden, lives for these kind of challenges. "I love to compete," he says, "and I love to teach."

"The job at USC is made for Pete, that's who he is," says Boomer Esiason, who was the quarterback in Carroll's first year as a head coach with the New York Jets. "I never want to see him back in the NFL. He can have a much greater impact on young peoples' lives where he is. There was Bear Bryant at Alabama, and Joe Pa at Penn State, and now there is Pete Carroll at USC. You watch all the other coaches out there, even guys like Bob Stoops at Oklahoma and Urban Meyer at Florida, and they always look so grim. Not Pete. He is always having fun. Life is great for Pete Carroll. I only wish I could be that happy all the time."

During Penn State's stay in Los Angeles for the Rose Bowl, Carroll marveled at the eighty-two-year-old Paterno, who openly talked of coaching for three, four, or maybe even five more years.

"There's no way I'll ever be like that," Carroll said, shaking his head. "When I'm that age, I'll hopefully be off on some beach somewhere, wearing a straw hat and sitting on the sand watching the waves come crashing in." I remember listening to those words and smiling to myself. "Yeah, right," I was thinking.

After a long, eventful year of madly chasing and closely observing this man of unparalleled energy, relentless enthusiasm, and surreal competitiveness, I have only one piece of advice for anyone who thinks Pete Carroll will be retiring any time in the next ten or fifteen years:

Don't bet on it.

Acknowledgments

First and foremost, I want to thank Pete Carroll for his time, his availability, and, most important, his trust. I would not have undertaken this project without his approval, and I was honored that he gave it. He and the members of his staff were as cooperative, patient, and understanding as they could be, considering they were in the midst of a heated and competitive football season.

The many friends, associates, players, and coaches from all over the country who have known and worked with Carroll were unfailingly cooperative. I would like to thank them for their time and their insight.

I want to express gratitude to my agent, Ian Kleinert of Objective Entertainment in New York, who happens to be an avid USC football fan, and to my friend and legal adviser, Sam Perlmutter, a longtime Trojans supporter who helped originate and complete the deal for the book.

USC Sports Information Director Tim Tessalone, one of the best in the business, was a huge help, along with his assistants, Paul Goldberg, Jason Pommier, and David Tuttle. Whether it was chasing down a player after practice for an interview or finding a desired statistic or fact, they always managed to come through.

Acknowledgments

I want to thank St. Martin's Press, my enthusiastic and supportive editor, Marc Resnick, and his assistant, Sarah Lumnah, for their faith and their commitment to this project.

Fellow author and former mentor, Loel Schrader, and friend and noted author Steve Springer both deserve thanks for their advice and encouragement. Scott Schrader was kind enough to assist in my recruiting research, and my Irvine neighbor and computer expert Josh Wertheimer was always there to help out in an emergency.

Finally, I would be remiss not to mention my wife, Marsha, who not only provided her usual love and support but her own tech knowledge, along with a keen copyreading eye that helped immeasurably.